RED SOX
VS.
YANKEES
The Great Rivalry

HARVEY FROMMER
AND FREDERIC J. FROMMER

SP
SPORTS
PUBLISHING
L.L.C.

www.sportspublishingllc.com

Mario Tama/Getty Images

ACKNOWLEDGMENTS

To all of the individuals and organizations, no matter which side of the rivalry they are on, who were of great help. Special thanks go to Mario Cuomo, Michael Dukakis, Ari Fleischer, Noah Amstadter, Maury Williamson, Kevin Shea, Lou Piniella, Mike Torrez, Johnny Pesky, Hawk Harrelson, Bob Watson, Ralph Houk, Eddie Yost, Dwight Evans, Fay Vincent, Marty Appel, Phil Rizzuto, Phil Pepe, Mike Geffner, Bill Madden, Alan Segal, Walter Mears, Sherwood Boehlert, Joe Pickering Jr., Clifford Kachline, Seth Swirsky, Phil Speranza, Wynn Bates, Chico Walker, David Szen, James Bontakis, Jason Giambi, Jeremy Giambi, Nomar Garciaparra, Tony Cloninger, Casey Fossum, Steve Karsay, Grady Little, Derek Lowe, Lou Meroni, Mike Stanley, Don Zimmer, Russ Cohen, Nick Anis, Leslie Epstein, Theo Epstein, Jim Kaat, Jerry Remy, Dan Shaughnessy, Willie Randolph, the late Charlie Lau, Til Ferdenzi, Bill Crowley, Irv Kaze, Sam Skoler,

Frank Messer, and all the rest of the voices, memoirists, fans and folks who provided a helping hand for this project; and special thanks to Kipp Wilfong, a caring and careful, on-the-mark editor. Also to Jennifer Polson, Michael Hagan, Susan Moyer, Kerri Baker, Holly Birch, Kevin King, Amanda Miller, and Dave Kasel of Sports Publishing.

We want to thank the Boston Red Sox, the New York Yankees, the Baltimore Orioles, the American League, the National Baseball Hall of Fame and Museum at Cooperstown, chief curator Ted Spencer, public relations director Brad Horn, vice president of communications and education Jeff Idelson. If we have left anyone out, the overlooking was unintentional.

And especially to the team on the bench—Jennifer and Jeff, Ian and Laura, Michele—thanks.

Director of production: Susan M. Moyer
Developmental editor: Kipp Wilfong
Book design, senior project manager: Jennifer L. Polson
Cover design: Kerri Baker
Imaging: Kerri Baker
Copy editor: Holly Birch
Photo editor: Erin Linden-Levy

Front endsheet: Photofest/Icon
Back endsheet: Frommer Archives

ISBN: 1-58261-767-8

Printed in Canada

Visit us on the Internet at sportspublishingllc.com

For Myrna Katz Frommer, wife and

mother extraordinaire, with much love.

CONTENTS

"In sports, the New England Patriots win the Super Bowl, thus using up all the sports luck that New England has been accumulating for decades, and thereby guaranteeing that the Red Sox will not win the World Series for another 150 years."

—From Dave Barry's 2002 year-in-review

•••

"I'm not a good loser. I believe in what Ernest Hemingway said: 'The way you get to be a good loser is practice and I don't want to practice.'"

—George Steinbrenner

•••

A BASEBALL FABLE

Three disconsolate baseball fans met in the woods. Each was very much concerned about the chances of his team returning to the World Series. Frustrated, they turned to God.

"When will my Cardinals return to the World Series?" the St. Louis fan asked.
And God replied: "Not in your lifetime."
"When will my Cubs return to the World Series?" the Chicago fan asked.
And God replied: "Not in your children's lifetime."
"When will my Red Sox return to the World Series?"
the Boston fan asked.
And God replied: "Not in my lifetime."

INTRODUCTION

I

I first stepped into Fenway Park in 1981, arriving hours early during batting practice. I had never been to a stadium that seated fewer than 50,000, and now I had this tiny, 34,000-seat ballpark to myself. Fenway Park felt like a backyard field to me.

It was September 6, a Sunday afternoon, the same day the Yankees fired manager Gene Michael and replaced him with Bob Lemon. A month before, the players had returned after a seven-week strike that split the season into two. The Yankees had won the first half, finishing two games ahead of the Red Sox. In the second half, Boston finished in fifth place and New York sixth, but the Yankees had a strong playoff and went on to win their fourth pennant in six years.

I was 14 years old, a huge baseball fan who was still a little bitter that half my summer had been ruined by the strike. But one look at Fenway's nooks and crannies pulled me back.

I watched batting practice from the first row behind the short right field wall, just inside the foul pole. Balls careened all over the field like pinballs.

Suddenly, one skipped along the outfield grass right at me. I reached over the wall and excitedly snagged it with my mitt. But my exhilaration turned to disbelief as I felt another mitt swat the ball out of mine.

I looked up, and saw a Red Sox outfielder smirking.

"Hey!" I said. "Why did you do that?"

"You're not allowed to come on the field," said Gary Hancock.

"I didn't come on the field," I protested. "I just reached over."

"Well, you can't do that," Hancock replied, looking over at the usher, who nodded in agreement.

"Come on, give me the ball," I pleaded.

"Give me one good reason I should."

"Well, I don't have any baseballs."

He shot me a look of disbelief.

"You don't have any balls?" he asked, laughing along with the usher.

"I'm from New York," I explained. "What chance do I have of catching a ball at Yankee Stadium or Shea Stadium, where there are 50,000 fans?"

"That's two things I don't like about you, kid," he said. "You are a liar, and you are from New York."

He walked away with the ball in his hand. Then suddenly, he turned around.

"Just don't let me see you here with another ball today," he said. And he tossed me the baseball.

But that was a promise I could not make.

Down on the field, my dad was interviewing Red Sox coach Johnny Pesky, who was hitting fungos to the players.

"That's my son out there, by the foul pole. Can you hit a ball to him?"

"No way," said Pesky, "What if it hits him in the head?"

"He'll catch it," my dad assured him, confident that the endless evenings he had spent hitting me fly balls would pay off.

"Sorry, I can't do it," Pesky said.

But a few minutes later Pesky must have had a what-the-hell thought because all of a sudden I heard a crack. A bunch of players in right field yelled, "Heads-up!"

I looked up, picked up the ball in the blue New England sky, and camped under it. Pesky had incredible aim. I didn't have to move as the ball landed in my mitt.

No one tried to strip it from me this time.

There was a reason Pesky had such good aim. The right field foul pole is known as "Pesky's Pole," because Pesky once hit a home run that just barely squeezed past the pole to win a game for Boston pitcher Mel Parnell, who in gratitude came up with the nickname.

"Hey, nice catch," some of the Red Sox shouted up at me. "We could use you out here, the way we're playing."

I must have given them some good vibes. The Red Sox beat the Seattle Mariners that day, 6-1, behind the pitching of Bruce Hurst.

Just before the game started, Pesky found my dad, told him to get the ball from me, and autographed it: "To Freddy, Nice Catch. Best Wishes, Johnny Pesky."

I still have that ball.

Frederic J. Frommer
Washington, D.C.
September 2003

II

My world and the universe of baseball have both changed a great deal since that September day in 1981 when Freddy caught the ball. Back then I was a professor in New York City and lived with my family on Long Island. Writing about sports, especially baseball, was my passion then. It still is.

I wrote for *Yankees Magazine* for almost two decades. I also have written two major books and many articles on the Yankees. So the pinstripes and all they represent have had a major effect on me.

But now I live in New England, and when I hear all the stories about "The Curse of the Bambino," it brings to mind the anguish many felt during my growing up days in Brooklyn and the plaintive cry of Dodger fans: "Wait 'til Next Year" echoed through the streets. It seemed "Dem Bums" could never beat the Yankees, just as the BoSox can't seem to prevail over the Bronx Bombers.

Red Sox vs. Yankees is a competition of teams, cities, owners, styles, ballparks, fans, media. Its roots reach back to Babe Ruth and Harry Frazee, even before, yet it is as contemporary as the next Red Sox-Yankees game.

The Boston Red Sox have finished second to the New York Yankees for six consecutive seasons through 2003, a combined total of 58 games behind in those years. They are restless and frustrated in New England; proud and confident in New York.

The historic rivalry between the two ancient rivals is at high intensity. So come, let us celebrate a storied baseball phenomenon— THE GREAT RIVALRY between the Red Sox of Boston and the Yankees of New York.

Harvey Frommer
Lyme, New Hampshire
September 2003

RED SOX VS. YANKEES
The Great Rivalry

I

MARCH OF RIVALRY TIME

1895

February 6—Babe Ruth is born at 216 Emory Street, Baltimore, Maryland.

1901

April 26—Boston's American League team, which will later be known as the Red Sox, makes its debut against Baltimore, a team that will later relocate to New York and become the Yankees. The Boston team loses that day, 10-6.

1903

April 22—The New York Highlanders play their first game and lose, 3-1, in Washington.

May 7—The first game between the two franchises is played. The Pilgrims nip the Highlanders, 6-2, at the Huntington Avenue Grounds in Boston.

December 20—In what would become a pattern for one-sided trades between the two franchises, the Highlanders trade southpaw pitcher Jesse Tannehill to Boston for right-handed hurler Tom Hughes.

1904

October 7—New York's Jack Chesbro picks up his 41st victory of the season, a 3-2 victory over Boston. The Highlanders take a half game lead over the Pilgrims.

October 10—In the final day of the season, the Pilgrims clinch the American League flag with a 3-2 victory over the Highlanders in the first game of a doubleheader. New York ace Jack Chesbro throws a wild pitch with a runner on third in the top of the ninth and allows the winning run to score.

1906

September 4—New York moves into first place by beating Boston 7-0 and 1-0, the team's fifth consecutive doubleheader sweep, a major-league record. But the team finishes the season in second place, while the Sox finish eighth.

1907

May 31—The Highlanders' pugnacious five-foot-five shortstop, Kid Elberfeld, steals home twice against Boston.

October 13—In a three-way deal, the Yankees ship second baseman Frank LaPorte to Boston and acquire Chicago White Sox first baseman Jake Stahl.

1908

June 30—At Hilltop Park, Boston's Cy Young hurls his third career no-hitter, an 8-0 gem against New York. Young gives up a leadoff walk to Harry Niles who is caught stealing. Then Young retires the next 26 batters. The 41-year-old Young is the oldest pitcher to record a no-hitter until Nolan Ryan hurls a no-hitter in 1990.

1909

September 11—The Highlanders sell Jack Chesbro, the team's first star hurler, to the Red Sox.

1910

April 14—On Opening Day, the Yankees and Red Sox battle for 14 innings at Hilltop Park in front of 25,000 fans before the game is called with the score 4-4.

Another Opening Day at Fenway, another first ball being thrown out. (Frommer Archives)

May 26—The Red Sox purchase the contract of New York catcher Red Kleinow.

1911

May 6—The Yankees record their first triple play, in a 6-3 victory over Boston at Hilltop Park. With Russ Ford on the mound, Bill Carrigan lines into a game-ending, ninth-inning triple killing.

1912

April 9—A spring snowstorm is the setting for the first game at Fenway Park. The Red Sox prevail in the exhibition game against Harvard University.

April 11—Opening Day at Hilltop Park sees the Yankees wearing pinstripes for the first time. The Red Sox win the game 5-3 as Joe Wood tosses a seven-hitter.

April 20—Just a few days after the sinking of the Titanic, the Yankees and Red Sox match up in the first major league game at Fenway Park. Boston Mayor John "Honey Fitz" Fitzgerald, the grandfather-to-be of John F. Kennedy, throws out the first ball. Boston ekes out a 7-6 win in 11 innings before 27,000.

1914

May 13—The Yankees purchase the contract of catcher Les Nunamaker from Boston for $5,000.

May 27—Right-handed rookie hurler Guy Cooper is sold by the Yankees to the Red Sox.

1915

May 6—Babe Ruth, pitching for the Boston Red Sox, hits his first major league home run off Yankee pitcher Jack Warhop at the Polo Grounds. Ruth picks up two more hits but loses the game, 4-3, in 13 innings.

May 8—Sixteen Yankees bat in the fourth inning as New York scores 10 runs, en route to a 10-3 romp over Boston.

June 2—The Red Sox conclude a 29-day road trip defeating the Yankees behind Babe Ruth's pitching, 7-1, at the Polo Grounds. After ripping his second major league homer, Ruth is walked intentionally the next two times he comes to bat. An infuriated and frustrated Ruth kicks at the bench and breaks a toe.

October 6—Boston sweeps a doubleheader from the Yankees, 2-0 and 4-2. The nightcap gives Sox pitcher Babe Ruth a 17-3 record since June 1.

1916

May 5—At Fenway Park, Babe Ruth is relieved by Carl Mays in the ninth inning with the Sox leading, 4-2.

New York ties the game on third baseman Larry Gardner's two-out error and ekes out an 8-4 win in 13 innings.

June 20—Tilly Walker hits Boston's only homer at Fenway Park the entire season of 1916. Red Sox shortstop Everett Scott, a defensive replacement, plays in the first of 1,307 straight games. Scott's streak comes to an end in 1925 when he is a member of the Yankees.

June 21—Boston pitcher George "Rube" Foster hurls a 2-0 no-hitter against the Yankees, the first no-hitter pitched at Fenway. Foster is rewarded with a $100 bonus; his teammates are each presented with gold-handled pocketknives with the no-hitter date engraved.

June 22—Boston's Babe Ruth allows but three singles and paces his team's 1-0 win over New York.

September 29—Pitcher Babe Ruth's season ends as he beats the Yankees, 3-0. It is the Babe's 23rd win, his ninth shutout, lowering his ERA to 1.75.

November 1—Harry H. Frazee, New York theater owner and producer, and Hugh Ward purchase the Red Sox from Joseph Lannin for $675,000 (one report puts the figure at $750,000). Sox manager Bill Carrigan says he will step aside as Boston manager to pursue other interests.

1917

April 24—George Mogridge is the first Yankee in history to hurl a no-hitter as he defeats Boston, 2-1, at Fenway.

1918

December 21—Boston ships pitchers Ernie Shore and Dutch Leonard and outfielder Duffy Lewis to the Yankees for four second-line players and cash.

1919

June 13—The Yankees sell outfielder Bill Lamar to the Red Sox.

June 28—Carl Mays of the Red Sox pitches two complete games against the Yankees. He wins the first game, 2-0, and loses 4-1 in the second game.

July 29—Boston pitching star Carl Mays is traded to the Yankees for pitchers Allan Russell and Bob McGraw and $40,000.

September 24—Boston's Babe Ruth breaks the single-season record with his 28th home run in a game against the New York Yankees. The ball clears the right-field roof of the Polo Grounds. Ruth will finish the season with a .322 batting average, 29 home runs and 114 RBIs.

September 27—Babe Ruth plays his final game for the Red Sox. On this day future Red Sox star shortstop and manager Johnny Pesky is born in Portland, Oregon.

1920

January 5—The Red Sox sell Babe Ruth, 24, to the New York Yankees for $125,000. Red Sox owner Harry Frazee is also given a $350,000 mortgage on Fenway Park by Yankee owner Jacob Ruppert. In four years as a pitcher, Ruth was 78-40. In 1919, he batted .322 with 29 home runs playing left field for the Red Sox. In 1919, he batted .319 with 22 home runs playing left field for Boston, and won nine games as a pitcher with a 2.97 ERA.

May 1—Babe Ruth hits his first home run as a Yankee. It clears the roof of the Polo Grounds and torques a 6-0 Yankee victory over the Red Sox.

October 29—Ed Barrow, former Red Sox manager, is appointed general manager of the Yankees.

December 15—Boston trades pitchers Waite Hoyt and Harry Harper, infielder Mike McNally and catcher Wally Schang to the Yankees. The Sox receive outfielder Sam Vick, third baseman Derrill Pratt, pitcher Herb Thormahlen, catcher Muddy Ruel and cash.

1921

September 5—New York's outfield makes a record five assists, four of them by outfielder Bob Meusel who will lead the American League in assists in 1921 and 1922.

October 2—Babe Ruth records his 59th home run as the Yankees beat the Red Sox, 7-6, in the 1921 season finale. Boston first baseman Stuffy McInnis plays in his 119th straight errorless game, while Red Sox shortstop Everett Scott plays in a Yankee team record 832nd consecutive game.

December 20—Boston trades pitchers Joe Bush and Sam Jones and shortstop Everett Scott to the Yankees for three pitchers, shortstop Roger Peckinpaugh and cash.

1922

July 24—The Red Sox trade third baseman Jumping Joe Dugan and outfielder Elmer Smith to the Yankees for outfielders Chick Fewster and Elmer Miller and shortstop John Miller. At the time, New York and St. Louis are in a close race for the pennant. St. Louis fans complain that the trade is too one-sided in favor of the Yankees. Baseball commissioner Landis rules that from now on, no trades except those that clear waivers can take place after June 15.

September 4—The Red Sox sweep a doubleheader from the Yankees, 4-3 and 6-5, dropping New York out of first place. Babe Ruth hits his last regular-season home run in the Polo Grounds.

September 30—The Yankees clinch their second American League pennant with a 3-1 win over the Red Sox at Fenway.

1923

January 3—The Yankees obtain minor league pitcher George Pipgras and minor league outfielder Harvey Hendrick from the Red Sox for backup catcher Al Devormer and cash.

January 30—The Yankees acquire pitcher Herb Pennock from Boston for pitcher George Murray, infielder Norm McMillan and outfielder Camp Skinner. The Red Sox also receive cash.

April 18—Yankee Stadium opens before a reported crowd of 74,200. In a ceremony before the game, Harry Frazee walks side-by-side with Yankees owner Jake Ruppert.

August 1—Harry Frazee sells the Red Sox to a syndicate headed by St. Louis Browns business manager J.A. Robert Quinn.

September 27—Lou Gehrig hits the first of his 493 home runs. It comes off Bill Piercy at Fenway Park in an 8-3 New York win.

September 28—En route to a 24-4 victory, the Yankees pound out 30 hits against Boston, an American League record.

1924

December 10—The Yankees trade infielder Mike McNally to the Red Sox for infielder Howard Shanks.

December 15—Boston sells the contract of catcher Steve O'Neill to the Yankees for $4,000, the waiver price.

1925

September 8—Red Sox pitcher Buster Ross gives up Babe Ruth's 300th career home run.

1926

May 26—New York runs its winning streak to 16, nipping Boston at Fenway, 9-8. The victory gives the Yanks a four-game sweep of the series, putting then ahead in the American League standings by eight and a half games.

1927

May 29—The Yankees rip the Red Sox, 15-7, in a game played at the Stadium. Scoring seven runs in the eighth inning, the Yankees coast to victory. Babe Ruth records his 13th homer.

June 23—At Boston, Lou Gehrig leads the Yankees to an 11-4 victory. He slams three home runs, a first at

Fenway Park. Gehrig hits a two-run homer in the second inning, and solo shots in the sixth and eighth innings.

June 30—At Yankee Stadium before a crowd of just 3,000, the Yanks beat the BoSox, 13-6. New York wins its fifth straight; Boston loses its 12th straight.

September 5—The BoSox outlast the Yankees, 12-11, in an 18-inning marathon at Fenway Park.

September 6-7—Ruth hits five homers in two days against the Red Sox. He wound up hitting 11 of his 60 homers against his old team in 1927.

1928

April 19—The Yankees are out of first for the first time since May 1926 as a result of their losing the morning Patriots Day game in Boston, 5-2. But the Yanks come back to win the second game, 7-6.

1929

April 23—The Yankees come to Fenway and are the first team to wear numbers on their road uniforms.

May 19—At New York, Babe Ruth and Lou Gehrig hit back-to-back homers off Boston's Jack Russell in the third inning. Two innings later a cloudburst sends a standing-room-only crowd scurrying for the exits. A stampede in the right field bleachers leaves two dead, 62 injured. The game ends with two outs in the fifth inning and the Yankees winning, 3-0. Jake Ruppert announces that never again will the Yankees sell more tickets than seats.

1930

January 29—Former American League home run king Ken Williams, a lifetime .319 hitter, is claimed on waivers by the Yankees from the Red Sox. But Williams will be released before the season gets underway.

May 6—Pitcher Red Ruffing becomes a Yankee when the Red Sox trade him for outfielder Cedric Durst. Boston also receives $50,000.

September 28—Babe Ruth returns to Fenway in a Yankee uniform and hurls a 9-3 complete game win over the Sox.

1931

April 22—Colliding at Fenway Park with Boston catcher Charlie Berry, an ex-professional football player, Ruth is carried off the field and rushed to a hospital. He had attempted to score from third base on a sacrifice fly.

May 4—Lou Gehrig and Babe Ruth, back in the lineup at the Stadium, switch positions to take the pressure off the Babe's lame leg. Babe Ruth plays first base. It is Gehrig's last game as an outfielder. Ruth and Gehrig combine for five hits, but lose to Boston, 7-3.

1932

May 30—A plaque in memory of former Yankee manager Miller Huggins is dedicated at Yankee Stadium. The Yanks then sweep the Red Sox, 7-5 and 13-3.

June 5—The Yankees acquire Boston pitcher Dan MacFayden for pitchers Ivy Andrews and Hank Johnson and $50,000.

July 3—The first Sunday game ever played at Fenway Park sees Boston lose to the Yankees 13-2. Sunday baseball was actually approved in Boston three years earlier, but not at Fenway because of its close proximity to a church. Red Sox Sunday games were played at Braves Field on Commonwealth Avenue before the law was changed.

August 3—The Red Sox trade pitcher Wilcy Moore to the Yankees for pitcher Gordon Rhodes.

1933

February 25—Multimillionaire sportsman Tom Yawkey purchases the Boston Red Sox from Robert Quinn for $1.5 million.

May 12—In a bit of role reversal, the Red Sox shell out cash for a Yankee player. Boston pays New York $100,000 for pitcher George Pipgras and rookie shortstop Bill Werber. Pipgras will be released two years later, and become an umpire in 1938.

June 6—Yankees pitcher Herb Pennock yields 11 hits but still shuts out the Red Sox, his former team, 4-0 at Yankee Stadium.

June 14—Lou Gehrig and his manager, Joe McCarthy, are ejected at Fenway Park for arguing that Boston's Rick Ferrell ran out of the baseline between first and second base. But Gehrig's consecutive-game streak is maintained at 1,249, as he goes one-for-three with a triple. The Red Sox romp, 13-5.

September 23—The Yankees overcome seven errors—three by Frank Crosetti—to beat the Red Sox, 16-12.

October 1—In his last game as a pitcher—and only his fifth since the Yankees bought him from the Red Sox 13 years earlier—38-year-old Babe Ruth hurls a complete game, defeating his former team, 6-5. He also homers.

1934

May 15—The Yankees trade infielder Lyn Lary to the Red Sox for infielder Fred Muller and $20,000.

August 12—A record 46,766 fans show up for Babe Ruth's final appearance at Fenway Park, and more than

Red Ruffing pitched for both the Red Sox and Yankees. (Photofest/Icon)

20,000 are turned away. In the first game of a double-header, the Babe singles and doubles. Walks limit him to one official at-bat in the second game.

1935

February 26—The Yankees release Babe Ruth, who returns to the city he started with, signing with the Boston Braves of the National League.

June 1—At Yankee Stadium, the Yankees smash a record six solo home runs to defeat Boston, 7-2. Bill Dickey hits two, and Frank Crosetti, Ben Chapman, George Selkirk, and Red Rolfe each hit one. Boston's runs come on a two-run homer by pitcher Mel Almedo.

June 2—Finishing his career in the city he started—only in a different league—Babe Ruth of the Boston Braves announces his retirement at the age of 40.

September 22—For the second straight year, Fenway's attendance record is broken in a Red Sox-Yankees double-header, as 47,627 fans jam into the Fens. The Yankees win the first game, 6-4, and then slam seven ground-rule doubles into the roped-off crowd to take the second game, 9-0. Such crowds will never be repeated. After World War II, more stringent fire laws and league rule prevent the overcrowding that was allowed in the 1930s.

1936

April 26—In one of the wildest games ever played between the rivals, the Red Sox score six times in the bottom of the first inning and the Yankees come back

with seven runs in the top of the second inning. New York goes on to win, 12-9.

August 21—Boston pitcher Wes Ferrell storms off the mound in the midst of a Yankees rally, only days after doing the same in a game against the Washington Senators. Red Sox manager Joe Cronin suspends the pitcher, fining him $1,000. "They can suspend me or trade me, but they're not getting any dough from me," Ferrell fumes. The suspension is lifted and the team trades him after the season.

1937

February 17—New York purchases the contract of first baseman Babe Dahlgren from Boston.

July 5—Joe DiMaggio hits his first career grand slam home run. It comes off Boston pitcher Rube Walberg.

September 8—The Yankees score eight times in the ninth inning with two out and defeat Boston, 9-6.

1938

May 30—A franchise-record crowd of 81,841 watches the Yankees sweep the Red Sox in a doubleheader at Yankee Stadium. More than 6,000 fans are turned away, and 511 are given refunds. New York's Red Ruffing ends Lefty Grove's eight-game winning streak in a 10-0 win. The Yankees win the second game, 5-4. Yankee outfielder Jake Powell and Boston player-manager Joe Cronin fight after Boston hurler Archie McKain plunks Powell. Charging to the mound, Powell is stopped by Cronin. Punches are thrown, and both combatants are ejected from the game only to continue the fight in an area beneath the stands.

1939

April 20—Prize Boston rookie Ted Williams racks the ball off the 407-foot sign in right-center field at Yankee Stadium for his first major league hit, a double. He had struck out twice in previous at-bats against Red Ruffing. The hit comes for Williams in the season opener in New York, delayed two days because of rain. It will be the only game Williams will play against Lou Gehrig.

July 9—The Red Sox triumph, 4-3 and 5-3, running their winning streak to 12 and sweeping a five-game series in Yankee Stadium. Joe Cronin drives in runs in both games, giving him 12 straight games with an RBI.

September 3—Stalling to avoid a loss as a Sunday baseball curfew looms, the Yankees incur the wrath of Fenway fans who bombard the playing field with debris. The game is forfeited to the Yankees by umpire Cal Hubbard, but AL President Will Harridge later overrules him. He also fines the Yankees for their tactics.

1940

April 26—Yankee third baseman Red Rolfe has nine assists but the Red Sox win the game, 8-1.

May 12—Red Ruffing's six-hit shutout trims Boston, 4-0, and halts New York's eight-game losing streak. The Red Sox, however, remain in first place in the American League while the Yankees are in last place.

1941

May 12—Boston hurler Lefty Grove stops Lefty Gomez and the Yankees, 6-4 for his 20th straight win at Fenway Park. A Jimmie Foxx two-run homer is the margin of victory.

May 25—Lefty Grove of Boston yields a single to Joe DiMaggio and becomes the first pitcher to take part in two of the greatest records in baseball history. The single locks Grove into DiMaggio's 56-game hitting streak. Grove had also given up one of the homers in Babe Ruth's 60-home run season 14 years earlier.

May 30—The Red Sox and Yanks split a doubleheader. New York wins the opener and Boston trounces New York in the second game,13-0. The Sox cap it off with a triple steal. Ted Williams laces six hits in the doubleheader, while Joe DiMaggio hits in both games, running his hitting streak to 16.

July 1—Joe DiMaggio ties Wee Willie Keeler's 44-game hitting streak with a single off Boston pitcher Jack Wilson. DiMaggio's three hits pace New York's doubleheader sweep over the Red Sox in front of 52,832 at Yankee Stadium. The second game is called after five innings.

November 27—Joe DiMaggio is named American League Most Valuable Player. He nips Ted Williams in the voting, 291 to 254.

1942

September 27—Tex Hughson of Boston wins his 22nd game as the Red Sox edge the Yankees. A Fenway Park crowd of 26,166, including 4,293 youngsters who gained free admission by bringing 29,000 pounds of scrap metal, watches Hughson space 11 hits. Ted Williams, in his final appearance before entering the war, singles and finishes the season at .356. The Sox great wins his second straight batting title.

1943

June 26—Boston pitcher Tex Hughson defeats the Yankees for the eighth straight time.

September 12—The first-place Yankees sweep a doubleheader from Boston, mathematically eliminating the Sox from pennant contention. The twin victory completes a five-game New York sweep of the Red Sox at Fenway.

1945

April 17—In a Yankee Stadium opener against the Red Sox, steady rain holds attendance down to 13,923 as mayor Fiorello LaGuardia throws out the first ball. New York scores seven runs in the seventh inning to clinch its 8-4 victory.

1946

April 25—The Red Sox beat the Yankees, 12-5, to start a 15-game winning streak.

May 10—Before a Friday Ladies' Day crowd of 64,183 Boston notches its 15th straight wins, edging the Yankees, 5-4, at the Stadium. New York scores all of its runs on Joe DiMaggio's grand slam.

May 11—The Yankees end Boston's 15-game winning streak with a 2-0 victory. Tiny Bonham beats Tex Hughson and Boo Ferriss at Yankee Stadium.

May 12—The Yankees and Red Sox record just three hits each. But New York gives up two unearned runs and loses the game, 3-1.

June 18—The Yankees sell 33-year-old right-handed pitcher Bill Zuber to the Red Sox.

July 7—Happiness pervades New England as the Sox lead the Yankees by seven and a half games in the standings at the All-Star break. Boston goes on to win the American League pennant, the team's first since 1918, but loses the World Series to the St. Louis Cardinals in seven games.

1947

April 14—The Red Sox sign pitcher Johnny Murphy after the Yankees release him.

May 26—The largest single-game crowd at Yankee Stadium to this date—74,747—is witness to a 9-3 Yankee win over the Red Sox.

September 3—The Yankees hit 18 singles against the Red Sox in a game played at Fenway.

September 29—Joe McCarthy, who led the Yankees to nine pennants, is convinced to "un-retire." He signs to manage the Red Sox. Joe Cronin becomes general manager.

October 1—Allie Reynolds of the Yankees scatters nine hits as New York defeats Boston, 10-3. Tommy Henrich's fifth-inning homer puts the game out of reach for Boston.

October 1—Ted Williams wins his second consecutive Triple Crown.

November 27—Setting off a storm of controversy, Joe DiMaggio is named American League MVP by a single point over Ted Williams. Williams, (.343, 32 homers, 114 RBIs) the Triple Crown winner, receives 201 points. A 10th-place vote would have given Williams the needed two points; however, writer Mel Webb leaves Williams off his ballot.

1948

March 29—In a spring training game, the Yankees and Red Sox play through four hours and two minutes to a 2-2 tie. Thirty-three players are used.

October 3—A 10-5 Boston win over the Yankees enables the Sox to tie Cleveland for the pennant and move into the first single-game playoff in American League history. The Red Sox will lose that playoff game to the Indians, 8-3.

1949

March 14—Joe DiMaggio signs a contract for $90,000. Ted Williams earns close to $100,000 a year.

June 29—Boston's Dom DiMaggio, bidding to break his brother Joe's record, has his consecutive-game hitting streak stopped at 34.

June 30—Joe DiMaggio completes one of his best series ever, winding up with four home runs and a single against Boston.

September 25—Seventy-one injuries kept players out of games, but the Yankee keep themselves in first place all season. The Yankees fall into a tie with Boston in a 4-1 loss at Fenway as Mel Parnell defeats Allie Reynolds. Parnell's 25th win gives him a 16-3 home record. Joe DiMaggio listens to the game from a hospital bed recuperating from pneumonia. The Yankees return to New York and are greeted at Grand Central Station by a huge crowd of fans, including Mrs. Babe Ruth, who predicts: "Whoever wins tomorrow should go all the way."

October 1—The Red Sox need to win just one of the season's final two games against the Yankees to clinch the pennant. They don't do it today, blowing a 4-0 lead and losing 5-4 in front of 69,551 at the Stadium. Yankee reliever Joe Page is virtually untouchable in five innings of work. A Johnny Lindell home run is the margin of Yankee victory.

October 2—The Yankees defeat Boston, 5-3, at Yankee Stadium in the final game of the season and take the American League pennant. Red Sox fans again are shocked and disappointed.

Bobby Doerr, Vern Stephens, Johnny Pesky. (Photofest/Icon)

1950

April 18—On Opening Day baseball commissioner Happy Chandler gives Ted Williams his MVP Award, and then governor Paul Dever tosses out the first ball, delighting 31,822 fans. Boston racks Allie Reynolds with a five-run fourth inning, driving him from the game, taking a 9-0 lead over the Yankees. But a nine-run Yankee eighth inning sends the New Yorkers to a 15-10 victory. Billy Martin becomes the first player to get two hits in one inning (eighth) in his first major league game. Tommy Henrich triples twice.

July 1—At Fenway, Whitey Ford makes his major league debut. It is one he says later he will quickly forget—in four and two-thirds innings, the rookie southpaw gives up seven hits, six walks, and five earned runs. Boston rookie Walt Dropo rips a grand slam homer in Boston's 13-4 route.

October 1—Ted Williams records four hits to pace Boston's 7-3 win over the Yankees. Williams has three RBIs to finish with 97 in just 89 games.

1951

April 17—Mickey Mantle makes his major league debut and goes one-for-four in a 4-0 Yankee win over the Red Sox at Yankee Stadium.

May 30—Yankee fans are depressed as rookie Mickey Mantle strikes out five straight times in a doubleheader. Red Sox fans are impressed as Ted Williams scores from second base on a sacrifice bunt and ties the first game with a home run. Boston wins the opener, 11-10, on a home run by Vern Stephens, then takes the nightcap, 9-4.

July 8—A Yankee pitcher fails to complete a game for the 20th straight time at Fenway Park.

July 13—Mickey Mantle strikes out four times in a doubleheader in Boston, and manager Casey Stengel sends him down to the minor league Kansas City Blues in Triple-A.

September 28—In the first game of a doubleheader against Boston at Yankee Stadium, Allie Reynolds tosses his second no-hitter of the season, defeating the Red Sox, 8-0.

1952

January 9—The U.S. Marines announce they will recall Ted Williams to active duty in the Korean War.

May 10—New York's Hank Bauer goes five-for-six in an 18-3 thrashing of Boston at Yankee Stadium.

September 2—The Yankees shut out the Red Sox in both games of a doubleheader, 5-0 and 4-0. Tom Gorman wins the first game, and Ewell Blackwell is the victor in the second.

1953

May 8—Boston snaps a 13-game losing streak to the Yankees, dating back to 1952, with a 2-1 victory at Fenway Park. Billy Goodman wins the game homering off Johnny Sain in the bottom of the 11th inning.

May 9—The first-place Yankees nip Boston at Fenway, 6-4. Mickey Mantle homers off Bill Werle. The Mick's bid for a second home run is denied as Jimmy Piersall makes a great catch in front of the Sox bullpen in right-center field.

1954

April 19—The Yankees sweep two games from the Red Sox on Patriot's Day in Boston. Jim MacDonald pitches a 2-1 one-hitter in the morning game. In the afternoon game, the Yankees roll over Mel Parnell, 5-0. Mickey Mantle hits his first home run of the year.

May 28—At Fenway, a ninth-inning walk to Joe Collins, the 20th of the game, is the winning run. The Yankees edge the Sox, 10-9, overcoming Boston's Jackie Jensen grand slam.

Outfielder Hank Bauer, a Yankee slugger. (Photofest)

September 6—The Yankees use 10 pinch-hitters in a 6-5 victory over the Red Sox.

1955

January 26—Joe DiMaggio is elected to the Baseball Hall of Fame.

April 14—Elston Howard, the first Yankee black player, singles in his first career at-bat in a game against the Red Sox.

July 4—Boston pitchers strike out four Yankee pinch hitters.

August 11—Ted Williams gets his 2,000th hit in a 5-3 Red Sox loss to the Yanks.

September 23—The Yankees beat the Red Sox, 3-2, to clinch the American League pennant.

1956

August 7—The Red Sox fine Ted Williams $5,000 for spitting at Boston fans at Fenway Park after he misplayed a swirling Mickey Mantle fly ball in the 11th inning. A bases-loaded walk to Williams in the bottom of the inning gave Boston a win over the Yankees.

September 21—Bill Skowron has five hits, but the Yankees strand a record 20 base runners, losing to the Red Sox in Boston, 13-9. A Mickey Mantle 480-foot homer into the centerfield bleachers lands a foot from the top. The Mick's three hits puts his average at .352, just four points behind Ted Williams.

September 30—Mickey Mantle nips Ted Williams for the batting title on the final day of the season to win baseball's Triple Crown. He finishes with a .353 average, 52 home runs and 130 RBIs.

1957

April 20—New York's Moose Skowron homers to the right of the center field flagpole out of Fenway, just one of only six balls ever hit out of there to that point in time.

November 22—Mickey Mantle is named American League Most Valuable Player, angering Red Sox fans who thought that Ted Williams should have won the award. Boston owner Tom Yawkey called sportswriters "incompetent and unqualified."

1958

September 2—Yogi Berra and Mickey Mantle hit back-to-back home runs breaking a scoreless tie with the Red Sox at Yankee Stadium. The Yankees go on to win, 6-1.

September 3—It's the Mickey and Yogi show again at Yankee Stadium. Mantle homers in the eighth, and Berra follows with a three-run shot in the ninth, as New York overcomes a 5-3 deficit to beat Boston, 8-5.

September 24—Mickey Mantle hits his 42nd home run of season in Boston's home finale. The Yankees win, 7-5.

1959

April 12—It's 42 degrees as the Yankees and Red Sox play their season opener in front of just 22,559 fans. New

Yankee pilot Casey Stengel, always making adjustments. (Frommer Archives)

York wins, 3-2, on Bob Turley's two-hitter. Norm Siebern homers for the Yankees in the eighth inning.

April 17—Boston pitcher Tom Brewer avenges an opening-day defeat to the Yankees and Bob Turley, throwing a two-hit shutout in Boston's 4-0 win at Fenway Park.

July 11—A 10th-inning grand slam home run by Boston's Don Buddin defeats the Yankees, 8-4.

July 13—Four days and 20 years after their historic 1939 five-game sweep of the Yankees, the Red Sox do it again, romping to a 13-3 win. Gene Stephens, who had come into the game as a pinch runner for Ted Williams, hits a grand slam home run as Boston bats around later in that inning.

August 14—The Red Sox defeat the Yankees, 11-6, aided by a pinch-hit grand slam by Vic Wertz off Ryne Duren.

1960

April 19—Boston mayor John Collins, wheel chair bound from polio, tosses the first ball, and Roger Maris makes his Yankee debut on Opening Day Patriot's Day at Fenway Park. Maris goes four-for-five with two home runs and four RBIs, and the Yankees win the game, 8-4, behind Jim Coates.

September 6—In his final game at Yankee Stadium, Ted Williams records his 518th career homer, pacing Boston's 7-1 win.

September 25—At Fenway Park, Casey Stengel clinches his 10th pennant in 12 years as Yankee manager. Ralph Terry pitches New York to a 4-3 win over the Red Sox.

September 30—The Yankees set an American League record for home runs as they defeat the Red Sox 6-5. Tony Kubek and Jesse Gonder hit New York's 191st and 192nd homers as the Yankees win their 13th straight game.

October 2—The Yankees win their 15th straight game closing out the 1960 season, beating the Red Sox, 8-7, on Dale Long's two-run homer in the ninth inning. Pittsburgh defeats New York in a seven-game World Series as Bill Mazeroski hits a home run in the bottom of the ninth inning of Game 7 for a 10-9 Pirates victory. There was much cheering in Boston.

1961

May 29—Mickey Mantle hits his first home run in two weeks, but the Yankees fall to the Red Sox, 2-1 at Fenway Park. Ike Delock out-pitches Whitey Ford for the victory.

May 30—Mickey Mantle and Roger Maris preview their historic race for Babe Ruth's single-season home run record. Both hit two home runs in a 12-3 drubbing of the Red Sox at Fenway Park. Moose Skowron also homers twice for the Yankees, and the trio ties a major league record for most players on a team, hitting multiple homers in a nine-inning game.

May 31—Mickey Mantle and Roger Maris homer in New York's 7-6 win over Boston at Fenway Park.

October 1—In the last game of the season, Roger Maris hits his 61st home run of the year, breaking Babe Ruth's single-season record. The historic shot comes off a 2-0 fastball from Boston pitcher Tracy Stallard. The home run gives the Yankees a 1-0 win, their 109th of the season, a victory shy of the franchise's 1927 record.

1962

September 9—Boston's Lou Clinton homers, triples and singles and makes four deft defensive plays. Still it requires 16 innings of baseball before the Red Sox claim the victory, scoring six times in the top of the 16th for a 9-3 win at Yankee Stadium. Dick Radatz pitches nine innings in relief for the winners.

1963

June 23—Boston first baseman Dick Stuart, known as "Dr. Strangeglove" for his ineptitude as a fielder, sets a major league fielding record. In the first inning Stuart snatches three first-inning ground balls and tosses to pitcher Bob Heffner for putouts, but the Yankees pound the Sox, 8-0, at Fenway Park.

1964

April 16—An 11-inning effort by Whitey Ford goes for naught as the Yankee left-hander loses to the Red Sox, 4-3, at Yankee Stadium. A Bob Tillman triple is the table setter as pinch runner Roman Mejias scores the winning run on a wild pitch in the top of the 11th.

April 17—At Fenway Park, in a JFK memorial game, the Red Sox nip the Yankees, 4-1.

April 20—Yankee rookie Bob Meyer debuts at Fenway Park and loses 4-0 to the Red Sox. Meyer is the last Yankee rookie pitcher in the 20th century to open in Boston.

1965

May 10—At Fenway Park, the ninth-place Yankees lose 3-2 to the Red Sox. Boston starter Jim Lonborg is lifted, and Dick Radatz gets the final out. It is Lonborg's first major league win.

July 20—Yankees pitcher Mel Stottlemyre hits an inside-the-park grand slam, the first pitcher to perform that feat in more than 50 years. The home run provides the margin of victory in the Yankees' 6-3 win over the Red Sox at Yankee Stadium.

1966

June 29—Mickey Mantle opens the scoring in the first inning with a three-run homer at Fenway. In the third inning the Mick homers between circuit clouts by Bobby Richardson and Joe Pepitone. New York wins the game, 6-5.

1967

April 14—Behind rookie pitcher Bill Rohr, 21, the Red Sox shade the Yankees, 3-0, at the Stadium. Rohr's no-hitter is broken up by Elston Howard's single with two outs in the ninth inning.

April 16—The Yankees in New York beat the Red Sox, 7-6, on Joe Pepitone's two-out single in the bottom of the 18th inning. The game lasts five hours and 50 minutes. Carl Yastrzemski and Tony Conigliaro each record five hits for Boston.

April 21—Red Sox rookie Bill Rohr continues to have the Yankees' number, defeating Mel Stottlemyre, 6-1, at Fenway Park. But Rohr won't win another game with the Red Sox, and is out of baseball within two years.

May 14—Mickey Mantle hammers his 500th career home run.

August 3—The Yankees, with no chance of success in 1967, send catcher Elston Howard to the Red Sox, who are in the midst of a pennant race. New York receives cash and two players to be named later. Down the stretch, Howard hits only .147 for the Red Sox but helps steady the pitching staff. All New England cheers as Boston goes on to win the pennant, finishing 20 games ahead of the ninth-place Yankees.

August 8—The Yankees purchase the contract of catcher Bob Tillman from the Red Sox for the $20,000 waiver fee.

August 29—For the second time in 1967, the Red Sox lose a game to the Yankees that goes at least 18 innings. This time, New York tops Boston, 4-3, in 20 innings, in the second game of a doubleheader. Boston had won the first game, 2-1.

1968

September 20—Mickey Mantle hits his last home run, number 536, off Boston pitcher Jim Lonborg at Yankee Stadium. The Red Sox win, 4-3, paced by Carl Yastrzemski's three hits.

September 27—Mickey Mantle flies out in his final plate at-bat at Fenway Park. He is replaced by Andy Kosko whose homer ties the score in the eighth inning. Joe Pepitone's home run in the ninth gives New York a 4-3 win.

September 29—In the "Year of the Pitcher," Carl Yastrzemski goes 0-for-five in the season finale against the Yankees but still wins the battle title with a .301 batting average—the lowest to ever lead the league. No one else hits .300 in the American League this season. The Yankees beat the Red Sox, 4-3.

1969

April 28—The Red Sox streak of home runs in consecutive games is snapped at 11. New York pitcher Fritz Peterson shuts them out,1-0, at Yankee Stadium.

1970

January 17—The Yankees draft super prospect Fred Lynn in the first round of the January phase of the annual free-agent draft, but the outfielder does not sign with the team from the Bronx and later joins the Boston Red Sox.

April 7—The Red Sox jump out to a 4-0 lead over the Yankees on Opening Day at the Stadium and eke out a 4-3 win. Mel Stottlemyre starts his fourth straight season-opener.

1971

April 6—The Red Sox win their second straight opener against the Yankees, a 3-1 victory at Fenway Park. Boston's Ray Culp beats New York's Stan Bahnsen.

1972

March 22—The Yankees acquire southpaw relief pitcher Sparky Lyle from the Red Sox for first baseman Danny Cater. It will prove to be one of the best New York trades ever. Posting a 1.91 ERA in his first season in the Bronx, Lyle leads the American League in saves with 35. In 1977, he will become the first American League reliever to win the Cy Young Award. He helps the Yankees win three straight pennants from 1976 to 1978.

September 7—Tommy Harper and Rico Petrocelli pace a 10-4 Red Sox victory over the Yankees with three-run homers. The victory puts the Sox in first place over the Tigers, but Boston will finish the strike-shortened season in second place, a half-game behind Detroit.

1973

August 1—Red Sox catcher Carlton Fisk and Yankee catcher Thurman Munson exchange blows at Fenway Park after a collision at home plate. Munson tried to score from third base on a missed bunt attempt. The Red Sox win the game, 3-2, although there is still doubt as to who won the fight.

1974

September 9—A 6-3 Yankee win over the Red Sox is New York's first triumph at Fenway Park since July 31, 1973.

1975

July 27—In the not-so-friendly confines of Shea Stadium (Yankee Stadium is being refurbished) Red Sox outfielder Fred Lynn's running, stumbling catch enables Boston to win the first game of a doubleheader against the Yankees. The Red Sox victory ends Yankee pennant hopes and closes out Bill Virdon's future as manager. For good measure the Sox win the second game for a shutout sweep.

1976

May 20—A spirited fracas takes place at Yankee Stadium after Lou Piniella barrels into Carlton Fisk at the plate. Red Sox lefthander Bill Lee injures his left shoulder in the melee.

1977

May 24—At Yankee Stadium, New York rallies to beat Boston, 6-5, thanks to back-to-back home runs by Carlos May and Graig Nettles.

June 18—Fenway Park is jammed with the largest Saturday afternoon crowd (34,603) in two decades. Boston cruises, 10-4, on five home runs, but the real story is the blowup in New York's dugout. Yankees outfielder Reggie Jackson dogs it on a Jim Rice bloop double, and is taken out of the game by manager Billy Martin. The two men almost come to blows in the dugout in front of national television cameras.

June 19—An 11-1 rout gives Boston a three-game series sweep over the Yankees. Boston is paced by five home runs, including Carl Yastrzemski's 460-foot shot that is the only ball to ever reach the right field roof facade. The Red Sox out-homer New York 16-0 in the series.

June 24—A 6-5 New York win at the Stadium breaks a seven-game Boston winning streak. Three Red Sox homers set a major league record of 33 home runs in 10 straight games.

September 28—Tiny Fenway Park draws its two-millionth fan of the season for the first time ever and becomes just the fourth stadium in the American League to break that attendance plateau. Boston makes a run for the division title but finishes two and a half games behind the first-place Yankees.

1978

January 13—Joe McCarthy, who managed on both sides of the rivalry, dies at age 90.

July 19—The Yankees trail Boston by 14 games in the standings.

September 7—The Yankees begin a four-game series with the Red Sox at Fenway Park, with Boston protecting a four-game lead. New York takes the first game, 15-3, setting the tone for the rest of the series.

September 10—New York completes its "Boston Massacre," a four-game sweep of the Red Sox that ends with the teams tied for first place after a ferocious stretch run by the Yankees. New York chases Boston pitcher Bobby Sprague after just two-thirds of an inning, and wins 7-4. The Yankees outscore the Bo Sox 42-9 during the series.

October 1—The Red Sox catch the Yankees on the final day of the regular season by beating the Toronto Blue Jays, 5-0, at Fenway Park, for their eighth straight victory. New York, with a chance to clinch the division, loses at home to the Cleveland Indians, 9-2.

October 2—The Yankees win the American League East, edging the Red Sox, 5-4, in just the second one-game playoff game in American League history. The day will always be remembered for Bucky Dent's three-run homer over the Green Monster. It's exactly 29 years to the date that New York won the pennant on the final day of the season with a 5-3 win over Boston. The Yankees go on to beat the Los Angeles Dodgers in the World Series for the second straight year.

November 7—Boston's Jim Rice nips New York's Ron Guidry, 353-291, to win the American League MVP Award. Rice led the league in hits (213), triples (15), home runs (46), RBIs (139), and slugging (.600), and became the first American Leaguer to accumulate 400 total bases in a season since Joe DiMaggio in 1937. Guidry had gone 25-3 with a 1.74 ERA.

November 21—After eight seasons with the Red Sox, pitcher Luis Tiant, 38, signs as a free agent with the Yankees.

Luis Tiant as a Red Sox pitcher. (Photofest)

York.

1979

July 1—Sliding home in a 6-5 loss to the Yankees, Boston speedster Jerry Remy, batting .304 on the season, injures a knee. He appears in only seven more games in 1979.

September 12—Carl Yastrzemski singles off Jim Beattie of the Yankees for his 3,000th career hit. Boston wins, 9-2, at Fenway Park.

November 8—Boston free agent first baseman Bob Watson is signed by New

1980

September 21—The Red Sox are eliminated from playoff contention when Yankee star pitcher Ron Guidry wins his 15th game of the season, a 3-0 shutout of Boston.

October 1—The Red Sox fire manager Don Zimmer who had guided Boston to a 411-304 record, a .575 percentage, from 1976 to 1980. Zimmer will go on to manage the Texas Rangers and Chicago Cubs before becoming Yankee manager Joe Torre's right-hand man.

October 27—Former Yankee manager Ralph Houk is named Red Sox skipper. He will last five seasons with Boston.

1981

September 12—Yankee catcher Rick Cerone hits a double in the bottom of the ninth inning to break up a no-hitter by Boston rookie Bob Ojeda. Dave Winfield follows with another double, but Red Sox reliever Mark Clear comes on to save the 2-1 victory.

September 19—The Red Sox score seven runs in the eighth inning and defeat the Yankees, 8-5, at Fenway Park.

1982

June 14—New York's Ron Guidry stops the Red Sox to run his record to 8-1. For the remainder of the season, however, Guidry manages a 6-7 record and a 4.47 ERA.

August 6—The Yankees trade shortstop Bucky Dent to the Texas Rangers for Lee Mazzilli. Dent, whose 1978 home run at Fenway Park led the Yankees to a dramatic victory over the Red Sox in a one-game playoff, is hitting only .169 at the time of the trade.

1983

July 4—Dave Righetti no-hits Boston. It is the first Yankees no-hitter since Don Larsen's perfect game in the 1956 World Series.

1984

September 14—The Yankees defeat the Red Sox 7-1, dropping Boston 16 and a half games back (with 16 remaining)—eliminating them from contention.

September 25—Ralph Houk, who managed both the Yankees and Red Sox, announces he will retire as Boston manager at the end of the season. Houk, 65, got his start with the Yankees in 1961, replacing Casey Stengel. He took over as Red Sox manager in 1981.

1985

April 8—At Fenway Park, 46-year-old Yankees pitcher Phil Niekro becomes the second-oldest pitcher to start an opening-day game. Niekro lasts only four innings, and the Red Sox go on to win, 9-2.

1986

March 28—In a trade of designated hitters, the Yankees send Don Baylor to the Red Sox for Mike Easler.

October 2—Breaking Earle Combs's team record set in 1927, Don Mattingly gets his 232nd hit of the season in a 6-1 win over the Red Sox.

October 4—Dave Righetti again makes history against the Red Sox, saving both games of a Yankees doubleheader sweep for a single-season major league record 46 saves.

1987

June 26—Boston ace Roger Clemens fails to hold a 9-0 lead against the Yankees, who win 12-11 in 10 innings. Boston's Wade Boggs has his 25-game hitting streak snapped.

September 29—New York's Don Mattingly sets a major league single-season record with his sixth grand slam, which comes off Boston's Bruce Hurst. The Yankees win, 6-0.

1988

June 13—Joining Ted Williams and Carl Yastrzemski, Boston's Jim Rice hits his 200th home run at Fenway Park, in a 12-6 loss to the Yankees.

1989

September 25—Boston's Wade Boggs gets four hits in a 7-4 win over the Yankees, becoming the first player in major league history to get 200 hits and 100 walks in four straight seasons. Boggs breaks a record he shared with Yankee Lou Gehrig.

1990

June 7—Greg Harris and Jeff Reardon combine on a one-hitter, as the Red Sox beat the Yankees, 3-0.

September 1—Boston's Mike Greenwell hits an inside-the-park grand slam in a 15-1 victory over the Yankees at Fenway Park. It's the third inside-the-park grand slam of the season, the first time that's happened since 1947.

1991

February 8—Red Sox pitcher Roger Clemens signs a four-year contract extension worth $21.5 million, making him the highest paid player in baseball at the time. Boston begins the 1991 season with the highest payroll in baseball.

1992

June 15—Red Sox reliever Jeff Reardon picks up his record-breaking 342nd career save in a 1-0 victory over the Yankees. The Sox will trade Reardon to Atlanta later that year, and the following season, Cardinals stopper Lee Smith will break Reardon's record a year before being traded to the Yankees.

August 7—Red Sox slugger Jack Clark, a former Yankee, files for bankruptcy. He lists debts of $11.5 million and assets of $4.8 million.

December 15—After his first season ever to bat below .300, a .259 batting average with the Red Sox, Wade Boggs signs as a three-year free agent deal with the Yankees after 11 seasons with Boston, which had refused to give him a long-term contract. He will rebound in 1993, batting .302 for New York.

1993

August 31—The Cardinals trade reliever Lee Smith to the Yankees for pitcher Richard Batchelor. Smith had pitched for the Red Sox from 1988-90.

1994

May 8—Danny Tartabull, Mike Stanley and Gerald Williams key an 8-4 Yankees victory over the Red Sox with consecutive home runs in the sixth inning at Yankee Stadium.

1995

May 2—Former Seton Hall University teammates Mo Vaughn and John Valentin hit grand slam home runs in consecutive innings, pacing Boston's 8-0 romp over the Yankees in the Bronx.

October 3—The division champion Red Sox and the wild card Yankees begin separate postseason playoff series. The Yankees overcome Ken Griffey's two home runs, winning their opener over Seattle, 9-6, only to lose the series, 3-2. The Indians defeat the Red Sox, 4-0, to start a three game sweep of Boston.

1996

July 1—Pitcher Roger Clemens of Boston loses for only the third time at Yankee Stadium, as Jimmy Key out-duels him, 2-0.

July 17—The Red Sox blow a 9-2, seventh-inning lead over the Yankees at Fenway and trail 11-9 after eight innings. But a three-run home half of the ninth gives the BoSox a 12-11 victory.

September 28—In his final appearance for Boston, Roger Clemens strikes out 10 but loses to the Yankees, 4-2, at Fenway Park. Mike Aldrete and Bernie Williams homer for New York.

December 13—Roger Clemens signs a three-year, $24.75 million contract with the Toronto Blue Jays.

1997

May 22—Collecting 19 hits, leaving 16 runners on bases, the BoSox rip the Yankees at the Stadium, 8-2 behind homers by Mike Stanley and Mo Vaughn and Will Cordero's five hits.

May 30—Mo Vaughn homers three times, and goes four-for-four, in Boston's 10-4 rout of New York at Fenway Park.

August 13—The Yankees trade minor league hurler Tony Armas and a player to be named later to the Red Sox for catcher-first baseman Mike Stanley and Randy Brown, a minor league infielder.

September 9—Boston shortstop Nomar Garciaparra drives in his 86th and 87th RBIs, breaking a 40-year-old major league record for leadoff men, but the Yankees beat the Red Sox, 8-6, at Fenway Park.

1998

September 29—Both the Yankees and Red Sox are in the playoffs again, despite finishing light years apart in the American League East. New York finishes 22 games ahead of wild card Boston. In their playoff openers, the Yankees nip Texas, 2-0, while the Red Sox win their opener over Cleveland, 11-3. Boston is eliminated in the division series while the Yankees go on to win the World Series.

1999

February 18—The Yankees acquire one-time Boston superstar Roger Clemens from the Blue Jays for pitchers David Wells, Graeme Lloyd and infielder Homer Bush. Clemens, who won two Cy Young Awards with Toronto, is coming off a 20-6, 271-strikeout year. He had left the Sox in 1997 as a free agent.

September 10—Pedro Martinez strikes out 17 Yankees, one-hitting New York, 3-1, at Yankee Stadium—the most strikeouts against a Yankee team ever. The only New York hit is a Chili Davis homer in the second inning.

September 12—The Red Sox beat the Yankees, 4-1, in front of 50,027 at Yankee Stadium. The win completes Boston's first three-game sweep at the Stadium since 1986.

September 21—Pedro Martinez strikes out 12 and breaks Roger Clemens's Red Sox team record of 291 strikeouts in a season.

October 13—For the first time since 1978, the Red Sox and Yankees meet in a playoff game—this time with the American League pennant on the line. New York, which won the division title over the wild card Red Sox by four games, takes the series opener, 4-3, on Bernie Williams's home run in the bottom of the 10th inning.

October 16—In a much anticipated pitching match-up of Boston ace Pedro Martinez and New York ace Roger Clemens, the Sox crush the Yankees, 13-1, at Fenway Park. Clemens lasts only two innings against his former team, giving up five runs on six hits. Martinez, meanwhile, gives up only two hits while striking out 12 in seven shutout innings. Boston cuts the Yankees' series lead to 2-1.

October 18—The Yankees beat the Red Sox, 6-1, to win the series, four games to one. Orlando Hernandez picks up the win and the ALCS MVP award.

October 20—In a celebration of Boston's first ALCS appearance in nine years, a rally is staged on the steps of City Hall. Two hundred and fifty fans are present.

December 10—In the same season that "the Curse of the Bambino" strikes again, an Associated Press panel votes Babe Ruth "Player of the Century."

2000

June 19—The Yankees beat the Red Sox 22-1, Boston's most-lopsided home loss ever. New York scores 16 runs in the last two innings of the game.

2001

January 12—Boston signs pitcher David Cone as a free agent. The right-handed hurler had rejected a Yankee offer to attempt to make the club as a fifth starter.

Cone, who struggled through a 4-14 season in 2000, will go 9-7 for Boston in 2001, his last season in the big leagues.

May 23—Behind Derek Jeter's five hits, the Yankees defeat the Red Sox, 7-3. Ex-Yankee David Cone is charged with the loss.

May 30—Pedro Martinez is victorious over the Yankees for the first time in more than a year. He had dropped five straight decisions to the New Yorkers. The next day Pedro made little of "The Curse," telling reporters: "Wake up the Bambino and let me face him—I'll drill him in the ass." Boston was defeated by the Yankees in the seven remaining games in 2001 after Martinez's comment.

September 2—Mike Mussina comes within one strike of a perfect game against the Red Sox, giving up a two-out, two-strike single to Carl Everett in the ninth inning. Everett's soft line drive falls between shortstop Derek Jeter and left fielder Chuck Knoblauch. Mussina ekes out a 1-0 win over ex-Yankee David Cone.

2002

August 28—Yankee pitcher Mike Mussina blanks the Red Sox, 7-0, at Fenway Park, a day after David Wells and Steve Karsay combine on a 6-0 shutout over Boston. It was the first time since 1943 that the Yankees had back-to-back shutouts at Fenway.

September 3—Roger Clemens fans ten Red Sox batters in seven and one third innings, recording his 100th win since leaving Boston.

November 20—Bucky Dent, 50, is named manager of the Columbus AAA Yankee farm team.

December 26—Red Sox President Larry Lucchino labels the Yankees the "Evil Empire" and says its tentacles extend even into Latin America. The comment is made after New York signs Cuban ace hurler Contreras, whom Boston was looking to add to its staff.

December 30—Yankee principal owner George Steinbrenner in a *New York Daily News* interview responds to Lucchino's comments: "That's B.S. That's how a sick person thinks. I've learned this about Lucchino: he's baseball's foremost chameleon of all time. He changes colors depending on where's he's standing. He's been at Baltimore and he deserted them there, and then went out to San Diego, and look at what trouble they're in out there. When he was in San Diego, he was a big man for the small markets. Now he's in Boston and he's for the big markets. He talks out of both sides of his mouth."

2003

August 22—New York Yankees owner George Steinbrenner makes a $10,000 donation to the Jimmy Fund, the longtime Boston charity that works with children with cancer.

August 31—Roger Clemens notches his 100th win at Fenway Park in his final regular-season start there as the Yankees coast to an 8-4 victory over the Red Sox.

October 17—An 11th-inning home run by Aaron Boone off Tim Wakefield gives the Yankees a 6-5 come-from-behind stunning triumph over the Red Sox and the American League championship.

October 25—Red Sox nation rejoices in the Florida Marlins' 2-0 triumph over the New York Yankees in the World Series.

October 27—The Red Sox let manager Grady Little go less than two weeks after Boston blew a chance to play in the World Series. Little paid the price for sticking with Pedro Martinez in Game 7 of the ALCS against the Yankees.

November 28—Curt Schilling, a five-time All-Star widely ranked among baseball's most dominant pitchers, agrees to waive a no-trade clause in exchange for a two-year, $25.5-million contract extension for 2005 and '06 with a $13 million mutual option to remain with the Red Sox in '07. The Schilling trade is viewed as a shift in the balance of power in the Red Sox-Yankees rivalry.

December 4—The Yankees match the Red Sox in the offseason arms race by trading for Expos pitcher Javier Vazquez. New York sends first baseman Nick Johnson, outfielder Juan Rivera and left-hander Randy Choate to Montreal. On the same day, the Red Sox hire Terry Francona as their new manager, replacing Grady Little.

December 17—The Yankees continue their offseason makeover by signing Atlanta slugger Gary Sheffield to a three-year, $39 million contract. Still, Yankees manager Joe Torre says he's not sure his team is the favorite over the Red Sox going into the 2004 season. "If we were better than them last year by a very narrow margin, they have certainly caught up at the very least because of their pitching moves, he said.

2003 PLAYOFFS: THE CURSE LIVES ON

The Curse of the Bambino taunted the Red Sox even before their showdown with the Yankees in the 2003 American League Championship Series. Playing in Oakland in the first round, the Sox were greeted with signs displaying the year 1918—the last time the team had won the World Series.

The mocking only accelerated when the team arrived at Yankee Stadium with the pennant on the line. Fans held up banners that said, "1918, What a Wonderful Year," and "The Curse Must Live On," along with pictures of Babe Ruth, whose sale to the Yankees in 1920 jinxed Boston for the rest of the century. Since that one-sided deal, the Yankees had out-championed the Sox, 26-0, and in 2003, for the sixth straight year, New York had finished first in the American League East, and Boston had finished second. In their last postseason match-up, the 1999 ALCS, the Yankees had knocked out the Red Sox, four games to one. But the 2003 teams were much more evenly matched. New York had taken the season series, 10 games to nine.

Many Red Sox fans trekked to Ruth's grave, at Gate of Heaven cemetery, 20 miles north of Yankee Stadium in Hawthorne, N.Y., pleading with him to lift the curse. Some brought beer. Yankee fans, meanwhile, urged the Bambino to leave the curse untouched.

The Sox were the sentimental favorites to advance to the World Series, along with the Chicago Cubs, whose championship drought had lasted even longer—to 1908. Even New York City's paper of record, *The New York Times*, endorsed a Cubs-Red Sox World Series.

"With all due respect to our New York readership—Yankee fans among them—to George Steinbrenner and to the Yankees themselves, we find it hard to resist the emotional tug and symmetrical possibilities of a series between teams that seem to have been put on earth to tantalize and then crush their zealous fans," read an October 8 *Times* editorial. "Cold reality favors the Yankees; warm sentiment, which is at the heart of baseball and to which we are always susceptible, favors one or the other of baseball's most reliable losers." The

editorial failed to mention that the New York Times Company held a 17 percent stake in the Red Sox ownership group.

Both teams approached the '03 series with anticipation. "I think it's the best rivalry in any sport," said Yankees shortstop Derek Jeter. "The fans, the history, the proximity. It seems like every time we play each other, there's a new story."

"This is like Magic and Bird," said Boston first baseman Kevin Millar. "This is an amazing series, all year long. Even the three-game series was like the postseason. We match up very well. This should be the World Series, Sox and Yankees." Millar, a Texan playing in the heart of New England, had kicked off a "Cowboy up" rallying cry for the team during the stretch drive. Then in the playoffs, his shaved head became an inspiration for teammates, who followed his lead in a show of solidarity.

Boston brought to the series one of the most powerful offenses in baseball history—a major league record .491 slugging percentage, besting the 1927 Yankees—against an aging New York dynasty with a talented and veteran pitching staff.

In the first round of the playoffs, the Yankees knocked off the Minnesota Twins, three games to one, earning two full days of rest before their meeting with Boston. The Red Sox, meanwhile, had to fight back from a 2-0 deficit to beat the As, three games to two. Derek Lowe, normally a Boston starter, came in to save the fifth and deciding game in Oakland. He fanned two batters looking with the potential tying and winning runs on base.

The Red Sox then boarded a red-eye flight to Newark and got to their New York City hotel at 8:30 a.m., 36 hours before their first game at Yankee Stadium. "Everyone in the clubhouse wants to go through the Yankees to get to the World Series, to battle them," said Red Sox general manager Theo Epstein.

Politicians from New England to New York City to Washington, D.C. got in on the act. New York mayor Mike Bloomberg, who grew up in Boston, quickly declared his allegiance to the Yankees. "I share a bond with Yankees past and present who have left Boston to find success in the greatest city in the world," he said, implicitly comparing himself to Ruth.

Presidential candidate Howard Dean, a New York City native who went on to become governor of Vermont, made it known that he had switched his allegiances from the Yankees to the Red Sox after Yankees ace Roger Clemens beaned Mike Piazza of the Mets in 2000. That didn't stop rival John Kerry, a Massachusetts senator, from trying to bait Dean into a bet over the series, which Dean declined. At stake was not so much the hearts of Bostonians, but the votes of neighboring New Hampshire, home of the first presidential primary the next year.

Movie stars and television personalities joined the bandwagon as well. Among those at the opening game at Yankee Stadium were Denzel Washington, Robin Williams, *Saturday Night Live*'s Seth Meyers, and Jerry Springer. Even the bald eagle Challenger made an appearance, nearly taking Jeter's head off as it flew toward the players in a pregame ceremony. Ruth was there, too, in spirit, as Yankee fans brought life-size cutouts of the famed slugger, hoping to spook the Sox.

Bernie Williams at work. (P. Speranza/behindthebombers.com)

"I don't think we're battling the Curse of the Bambino here," said Boston manager Grady Little, his laid back North Carolina accent a little out of place in New England. "We're battling the New York Yankees, and this group of renegades that I'm putting out on the field, they don't care. They care about their Harley-Davidsons running good enough that they won't run off the Tobin Bridge over there in Boston, and playing baseball."

"It's different people, different personalities, different chemistry and different karma," said Larry Lucchino, the Red Sox's chief executive. "Oh, and better hitting."

The loose Red Sox took the first game, 5-2 victory, as knuckleballer Tim Wakefield, barely breaking 70 mph on the radar gun, defeated Yankees ace Mike Mussina. David Ortiz, a player that George Steinbrenner had sought during the off season, hit an upper deck home run for the Sox.

New York took the second game, 6-2, behind the pitching of its playoff stopper, Andy Pettitte. First baseman Nick Johnson's two-run homer erased a 1-0 deficit to put the Yanks ahead. In the seventh, the Yankees brought in Jose Contreras, a Cuban pitcher they had signed to a $32 million contract, outbidding the Sox. Contreras got Nomar Garciaparra to pop up to end the inning, then struck out Manny Ramirez and popped up Ortiz and Millar in the eighth. "I love the way the young Cuban pitched," Steinbrenner gloated after the game. "I thought that was the best part of the night." Contreras's signing had provoked Lucchino to label the Yankees the "Evil Empire."

That set up the game and match-up everyone had been waiting for: Pedro Martinez against Roger Clemens, Game 3, Fenway Park. In 1999, these two had also squared off in Game 3 of the ALCS at Fenway, but the Yankees had carried a 2-0 lead into that showdown. With the '03 series tied up, and their ace going against an aging star, New England fans liked their chances. And for once, they had a bit of history on their side. In that 1999 game, the Sox had rocked Clemens on their way to a 13-1 drubbing. Boston was also getting back its sparkplug centerfielder, Johnny Damon, who had missed the first two games after suffering a concussion in a collision with second baseman Damian Jackson in the Oakland series.

Clemens, 41, was making what was billed as his final start at Fenway Park, where he had pitched for 13 seasons as a member of the Red Sox. Martinez, 31, was in the prime of his career, coming off a league-low 2.22 ERA and a 14-4 record. The front page of the *Boston Herald* the day of the big game read, "Fight of the Century," with Martinez and Clemens squaring off in a boxing pose. Earlier that season, Pedro had nailed Jeter and Alfonso Soriano, sending both to the hospital for X-rays. Clemens dismissed much of the hype, saying, "We are not in a boxing ring." But the tabloid headline writers got it right.

The Sox jumped out to a quick 2-0 lead in the late-afternoon shadows, on a first-inning single by Manny Ramirez. Jeter tied it up on a solo homer in the third. The Yankees went up 3-2 in the fourth on ground-rule double by Hideki Matsui, putting runners on second and third with nobody out against the struggling Martinez. Up came right fielder Karim Garcia, who had driven in New York's

first run earlier in the game. Pedro came in high and hard, his fastball screaming towards Garcia's head. The Yankee batter ducked, and the ball caromed off his back. Garcia glared and yelled at Martinez on his way to first base. Moments later, the burly Yankee took Boston second baseman Todd Walker out with a late, hard slide, and then jawed with both Walker and Martinez as he trotted back to the dugout.

Then things really spun out of control. Yankees catcher Jorge Posada yelled at Martinez from the New York dugout. Martinez took his finger, pointed at his own head, and yelled, "I'll hit you in the head, too!" That prompted Yankee bench coach Don Zimmer, who had been Red Sox manager during their 1978 collapse to the Yankees, to yell out at Pedro.

When the Red Sox came to bat in the bottom of the fourth, now trailing 4-2, Clemens threw a pitch high, but not particularly inside, to Manny Ramirez. The Boston slugger ducked, then went into a rage, yelling out to Clemens, "Fuck you!" while holding his bat menacingly. Clemens repeated the phrase right back at Ramirez. Benches emptied from both teams as players restrained a snarling Ramirez.

But no one thought to put a block on the portly, even cuddly, Zimmer, who, as a player 50 years earlier, had spent nearly two weeks in a coma after getting hit in the head with a pitch. Sprinting around the scrum at the speed of a turtle, Zimmer finally made it over to Pedro, and threw a left hook in the pitcher's general vicinity. Martinez grabbed at Zimmer's head with both hands and threw the 72-year-old man down. Zimmer went flying, tumbling end-over-end a few times, before

Frommer Archives

Boston police and Yankees gathered around to make sure he was OK. The umpires huddled during a 15-minute break, but nobody was thrown out. As a precaution against an incensed crowd, Fenway Park stopped selling beer. Meanwhile, both pitchers settled down after that, each pitching three scoreless innings before being pulled.

Most observers agreed that Pedro had hit Garcia on purpose. "You saw it," Jeter said. "He didn't miss with many spots with the rest of his pitches, did he?"

"He was absolutely trying to hit me," fumed Garcia. "He's got good control, and all of a sudden he throws at my head." Martinez said he was trying to get his fastball "up and in."

Yankee players also criticized Martinez for tossing Zimmer to the ground. "What Pedro did was ridiculous, way out of line," said Yankee relieve Jeff Nelson. "This guy is a senior citizen. It's not just a question of respect, but whether he runs at you or not. How much can he hurt you? You can't duck out of the way?" From New York City, Mayor Bloomberg said Martinez would have been arrested had he done the same thing at Yankee Stadium.

Martinez expressed remorse over the incident with Zimmer, although he didn't apologize. "I would never raise my hand against

him," the pitcher said. "I was just trying to dodge him and push him away."

"If you look back at the whole incident, I don't see why he had so much [anger] with what went on in the game," he added. "I'm trying to pitch and actually to get outs, because I needed outs at that point. I was the one in trouble. I didn't want to dig myself a bigger hole."

Red Sox second baseman Todd Walker defended his pitcher. "We have the utmost respect for Don Zimmer," Walker said. "He put himself at risk by charging Pedro the way he did. And that's a sad thing. Nobody in this clubhouse blames Pedro for what he did."

The game looked liked it would finish uneventfully until a ninth-inning fracas in the Yankee bullpen. Boston grounds crew member Paul Williams, 24, standing in the Yankees bullpen to remove debris, either pumped his fist in the air, as the Red Sox claimed, or waved a rally flag to irritate New York's relievers, as the Yankees insisted. In any event, he got into a tussle with Yankee reliever Jeff Nelson, and then right fielder Garcia, already hot from the beaning, hopped over the short right field wall to get a piece of the action. Afterwards, the Red Sox took Williams to a hospital, claiming he had cleat marks on his backs and arms. The team, trying to win the public relations war with the Yankees, said that Williams was a teacher who taught children with disabilities, prompting reporters to burst out laughing.

Two Boston police officers who saw the incident—one from each bullpen—issued a

AP/WWP

report saying the Nelson and Garcia had engaged in "an unprovoked attack" on Williams, and announced that summonses would be sought for the two Yankees for assault and battery. "Nelson was observed pushing/grabbing the victim in the chest area, at which time both parties fell to the ground, where Jeff Nelson began punching and flaring his legs at the victim," the report said. Given the emotions in the partisan city, police may have considered handing the case off to federal authorities.

"When this series began, everyone knew it was going to be a battle," Red Sox manager Grady Little said after the game. "But I think we've upgraded it from a battle to a war."

"It's pathetic, it's shameful and, the worst part, it was anticipated," said Yankees president Randy Levine. "This is unacceptable. There was an atmosphere of lawlessness that was allowed to be perpetrated all day long and that needs to be corrected quickly. I'm very concerned."

Although the next day's game was rained out, there was even more fodder for the rivalry. Commissioner Bud Selig said he was "very disappointed" in the behavior of the participants. "I have told the clubs that any

further misconduct by either team will not be tolerated and will be dealt with severely." Major League Baseball fined Martinez $50,000, Ramirez $25,000, Garcia $10,000 and Zimmer $5,000.

Boston owners mocked Levine's call for an apology. "I spoke with Randy this afternoon," said Sox principal owner John Henry. "I didn't feel it was necessary for him to apologize for his remarks or for the attack last night." Added Lucchino: "I think that once again, perhaps an incomplete knowledge of the facts, if I can put it diplomatically, might be at the root of Mr. Levine's comments. But we'll leave it to Major League Baseball to address the inflammatory comments." Reporters asked Lucchino if he had talked to Steinbrenner. "Who?" the Sox CEO said, laughing. "You can bet I haven't."

Zimmer, meanwhile, issued a tearful apology. "I'm embarrassed for the Yankees, I'm embarrassed for the Red Sox, I'm embarrassed for the umpires and my family," he said, before he had to leave the podium, overcome.

Game 4, much hyped, was rather uneventful. The Red Sox, taking advantage of the rainout, moved scheduled Game 5 starter Tim Wakefield up a day. For the second straight

time, Wakefield handcuffed Yankee batters with his knuckleball, even striking out the side in the sixth inning, as the Red Sox evened the series with a 3-2 win at Fenway Park. Todd Walker and Trot Nixon homered off Mussina, who lost for the second time in the series. Mussina pitched well, but irritated some Yankees fans by shifting the blame to teammates.

"I can only control 60 feet, six inches, that's the best I can do," Mussina said. "That's about as good as I got. The other stuff has to be attended to by other people." New York had scored a total of four runs in Mussina's two starts.

The Yankees sent lefty David Wells to the mound for Game 5 at Fenway Park against Lowe. The 40-year-old Wells helped stoke the rivalry before his start, declaring on his web site, "Bostonians are Psycho!!" Wells shut down the Sox, giving up only one run in seven innings, as the Yankees won, 4-2. New York got all the scoring it needed in the second inning, on a two-RBI, bases-loaded single by Karim Garcia and an RBI base hit by Alfonso Soriano. "It was very emotional; the teams hate each other and the fans, too," Soriano said after the game.

Wells shared the credit with the Curse of the Bambino.

"I believe in it," Wells said. "That's just one man's opinion. I'm going out there and doing what I love to do, especially in this ballpark, where it's pretty rare. I just try to follow suit and keep that theory alive."

Actually, it seemed as if two curses were alive that day. A few hours later, a thousand miles away, the Chicago Cubs were five outs away from their first World Series appearance since 1945. Leading 3-0 with one out in the eighth at Wrigley Field, the Cubs missed an opportunity for an out when a fan tipped a pop foul away from Chicago leftfielder Moises Alou, then blew a potential double play when shortstop Alex Gonzalez muffed an easy grounder. The Marlins rallied for eight runs, tying the series at three games, then won game seven the next night.

The Cubs' demon? The Curse of the Billy Goat. According to legend, Cubs fan Billy Sianis would bring his goat to games to taunt opposing players. But he and his goat were turned away from Game 4 of the 1945 World Series with the Tigers, prompting Sianis to curse the Cubs that they would never appear in the World Series again.

The biggest mystery for Red Sox fans was not a goat or a curse, but their shortstop, Nomar Garciaparra. The 30-year-old superstar was coming off another excellent season, batting .301 with 28 home runs, 13 triples, 37 doubles and 105 RBIs, and he hit .300 in the division series. But after five games in the ALCS, Garciaparra was batting only .105, and he missed a crucial RBI opportunity in Game 5 by striking out with runners on second and third and two outs. He was due to find his stroke, and he would soon enough.

The Red Sox and Yankees returned to the Bronx for the final two games of the series, with New York needing just one win to claim the pennant. The Red Sox, as if tempting fate, sent John Burkett to the mound against Andy Pettitte. Burkett entered the game with a lifetime regular season record of 0-6 against the Yankees, with an 8.49 ERA, and his team was averaging only 3.2 runs per game in the se-

OPPOSITE: *As Yankee player and coach, Willie Randolph has seen it all. (Photofest)*

Lee Smith and Don Zimmer (Frommer Archives)

ries. Pettitte, meanwhile, had shut down the Red Sox in Game 2 of the series, and had been New York's most dependable playoff starter.

But Pettitte didn't have it that day, falling behind 4-1, and lasting only five innings. Jason Varitek, the ninth-place hitter, homered in the third, and leadoff man Damon followed with a walk. A Todd Walker single and Manny Ramirez walk loaded the bases, and Ortiz and Millar cleared the bases with back-to-back singles.

New York scored four runs in the fourth to take the lead, with two unearned runs coming after a Garciaparra error. Posada made it 6-4 with a solo homer in the fifth, and the Yankees turned it over to their postseason bullpen sensation, Contreras. The strategy was simple: Contreras would pitch three innings, and Mariano Rivera would ice the game and the series in the ninth inning.

Everything worked according to plan in the sixth, when Contreras struck out three of the four batters he faced. Things looked bleak for the Red Sox, as the sky darkened, the wind whipped up, and plastic bags and other debris flew around Yankee Stadium. But in the seventh, Boston sent the heart of its lineup—batters three, four, and five. Garciaparra led off with a shot over centerfielder Bernie Williams, the third of his four hits that day. The ball caromed off the wall past Williams, and left fielder Hideki Matsui had to chase it down. As Garciaparra raced to third, Matsui uncorked a wild throw that landed up the left field line and bounced into the seats. Garciaparra was awarded home, and the lead was now 6-5.

Ramirez, the cleanup hitter, hammered a double to centerfield, and scored the tying run on a single by Ortiz that bounced off first base. One out later, Bill Mueller singled, chasing Contreras. In came lefty pitcher Felix Heredia, an August pickup from Cincinnati. Heredia was both unhittable and out of control. He tossed a wild pitch to put runners at second and third, then struck out Nixon for the second out. After intentionally walking Varitek to load the bases, however, he quite unintentionally walked Damon, giving the Sox a 7-6 lead they would never relinquish. Boston tacked on two more runs on a ninth-inning, two-run homer by Nixon, and Red Sox

relievers Todd Jones, Alan Embree, Mike Timlin and Scott Williamson combined to pitch four scoreless innings. The Red Sox finished with nine runs on 16 hits.

"We know if we want to get to the World Series we have to get through the curse and the Yankees," said Damon. "We feel pretty good we can do that. We're going to have a couple of cocktails, get some rest and be ready to take on the Babe and the rest of the Yankees."

Added Sox GM Theo Epstein: "We've been on a collision course for a hundred years."

"I guess it was supposed to come down to seven games, as much as you hate to think about it," Torre said. "But they battled like we've battled each other all year. And tomorrow, at least we know tomorrow will be the last day."

Technically, Torre was incorrect. Because as midnight struck the following day, there was still no winner, no American League champion. The teams were locked in 5-5 tie when Thursday night turned into Friday morning at Yankee Stadium. The starting pitchers in what was billed as a historic rematch, Pedro and Clemens, were both gone from the game. Clemens was yanked in the fourth after giv-

Alfonso Soriano (Flair)

ing up four runs, Pedro was lifted in the eighth.

The Red Sox had jumped out to an early 4-0 lead, silencing the crowd of 56,000 Yankee fans. Martinez held New York at bay except for Jason Giambi, who had been dropped to seventh in the lineup after hitting only .216 in the postseason. The slugging DH responded with two solo home runs, and the Yanks drew to 4-2 in the seventh. A David Ortiz homer for the Sox made it 5-2 in the eighth.

"When the Yankees were losing, there were times that I thought the Red Sox would finally win it," conceded former New York City Mayor Rudy Giuliani, who was at the game. "Having watched what happened in the loss to Arizona in the 2001 World Series, when we asked Mariano Rivera to do it for the hundredth time in a row, and you can't quite do it for the hundredth time in a row, you think, maybe the string is up."

Martinez retired the first batter in the bottom of the inning, and the Red Sox found themselves in the identical position the Cubs had been earlier that week: up by three runs, nobody on base, and only five outs away from the World Series.

For those who believe in curses, it wasn't a good place to be.

The Yankees added a run, put two more on base, and then tied the score on a two-out, two-run bloop single by Posada. Pedro was done. The teams went to the ninth, the outcome uncertain. "If you are from New York or New England, this is a dream series," Lowe had said after Game 6. "You would love to see this one go to Game 7 and the ninth inning."

With the season on the line, both managers turned to pitchers unaccustomed to their roles. In the ninth, Torre sent in Rivera, the

OPPOSITE: *David Wells in an upbeat Yankee moment. (Photofest)*

closer who normally pitched to protect a lead. Grady Little asked for some more magic from Wakefield, a starting pitcher, in the 10th. In his two starts in the series, Wakefield had surrendered just three runs.

After 10 innings, the score was still tied. Rivera went out to pitch in the top of the 11th, his third inning of relief, the first time he had pitched that much in seven years. He struck out two batters in the 11th, but Torre knew he would have to turn to another pitcher if the Yankees didn't score in their half of the inning.

In stepped Aaron Boone. Like Bucky Dent a generation earlier, Boone was an unlikely hero. He was batting only .125 in the series. But the Yankee third baseman crushed the first pitch into the left field stands, and ghosts, mystique, the curse—whatever you want to call it—had prevailed once again.

"I believe in ghosts," Jeter said. "And we've got some ghosts at this stadium."

"After Boone's home run, I went into the Red Sox clubhouse, and I congratulated them on having a very good season," former New York City Mayor Rudy Giuliani said. "I thought they had played well enough to win. I went up to about eight or nine players, including Johnny Damon, Jason Varitek and Pedro, as well as manager Grady Little. I got a wonderful reception. They were very generous, they were very nice.

"When a team gets itself to that stage, and then loses a big game, they tend to think the whole season is a waste," he added. "It's like what happened to the Yankees when they lost in the sixth game of the World Series. When the reality is, at the beginning of the season, any team would give anything just to be playing in that game. You just passed the rest of baseball by the mere fact that you're in that game. And luck does play a part in this. And that's why, during the game, I worried, well, would the Red Sox win? Because how often can we be lucky? How often can Derek Jeter make a throw going down the first baseline backwards, and get somebody out at the plate, like he did in the 2001 playoffs? That play was a great athletic play, but it also had to work just right."

Red Sox fans would get a small consolation prize a week later, when the Yankees lost the World Series to the Florida Marlins, the first time a visiting team had eliminated the Yankees at the Stadium in 22 years. Two days later, Boston let manager Grady Little go. Many Red Sox fans had blamed him for the Game 7 loss, arguing he had left Pedro Martinez in too long.

The man they call "The Godfather" in New York, Yankee manager Joe Torre. (Photofest)

*One of the great relievers—
New York's Mariano Rivera.
(Photofest)*

COLLISION

In 1976, the New York Yankees finished the season with a 97-62 record and won the American League East title. The Red Sox of Boston finished in third place, 15 and a half games behind. In 1977, the Yankees won 100 of the 162 games they played and repeated as division title winners. Boston won 97 games and tied for second place with Baltimore. Both teams trailed the Yankees by two and a half games.

It was during these two seasons that more and more Yankee fans began to sport "Red Sox Suck" tee shirts. And it was during this time that Yankee principal owner George Steinbrenner kept wheeling and dealing, embellishing the Yankee image, his team's skills and the Red Sox failings.

The start of the 1978 season gave Boston fans hope. Over the winter the team engineered several key moves to strengthen itself. Mike Torrez, winner of two World Series games for the Yankees in 1977, was signed as a free agent. Dennis Eckersley, just 23, was acquired from the Cleveland Indians. It was

felt that the combination of the veteran Torrez and the youthful Eckersley would shore up Sox pitching. Another key Boston acquisition was Jerry Remy, a sure-handed speedy second baseman obtained from the California Angels. Remy's promise was added speed on the base path and an effective contact hitter near the top of the Boston batting order.

With Remy at second base and Rick Burleson at shortstop, Boston fans felt their team had a double-play combination to rival if not surpass the Yankee tandem of Bucky Dent and Willie Randolph. George Scott, the Sox first baseman, recorded 33 homers in 1977—almost twice the total of Yankee first baseman Chris Chambliss. Slugging Butch Hobson was a fixture at third base. Nettles of New York was peerless with a glove, but Sox fans argued that Hobson outmatched the Yankee third baseman when it came to hitting. Hobson had rapped 30 homers and driven in 112 runs in 1977.

Both teams boasted top-flight catchers. Most baseball experts rated Boston's Carlton

Catcher Thurman Munson
was a Yankee captain. (The
Topps Company, Inc.)

Fisk and New York's Thurman Munson among the two best backstops in all of baseball.

Both teams had powerful clutch-hitting outfielders, capable of making crucial defensive plays. Carl Yastrzemski, Dwight Evans, and Fred Lynn would be Boston's picket line, augmented by perhaps the best potential designated hitter in all of baseball—Jim Rice. The Yankees had steady Roy White, flamboyant Mickey Rivers, and dramatic Reggie Jackson, buttressed by Paul Blair, Lou Piniella, and, if needed, Cliff Johnson.

If there was a difference, it was in pitching. Over the winter George Steinbrenner had signed Rich Gossage, Rawly Eastwick, and Andy Messersmith. This trio joined Catfish Hunter, Don Gullett, Sparky Lyle, Ed Figueroa, Ken Holtzman, Dick Tidrow, and Ron Guidry (16-7 in 1977 and getting better, much better).

Against this array of all types of pitching talent, Boston had its Latin duo of Luis Tiant and Mike Torrez, Eckersley, Bill Lee, and Bob Stanley. Bill Campbell had saved 31 games in 1977, and it was felt that he could repeat that performance in 1978.

Seven straight wins at Fenway Park launched Boston on a fine start as the season got underway. By May 18, the Yankees (19-13) trailed the second-place Sox (23-12) who were a half game behind the surprising first-place Detroit Tigers. On May 24, the Sox moved into sole possession of first place. They would remain there for 113 days, to the delight of their adoring and rabid fans.

At the All-Star break, powered by a combination of good pitching and power hitting, Boston had a record of 57 wins against just 26 losses, a .687 winning percentage, the best in baseball. More enjoyable to some Red Sox fans was the record of the New York Yankees. The hated rivals were mired in third place, way back off the pace.

"George came into the clubhouse one day," Reggie Jackson recalled, "and said 'I'm going to back

Current Boston broadcaster
Jerry Remy shown in his playing days. (The Topps Company, Inc.)

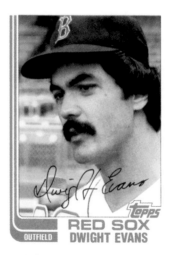

Dwight Evans
(The Topps Company, Inc.)

Red Sox fans waiting for autographs. (Frommer Archives)

up the truck and get rid of all you guys, everybody, if we don't get it turned around.' It was an unbelievable tirade. Whether that motivated us or not, I don't know. I think it made us mad. George yelled at us. Told us we were terrible, that he was going to break up the club and nobody was above being traded."

Emanating daily from New York was news of controversy, sore-armed pitchers, bruised infielders, battered egos, unhappy coaches. In Boston, for a change, there was relative harmony.

On July 18, the Sox stretched their lead over the Yanks to 14 games. "Even Affirmed couldn't catch the Red Sox now," snapped Reggie Jackson, referring to the horse that had won the 1978 Triple Crown.

Off the field Yankee activity was more explosive than anything the team was doing on the field. Dissension prevailed. Sparky Lyle was fined $500 for taking himself out of a game, but the fine was later dropped. Reggie Jackson was suspended indefinitely on July 17 for refusing to bunt in a game against Kansas City. Jackson struck out and this rather than the bunt refusal instigated the suspension lev-

ied by manager Billy Martin that lasted five days. It was reported that Steinbrenner ordered Martin to reinstate Jackson to the lineup.

A piqued, infuriated, frazzled Martin delivered a long monologue to reporters. The phrase that received the most publicity was: "The two of them [Jackson and Steinbrenner] deserve each other. One's a born liar, the other's convicted."

One day after his outburst, Martin bowed out as Yankee manager. He was replaced by Bob Lemon, who just a few weeks before had been fired as Chicago White Sox pilot. A low-keyed Lemon proved a dramatic counterpoint to the short-fused, heavy-drinking Martin. He was a soothing balm for the Yankees.

"Lemon was the guy," Willie Randolph noted. "He didn't even know the names of the guys. He'd call everyone 'Meat,' 'Hey, Meat, how you doing? Way to go, Meat.' That was very instrumental in us getting a nice little focus, a little groove."

With the Hall of Fame pitcher managing mildly and carefully, the Yankees started to move up in the standings. Boston, battered by injuries, started to fade. With Rick Burleson and Carl Yastrzemski sidelined with physical ailments, with Mike Torrez and Bill Lee suddenly ineffective, the Sox saw their lead drop to seven and a half games on July 30. Lee, 7-0 at one point, couldn't buy a win. His downward spiral continued throughout the season, and he finished with a 10-10 record and a 3.46 ERA.

On August 3 the Yanks and Sox met in a two-game series. Boston's lead had dropped to six and a half games. New York had copped 12 of its last 16 contests while Boston been victorious in just three of its last 14 games. To the delight of their fans, the Sox swept the Yankees, 7-5 and 8-1 and increased their lead over the New Yorkers to eight and a half games. But it was a Pyrrhic victory. The double-loss seemed only to give the Yankees more motivation.

Down through the humid weeks of August, in the hot sun of the day and through the cool breezes of evening, the two teams played out their strange seasons.

"The 1978 season was like two seasons in one," noted sports writing stalwart Phil Pepe, who began covering the Yankees regularly for the *New York Daily News* in 1971. "The Sox had made just two roster changes in the first half of the season; the Yankees had all kinds of physical problems. The second half of the season was just the reverse."

Catfish Hunter, who had slumped, suddenly regained his pitching rhythm. Bucky Dent, who had been sidelined with injuries for almost a month was well again.

Reggie Jackson, enraged and driven, began to take out his fury on opposing pitchers. On August 10 he went on a tear that saw him pound 13 homers, drive in 49 runs and notch a .288 average over the last 53 games of the season.

For Boston, the season regrettably continued on a downward slide. Steady Jerry Remy chipped a bone in his left wrist on August 25. Sox fans gasped at the prognosis: "Quick return doubtful." Five days later Dwight Evans was beaned. He would not be the same again in 1978.

As the season turned into September, it was almost as if the first-place Sox were chasing the second-place Yankees.

Lou Piniella remembers the time: "You fall back 14 ball games and a lot of teams would have packed it in. Well, this team didn't. We had confidence in ourselves. It was a special group of players. A team that in the clubhouse didn't always get along so well. For us to be world champions we had to beat Boston five straight times in their own ballpark—and that's exactly what happened."

On September 7, Boston's lead was just four games over the energized and charging Yankees as the rivals prepared for a four-game series at Fenway Park. Boston had played 25-24 ball since its July 24 14-game lead.

New York had won 35 of 49 games, a .714 clip, in the same time span. Writers billed the Yankee drive as the "Great Comeback." Boston's behavior was dubbed the "Great Collapse." Red Sox fans clamoring for tickets, hovering around their TV sets and radios had earthier expressions.

"Before the series got underway, the managers were talked to by the umpires," noted the late American League arbiter Ron Luciano. "Throughout 1978, the entire Boston-New York series was handled like a playoff because of the history of bad blood between the two teams."

Mike Torrez opposed his former team in the first game; Catfish Hunter started for the New Yorkers. Torrez didn't have it. He was touched for two runs in the first inning as Munson and Jackson both padded their RBI records. In the second inning, Torrez was lashed for four straight singles and left the game muttering to himself. The handsome right-hander's last victory had been on August 18. After two innings, the score was 5-0, Yankees. After three innings, it was 7-0, Yankees. After four innings it was 12-0, Yankees.

A Boston reporter quipped: "There was a traffic jam outside of Fenway as fans fought with each other trying to get home in time for *Hawaii Five-O.*"

The standing-room-only crowd at Fenway was shocked and sour. They could not believe the mauling their favorites were experiencing. When the debacle finally ended, the Yankees walked away with a 15-3 triumph. They had treated their fans to a fireworks display of their offensive might by cracking out 20 hits to all parts of the little ballpark. It was a humbling experience for the Sox and their fans. There was more to come, and soon.

Rookie Jim Wright (8-4 in 1978) opposed Yankee rookie hurler Jim Beattie (6-9 in 1978). The pounding inflicted on the Sox by the Yankees the day before was immediately evident.

The Hub players were tentative, while the team from the Big Apple was tenaciously aggressive. Mickey Rivers led off the game with a single, stole second, moved to third on a Fisk throwing error. The Yankees led 2-0 after one inning and then opened up their offensive engine full throttle in the second.

A Lou Piniella triple and a Roy White single scored one Yankee run. White swiped second base and wound up on third as Fisk committed yet another throwing flub. Dent brought White home with a sacrifice fly for New York's second run of the inning. Tom Burgmeier replaced Wright on the mound for Boston. Rivers rapped out another single. Munson walked. And then Reggie Jackson smashed a home run to score three more Yankee runs. Chris Chambliss singled. Burgmeier mishandled a bunt by Nettles. Piniella smashed his second extra-base hit of the inning—a double that drove in the sixth Yankee run in the second and increased the lead to 8-0. The final score was Yankees 13, Sox 2.

In two games Boston had committed nine errors. That made 23 errors in the last nine games, leading to 19 unearned runs. The Yankees had pounded out 28 runs to Boston's five and out-hit the Sox, 38-14.

"I can't believe this is happening," said Yankee super-scout Clyde King. "I could understand if an expansion team fell apart like this, but Boston's got the second-best record in all of baseball. It can't go on like this."

A shaken Boston press reacted with jibes and worse against the BoSox. "If you need directions to home plate at Fenway Park," proclaimed a *Boston Globe* story, "just stop and ask any New York Yankee. They've all been there already."

Boston manager Don Zimmer tabbed Dennis Eckersley to pitch the third game of the series on September 9. Bob Lemon, confident but not complacent, chose Ron Guidry. The Red Sox were staggering but they were playing on their own home ground, and Lemon went out of his way to point out how, while pitching for Cleveland, he once was leading 11-1 at the Fens and wound up losing the game.

OPPOSITE: *Lou Piniella running bases. (Photofest)*

Red Sox

DON ZIMMER

Don Zimmer (The Topps Company, Inc.)

Eckersley was the best pitcher the beleaguered Zimmer had to call on. His record was 16-6, and he was unbeaten in nine decisions in his home park. But Ron Guidry was the best pitcher in all of baseball. The Gator boasted a glittering 20-2 record, a popping fastball and a dancing slider.

There were 33,611 fans at the park, most of them strong Sox zealots. The Yankees failed to score in the top of the first inning and the huge partisan crowd sounded off with a mock roar of approval for Eckersley's efforts.

Rick Burleson singled to center to lead things off for Boston. His line drive buzzed perilously close to Guidry's head. A sac bunt by Fred Lynn moved Burleson to second. Jim Rice swung hard but grounded the ball to short, to the dismay of the Fens faithful. But Bucky Dent had difficulty getting a handle on the ball and Rice beat the throw to first.

Yaz faced Guidry. With runners leading off the corners and with just one out, it seemed the Sox had the 'Ragin Cajun' on the ropes.

But Yaz grounded out weakly and then Fisk struck out looking and the inning was over.

It was not only the end of the inning, it was also the end of the Red Sox chances for victory that day. Guidry did not allow another hit. Eckersley matched the Yankee star until the fourth inning.

Then Thurman Munson popped a single to right field to open things up for the Yankees. Jackson smacked the ball to the left field corner. Yaz chased it down for the catch, and fired in a deft relay throw to second baseman Frank Duffy who pegged the ball to Scott at first. Munson was doubled off. Streamers, scorecards, whistles and waving Red Sox caps vied with each other as the Fens rocked with joy at the heroics of the home team's reclaimed defense.

But a Chris Chambliss double quieted things down. With one on and two out, Nettles was intentionally walked. Zimmer made the decision that he would pitch to Piniella. Later the embattled BoSox skipper would be severely criticized. Piniella was the only Yankee batting over .300—he was a deadly clutch, professional batter.

Lou lofted a short fly ball to right center field. There were five Red Sox giving chase. The wind played with the ball, and it dropped in out of reach of anyone. Chambliss scored. Nettles moved to third base. Elated, Piniella stood on second base where his gift fly ball double had placed him.

Zimmer intentionally walked Roy White. Bases loaded. With a 1-2 count, Bucky Dent kicked at the dirt and readied himself for Eck's fourth pitch—a high fastball. Dent slammed it to left. Nettles scored. Piniella scored. White chugged into third base, and Dent cruised into second as Yaz mishandled the ball. "It was that hit," Eckersley would admit later, "that broke my back."

Roy White then poked a single to left. He and Dent would score the Yankee fourth and fifth runs of the inning. When the scoring was finally ended the Yankees had racked up seven runs and driven Eckersley to the showers.

Incredibly, the Yankees had won three straight at Fenway Park and demoralized the entire city of Boston. "I've had my heart broken by the Sox many times," said one fan. "But what happened in those three games just ripped my heart to shreds."

Fred Lynn attempted to soften the shock with a joke: "They must be cheating," he said. "These aren't the same Yankees we saw before. I really think George Steinbrenner used his clone money. I think those were Yankee clones that were being used out there from the great Yankee teams of the past."

A Boston writer groaned, "It's the first time a team has been in first place by a game and trailing."

The real mood of the Boston team was captured by Carlton Fisk. "How can a team get thirty-something games over .500 in July and then in September see its pitching, hitting and fielding all fall apart at the same time?"

Guidry's 7-0 whitewash was only the second complete game turned in by a left-hander against Boston in 1978, and the first southpaw to blank them at Fenway since 1974.

"This team is loaded with tough guys," said Reggie Jackson, attempting to explain the Yankee turnaround. "This team is loaded with professionals."

Game 4 pitted Bobby Sprowl against Ed Figueroa. A couple of months earlier Sprowl

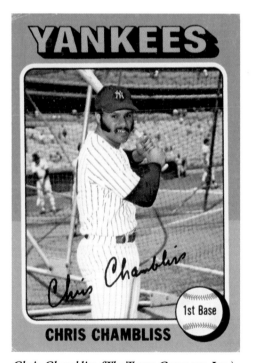

Chris Chambliss (The Topps Company, Inc.)

A frustrated Boston batter, Fred Lynn, 1977. (Photofest)

had been a hit pitching in the minors for the Bristol Red Sox. Sprowl articulated Don Zimmer's instructions: "My only objective is to keep us in the game. I am not expecting to pitch a shutout." No one expected him to pitch a shutout either.

For Boston fans and players, what happened in the first inning was like an old-time horror movie replayed. Sprowl walked Mickey Rivers. Sprowl walked Willie Randolph. Things looked hopeful for Boston when

Munson grounded into a D.P., but there was Reggie to contend with. Jackson singled in Rivers. Sprowl had lost his shutout. He walked Piniella. He walked Chambliss. Zimmer walked, too. The harried Boston pilot walked out to the mound and replaced the even more harried Sprowl with Bob Stanley, who gave up a two-run single to Nettles. The inning finally ended with the Yankees leading, 3-0.

By the fourth inning, the Yankees led 6-0. The final score of the game was Yankees 7,

Sox 4. "HOLY COW," one newspaper headline declared, summarizing the entire frenetic turn of events in the standings, "IT'S TIED."

The statistics for the four games were completely lopsided. The Yankees pounded out 42 runs and collected 67 hits. Boston eked out just nine runs and 21 hits. A dozen errors also contributed to what they were calling "the Boston Massacre."

The record of the two teams from July 19 to September 10 was:

Boston 25-28 .472

New York 39-14 .736

Carl Yastrzemski responded to all the flak by claiming, "It's never easy to win a pennant. We've got three weeks to play. Anything can happen. We've got three games at Yankee Stadium next weekend."

For Yaz, it was easier to look ahead than back at the four-game Yankee sweep—the first time since 1968 that the Sox had been swept in a four-game series at Fenway.

The next day, Jim Rice's 39th and 40th home runs of the season gave Boston a 5-4 triumph over Jim Palmer and Baltimore. It was the first errorless game played by the Sox in 11 attempts. The win enabled Boston to climb back into first place, a half game ahead of the idle Yankees. "This win can turn us around," said Rice. "But we can't let up."

But they did let up. There was a loss to Baltimore and two losses to Cleveland. Boston, trailing the Yankees by one and a half games, came into Yankee Stadium on Friday, September 15 for a three-game series. The dissension and disharmony that had afflicted the Bronx Bombers like a bad summer cold had now seemingly been passed on to Boston.

Rick Burleson's griping typified the disharmony that hung over the Sox. "The Yan-

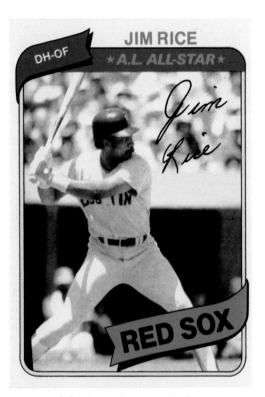

Jim Rice (The Topps Company, Inc.)

kees are together as a unit and we are not," he said. "We don't know who's going to be in the lineup when we come to the park and that's a bunch of *bleep*. The way I see it, the Yanks had a guy, Jackson, who comes out of the hospital to play in the series against us. That's how much it meant to them. We have a guy who pulls himself out of a game after making a couple of errors [a reference to Dwight Evans, who removed himself from the third game at Fenway Park after he had committed two miscues against the Yankees]. Just having Evans in there would have been helpful to the last two games."

Former Boston announcer Ken Harrelson remembered arriving at the Stadium with the Sox: "It was kind of unbelievable com-

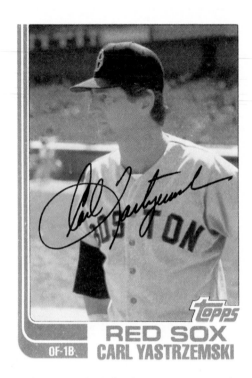

Carl Yastrzemski (The Topps Company, Inc.)

ing off the bus and walking through the crowd out there with so many of them screaming out four-letter words and witnessing all that aggression against the Red Sox. There were a lot of sick people."

The greatest rivalry in baseball was once again at fever pitch. Amid extensive media coverage and extra security personnel, Yankee Stadium crackled with tension as Luis Tiant warmed up for the Sox and Ron Guidry readied himself for the Bronx Bombers. Thousands of BoSox loyalists had made the trek to New York City to support their team. "The damn guy's not Superman," one of them yelled at a Yankee fan. "Guidry's gonna lose today."

If he wasn't Superman, he was managing to perpetrate a good impersonation. Guidry

allowed but two hits as he went the distance in a 4-0 shutout. It was the 42nd win in 56 games for the Yanks. The "Big Push" was a steamroller. The Yanks had extended their lead over Boston to two and a half games.

Catfish Hunter opposed Mike Torrez in the second game of the series. Jim Rice's 41st home run of the year gave the Sox a 2-0 lead in the first inning. A Reggie Jackson single brought the Yankees within a run of the Sox in the bottom of the first and then the outspoken outfielder homered in the fifth to tie the score. Jackson had been revived since Martin's exit and batted .317.

The game moved to the bottom of the ninth inning with the score tied, 2-2. Torrez and Hunter had matched each other virtually pitch for pitch. With two strikes on him, Mickey Rivers smacked the ball over the head of Yastrzemski, who was playing a shallow left field and shading the foul line. Rivers turned on the speed and wound up on third base with a triple. A Munson RBI drove Rivers home and gave the Yanks a 3-2 triumph.

"If it had been me," Rivers said later, "and it was that late in the game that means so much, I would have played a lot deeper than he did." Rivers was underscoring the acrimony between the two clubs.

Bob Lemon, grandfatherly, kindly, unassuming, emerged more and more as a Yankee folk hero. It was reported that he called up his wife after the 3-2 victory and told her how much fun he was having winning. "This is even better than sex," he quipped.

Carl Yastrzemski was not in a joking mood. The soul and spirit of the Boston team, he was the media's designated goat for the way he had "non-played" Rivers. Before the fatal pitch to the Yankee outfielder, Yaz had moved in about a half dozen steps and crowded the left-field foul line.

"I didn't want Rivers on base," he said, defending his move. "I thought he might bloop one in or hit a line drive that I would not be able to catch. I wanted to keep him off base. He could steal off Mike's big windup." And then underscoring the confusion, the pulling in opposite directions that many complained about the Red Sox, Yaz added: "The pitch was supposed to be low and inside. It wound up over the plate where he could go with it to left."

With 14 games to play, the Yankees led by three and a half games. "We have to win them all," said Yastrzemski.

Burleson was not so upbeat. "The abuse we've taken and the abuse we must be prepared to take we richly deserve."

One Yankee player provided this perspective: "Boston is so tight that you couldn't get a needle up their asshole, they choke."

But they didn't choke in the third game of the series. Behind Dennis Eckersley they pounded out a 7-3 win. Even George Scott contributed. With no hits in his last 36 at-bats, Scott snapped out of the deep slump with a double in the eighth. The Yankee lead was whittled down to two and a half games. Sox loyalists had hope.

But the Boston press battered the home team daily and fair-weather fans kept on second-guessing. Charges that the Sox were choking, flinching, losing their nerve—these were main topics of conversation all over New England.

But incredibly, the abuse seemed to act as a stoker for harried BoSox. Instead of folding up their tents and sinking further down in

George Scott (The Topps Company, Inc.)

the American League East standings, the Red Sox caught fire. It wasn't that the Yankees faltered, it was just that Boston went on a tear as the following table reveals.

BOSTON   (GAMES BEHIND)

September 19
Boston 8, Detroit 6
Milwaukee 2, New York 0   1 1/2

September 20 (double header):
Toronto 8, New York 1
New York 3, Toronto 2
Detroit 12, Boston 2   2

September 21
New York 7, Toronto 1
Boston 5, Detroit 1   2

September 22
Cleveland 8, New York 7
Toronto 5, Boston 4   2

September 23
Boston 3, Toronto 1
Cleveland 10, New York 1   1

September 24
New York 4, Cleveland 0
Boston 7, Toronto 6   1

September 26
Boston 6, Detroit 0
New York 4, Toronto 1   1

September 27
Boston 5, Detroit 2
New York 5, Toronto 0   1

September 28
Boston 1, Detroit 0
New York 3, Toronto 1   1

September 29
Boston 11, Toronto 1
New York 3, Cleveland 1   1

September 30
New York 7, Cleveland 0
Boston 4, Toronto 1   1

October 1
Cleveland 9, New York 2
Boston 5, Toronto 0   —

The season came down to the final three games for both the Yankees and Red Sox. Only one game separated baseball's greatest rivals. No longer were the "choke" charges being tossed about at Boston. All of New England was in a frenzy. Every pitch of Yankee and Red Sox games was being labored over by millions of fans. Like two punchy fighters, neither willing to quit, or knowing how to quit, the archrival Red Sox and Yankees played out the string.

Boston took two games from Toronto while New York (with its eyes on the scoreboard) won two games from Cleveland to close out September.

On the first day of October, the last day of the regular season, the Yankees still clung to a one-game lead over Boston. A Red Sox defeat or a Yankee victory would clinch the division for the Bronx Bombers. But the Yanks went down to a 9-2 defeat as the Indians pounded Catfish Hunter and his successors.

At Fenway, the Sox racked up their eighth straight win, and their 12th victory in 15 games, with a 5-0 win over Toronto. Both rivals concluded the season with an identical record: 99-63, a .611 winning percentage. The stage was set for only the second one-game playoff in American League history.

All those years of coming in second behind the Yankees were evoked as the city of Boston and the Sox faithful girded for the 1978 playoff game. There were many in New England who through the years had been beset by bitter memories: they wondered if they would have one more nightmare to add to their collection that woke them up in the middle of the night with a vision of a Yankee crossing home plate with a winning, heartbreaking run scored against their beloved Sox.

"Coming into Fenway," Phil Pepe recalled, "the Yankees were sky-high for that final game. They had wiped out Boston in those four games. They had momentum. They had Ron Guidry pitching—they thought he was invincible, and there was Gossage to back him up. The only thing that I guess was in everyone's minds amidst the tension and excitement was that it was a game in Fenway Park and anything could happen."

The scene was out of Hollywood casting: October 2, 1978, Yankees versus Red Sox at Fenway Park. Boston's 1978 home attendance was 2,320,643—just 15,000 behind the Yankees, who led the American League playing in a much bigger park. New York had triumphed in nine of the 16 games played between the two teams to take the season series, but the Sox had performed at a .728 clip on their home field, going 59-22 at Fenway. The Yankees were only 44-37 (.543) on the road that year.

Boston was the "hot team" and had the home field advantage, but the Yankees had Guidry (24-3) and, if necessary Gossage (26 saves). Much was made of the fact that Guidry was going to pitch with only three days' rest. "It's only one game," he said. "And one game is enough. I can pitch one game."

Also out of Hollywood casting was Guidry's opponent, Torrez, who just the season before had worn Yankee pinstripes. He was determined to beat his former teammates.

Almost 33,000 crowded into Fenway to watch the action and millions saw the game over national television or heard it on their local radio stations. "That one game surpasses any other one I've ever been connected with," recalled Frank Messer. "Those two teams—and the whole season boiling down to one game at Fenway—it was quite a moment for everyone who was there or watched it on TV."

In the second inning, Yaz stoked a home run down the right field line. Boston led, 1-0.

"Guidry wasn't the same guy we saw earlier," said Fred Lynn.

"I thought that when the old man [Yaz] hit the home run that was going to do it. Mike [Torrez] was throwing the ball real well and he wanted that win," said former Boston announcer Hawk Harrelson.

In the third inning Scott doubled off the left-field wall, giving Guidry another lump. Boston failed to score but its batters were making contact against the invincible man and gaining more confidence with each at-bat. There was more offense generated in the fourth and fifth innings. Then in the sixth, Burleson cracked a double and Remy's bunt moved him to third. The score became 2-0 Boston as Jim Rice singled Burleson home.

Fred Lynn was next. He mashed Guidry's pitch deep to right field. "I lost the ball for a moment in the sun," Piniella recalled. "But I recovered and fortunately was able to make the catch." The Gator had been on the ropes a couple of times, but Boston could not deliver the knockout punch.

As the Yankees came to bat in the seventh inning, there was a swelling of confidence among Boston rooters. Torrez had been sharp—no runs, just two hits to this point in the game.

But Chambliss singled. White singled. Lemon yanked Brian Doyle and inserted Jim Spencer as a pinch hitter. He flied out. The tension eased a bit for Boston fans. The light-hitting Bucky Dent was up next.

Dent stepped in. Just hoping to make contact, the five-foot-nine Yankee peered out at Torrez, the six-foot-five Red Sox pitcher. The two were locked in, locked up.

Earl Russell Dent out of Savannah, Georgia was a fine defensive shortstop, but not

much of an offensive threat. He had hit but .243 for the season, just .140 in the final 20 games of the season. He had hit only four home runs in 1978.

Dent stood in, choking up on the bat. He fouled the second Torrez pitch off his left foot. The shot stung an old injury from battles earlier in the season. Dent moved about in front of the visitors' dugout attempting to shake off the sting. There was a brief delay as the Yankees trainer tended to Dent.

"Mickey Rivers was on deck," recalled Messer, "and he noticed a crack in Bucky's bat. He called it to Bucky's attention." Dent decided to switch bats, and he stepped back in to face Torrez with a Mickey Rivers bat.

First base coach Gene "Stick" Michael recalled: "Roy White was the runner on first base, and when Bucky went to get another bat I said to Roy, 'Can Bucky handle this guy?' Roy said: 'If he hangs him a slider, I think he could.'"

In their dugout the Yankees were screaming out encouragement to their shortstop. In the stands fans were exhorting Torrez to greater effort, beseeching him to strike out Dent.

"Hit the tin, Bucky," screamed Reggie Jackson, encouraging Dent to pound the ball off the left-field wall and drive in the two runners who were on base. The pitch came in and Bucky swung, getting good wood on the ball.

"The fact that it was at Fenway Park," recalled Messer, "as soon as it left the bat I thought it had a chance. Any time you hit a fly ball in Boston, there's a chance."

The ball cleared the infield and climbed in the outfield toward the left-field wall—the Green Monster. Yaz, who had been in that position many times before, backed up, back, back toward the wall.

"Deep to left!" Bill White, Yankees broadcaster shouted, "Yastrzemski will not get it!"

Yaz had been in this position before. But he knew it was hopeless. The ball sailed into the 23-foot net above the Green Monster, the 37-foot wall in left field. Three-run home run!

"When I hit the ball," Bucky Dent recalled, "I knew that I had hit it high enough to hit the wall. But there were shadows on the net behind the wall and I didn't see the ball land there. I didn't know I had hit a homer until I saw the umpire at first signaling home run with his hand. I couldn't believe it."

Neither could the Red Sox.

"I was so damn shocked," Torrez said. "I thought maybe it was going to be off the wall. Damn, I did not think it was going to go out."

The ball went over the "tin." As Bucky raced around first base he knew the shot had landed in the left-field net.

White, Chambliss and the entire Yankee bench were there waiting at home plate. It was all Bucky Dent that October day.

"I had a dream as a kid," Dent said later. "I dreamed some day I would hit a home run to win something."

"God was kind to me, God was kind to me," recalled Ted Spencer, chief curator of the National Baseball Hall of Fame and Museum, who was born in Quincy, Massachusetts into a Red Sox obsessed family. "I was working in Philadelphia. I had the game on at my desk and when I left the Red Sox were ahead. When I got into my car at the other end of the subway Dent had already hit the home run. But I did not have the instant pain of seeing that ball land in the screen. I did get home in time to see Yaz make the last out."

OPPOSITE: *Ron Guidry, "Louisiana Lightning," letting it go. (Photofest)*

Willie Randolph (The Topps Company, Inc.)

Johnny Pesky, coaching at first base, had the instant pain of the Dent homer and the Yaz last out. "I wanted to shoot him. I called him after that 'Eugene Vernon Bucky [bleeping] Dent.' But he was a nifty player." Don Zimmer, then Boston's skipper, also changed the Yankee shortstop's name to "Bucky [bleeping] Dent." Red Sox fans had even more salty phrases.

With the Yankees now leading, 3-2, Fenway Park was silent. Suddenly stunned Boston fans could not believe what had taken place. An instant before it was all Red Sox— now the hated Yankees had taken control of the game.

Willie Randolph had a hamstring and did not play in that legendary game: "I just remember that when Bucky hit the ball there was a deafening hush over the crowd. Thirty thousand people just totally shocked. There was a group of maybe 20 to 30 Yankee wives and the Yankee brass there and they were going nuts. You could hear this hush come over the crowd and then this small group going ballistic."

"So much has been made of that home run," said Jerry Remy, "and it's because of who hit it. That ball was not exactly crushed. Going through the game I was upset that they

had taken a lead but I did not think the game was anywhere near being over. The fact is we still had nine outs to go."

So unnerved was Torrez that he went to a full count on Rivers and then walked him. That was all for Torrez. He was removed from the game. Bob Stanley took over. Rivers stole second base and scored on a Munson double to deep center field. It was Yankees 4, Red Sox 2.

In the bottom of the seventh inning a George Scott single ended Guidry's stint on the mound. Burly "Goose" Gossage came in to pitch. He had a string of 30 appearances during which he had given up no home runs while recording 15 saves and six wins.

Out of Colorado Springs, Colorado, Richard Michael Gossage was one of the most consistent relief pitchers ever. A glarer on the mound, always staring a batter down, Gossage's big cowboy-style moustache, wild mane of hair, thick stubble and wide body made him an intimidator. The Goose threw wicked heat, making him usually unhittable.

"Gossage was this big hulking guy," recalled the late Irv Kaze, who was on the scene then as publicity director for the Yankees. "He had that fumanchu moustache—and there he was 60 feet away with seemingly the ability to throw a ball through a wall. But he was a gentle man."

The Sox did not score off the Goose in the seventh.

"That '78 playoff game is something I'll never forget," said Lou Piniella. "I can still vividly recall standing out in right field in the latter part of the game wanting the game to get over. We had the lead on Bucky's home run. We had the Goose in there to short-circuit them. But we knew that Boston was at home and that Boston was going to come back

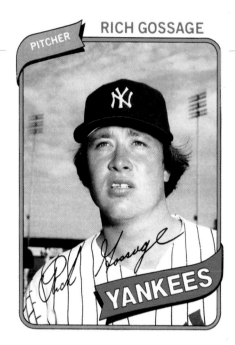

PITCHER

*Richard Michael Gossage (The Topps
Company, Inc.)*

at us. It was probably the most exciting game I ever played in."

In the Yankee eighth, Reggie Jackson tagged a Bob Stanley fastball deep into the centerfield bleachers. The Yankees now led, 5-2. Time and outs were disappearing for the Red Sox.

"When it wound up in the bleachers," Jackson said, "I just thought it was an extra run."

The game moved to the home half of the eighth inning. Fenway was a frenzy of Boston fans cheering on the Sox. Remy doubled off Gossage. Bedlam was on parade. Yaz singled him home. The little ballpark literally rocked. Carlton Fisk singled. Lynn singled to score Yaz. The Sox were now within one run of the Yankees.

Gossage managed to get Hobson on a fly ball. Scott was next. Thousands were on their feet, cheering, imploring the powerfully built batter to hit the ball out. Lemon was calm while all around him there was hysteria. He stayed with Gossage, who reached back and struck out Scott with one of his fiery fastballs.

The Yankees went down quickly in the top of the ninth, and the entire season for the two archrivals came down to the Sox' last three outs in the bottom of the ninth inning.

With one out, Burleson managed to work a walk against Gossage. Remy, the contact hitter, stepped in. Gossage pitched carefully—some would say cautiously. The Goose seemed to aim his pitch to the plate and Remy slashed the ball to right field. It kept sinking. The sun and the moment bore down on Piniella, who lost the ball for a moment. It dropped in front of him. Trapping the ball at the last moment, he picked it up and fired it to third base. Eddie Yost, screaming from the coach's box at third

for Burleson to come on, watched in both horror and amazement as the runner hesitated and finally remained at second base.

"We had a damn good chance to win it in the ninth inning," Remy still remembers the time. The Yankees were not out of it just yet. Powerful Jim Rice, who had connected for 28 home runs that season at Fenway Park, came to the plate. He was lusting for Number 29. Overanxious, he was a tick tardy on a Gossage fastball. He didn't get it all. Piniella did in deep right field. Burleson could have scored on that shot had he followed Yost's pleadings. He did move up to third on the out.

But the Red Sox were now down to their final out. Out of Central Casting—it was Gossage vs. Yastrzemski, in his 18th season with Boston.

Durable, dependable, the darling of fans all over New England, Yaz played through wrists and back problems that had vexed, hobbled him throughout the season.

It was the stylish slugger vs. the brutish power pitcher.

Burleson took his lead at third base. Remy took his lead at first base. Gossage took

Lou Piniella (The Topps Company, Inc.)

his signs from Thurman Munson. The signs were for show, academic.

"I wasn't going to mess around with breaking junk," Gossage said later, "and get beaten by anything but my best. Yastrzemski's the greatest player I've ever played against. I just wound up and threw it as hard as I could—I couldn't tell you where."

Yaz took the first pitch for a ball. He was honed in. Burleson, the potential tying run, was edgy at third base. Remy, the potential winning run, was stretching his leg muscles at first base. Reggie Jackson's home run, which seemed superfluous at the time, was all that stood in the way of the Sox.

Two on, two out. Gossage went into his windup. Around came the right arm, and a fastball tailing away from Yaz's strength and power came to the plate. The Sox legend swung with full force, but all he could manage was to hit the ball in a gentle arc toward third base. Nettles gloved it near the coaching box at third. Yankees poured out onto the ancient turf of

Fenway; Nettles jumped into the arms of Gossage.

The Yankees had their victory, 5-4. Ron Guidry was credited with the win, and his record moved to 25-3. Guidry's .893 winning percentage set a major league record for a 20-game winner. For Boston, the end was very bitter. Yaz marched back to his dugout, totally disgusted.

"Probably one of the biggest disappointments I ever had was losing that game," said Don Zimmer, who still feels the pain. "After the game was over it was pretty tough to walk into the clubhouse and see grown men cry."

For New York, the end was sweet. They Yankees were whooping it up in their dugout. They had overcome a 14-game lead and beaten the Sox on their own turf in the most significant game of the season—the most crucial game of all the supercharged contests played by the two clubs over the years.

A dejected Jim Rice retreated to the trainer's room and refused to speak to the press. That season had seen him pound out 46 homers and drive in 139 runs, but his team was the loser.

Yaz, disappointed but hopeful, said: "Someday, we're going to get that cigar. Before Old Yaz retires, he is gonna play on a world champion."

Fisk, angered and exhausted, said: "They caught us this time at our lowest ebb. We were hurting and our pitching was not consistent. When they came back they found out that we were the team with momentum. We had won eight in a row, and to think that it came down after a 162-game schedule to one game. But we never quit—not once."

OPPOSITE: *A youthful Reggie Jackson showing off his batting pose. (Photofest/Icon)*

PAST AS PROLOGUE

The Boston Red Sox came into exist ence in 1901 and remained one of the most successful of all baseball franchises through the first 19 years of the team's existence. They were known briefly as the Americans and Somersets and then the Pilgrims. Boston won the first "modern" World Series in 1903 and repeated as champions of the American League in 1904.

But the rough and cynical manager of the New York Giants, John J. McGraw—born in Truxton, New York, one of nine children of a father who was a nine-dollar-a-week railroad man—refused to allow his team to face Boston in postseason action. The Giants manager deemed the American League an inferior organization. He wasn't right about everything, despite his often saying he was.

By the early 1910s the nickname for the Boston American League team was the Red Sox. They moved into Fenway Park in April of 1912, and that initial campaign in the little ballpark was a momentous one. Boston captured the American League pennant and won the World Series.

Those were the glory years for Boston's Red Sox. In 1915, 1916, and 1918, the franchise repeated as pennant winners and won postseason championships. Those teams were built around a great pitching staff and terrific hitting, especially from the outfield of Tris Speaker, Harry Hooper and Duffy Lewis. The rest of the supporting cast fit in quite well.

Manager Bill Carrigan, Boston manager from 1913-16, made the most of pitchers like Joe Wood, Carl Mays, Dutch Leonard, Herb Pennock, Waite Hoyt, Ray Collins. Pitcher Babe Ruth was on the scene for the 1915 and 1916 triumphs.

The New York Highlanders (they officially became the New York Yankees in 1913) were a sad counterpoint to the attractive, successful and glamorous Red Sox. In their first 16 years of existence, the New Yorkers finished under .500 10 times and last in the league twice.

After the Red Sox won the 1916 World Series, Harry Frazee, a former Peoria, Illinois billposter, purchased the club from Joe Lannin.

OPPOSITE: *Ted Williams, Yogi Berra, Mickey Mantle. (Photofest)*

All agreed that the future looked bright for Frazee and the Bostons.

"Nothing is too good," declared Frazee who hadn't even paid Lannin for the purchase of the team, "for the wonderful fans of the Boston team." Hub zealots should have taken Frazee at his word. For as the future was to show time and time again—Frazee meant exactly what he said.

He had a home in Boston, but Frazee's main residence was on Park Avenue. He had made the comment that the "best thing about Boston was the train ride back to New York." A show business wheeler-dealer who owned a theater on 42nd Street in Manhattan, close by the New York Yankees offices, Frazee was a gambler. And he was always hustling, scuffling about for a buck, always overextended in one theatrical deal or another.

The World War I era had a very negative effect on attendance at Fenway. The wartime economy also hindered some of Frazee's show business ventures. Hurting in the pocketbook, the Sox owner looked to the Yankees for a silver lining. Dispatching pitchers Ernie Shore and Dutch Leonard and outfielder Duffy Lewis to the Bronx Bombers four days before Christmas of 1918, Frazee pocketed $50,000 for the trio—a very nice Christmas present.

After their 1918 World Series triumph over Chicago, Boston was baseball's top dog—winners of four titles in seven seasons. But the future was not so bright. Owner Harry ("Who did you send to the Yankees today?") Frazee more and more began to dismantle his ball club by shuttling stars and serviceable players to New York.

Carl Mays, a submarine-ball hurler, had back-to-back 20-win seasons in 1917-18 for the "Red Sawks." But by mid-season of 1919, his won-lost record was 5-11. And his attitude was as depressed as his pitching stats.

"I'm going fishing," he snapped on July 13, blaming his poor fortune and poorer pitching record on his teammates and their inept fielding skills. Mays followed this statement with another and more definitive one a few days later.

"I hate the Boston team. I'll never pitch another game for the Red Sox again."

Harry Frazee really had no part to play in the malaise that had attached itself to Carl Mays. But Frazee was not one to let any opportunity to make an extra buck pass him by. A good friend of Yankees owners colonel Jacob Ruppert and colonel Tillinghast l'Hommedieu Hutson, Frazee started wheeling and dealing again with the rich New Yorkers who had purchased the franchise in 1915 and were most anxious to produce the first New York Yankees championship team.

On July 29, 1919, two weeks after Mays "jumped" the Boston team, he was shipped to New York for $40,000 and pitchers Allan Russell and Bob McGraw. Boston was in an uproar, a condition that generally applied when it came to Yankees-Sox dealings.

American League president Ban Johnson made a very pronounced and principled announcement: "Baseball cannot tolerate such a breach of discipline. It was up to the owners of the Boston club to suspend Carl Mays for breaking the contract and when they failed, it is my duty as head of the American League to act. Mays will not play with any other club until the suspension is raised. He should have reported to the Boston club before they made any trade or sale."

Pitcher Babe Ruth (standing, far right) won 18 games for the 1915 Boston team. (Photofest / Icon)

The Johnson proclamation was followed by lawsuit and counter lawsuit and increasing controversy. In the end, Mays, like Leonard, Shore and Lewis before him—and the many who would follow after him—became a New York Yankee. In 1921, the Yanks won 98 games. They also won their first pennant. Carl Mays chipped in with 27 victories.

If Boston fans were alarmed and agitated by the loss of Carl Mays—what lay ahead would give them heartburn, nausea, and put them into fits of rage. What would be known in later years as the "The Curse of the Bambino" was on the horizon.

George Herman Ruth was born on February 6, 1895 in Baltimore. When he was eight years old he was placed in St. Mary's Industrial School for Boys, an institution that had a reputation for its effective treatment of "in-corrigible behavior." The Babe's "incorrigible" behavior included: stealing, truancy, chewing tobacco and drinking whiskey. Ruth's entire youth was spent at St. Mary's, and it was there that his awesome baseball talent was developed.

At age 16, Ruth was permitted to leave St. Mary's and pursue a career as a member of the Baltimore Orioles baseball team. A highly talented pitcher, a premier power hitter, the southpaw Ruth was purchased from Baltimore by the Red Sox in 1914. He was an 18-game winner in 1915, a 23-game winner in 1916, and a 24-game winner in 1917. With each passing season of success as a hurler, Ruth was given more and more time to ply his trade as a slugging outfielder. In 1918, he batted 317 times and tied for the league lead in home runs with 11.

Harry Frazee was thrilled with the all-around accomplishments of his slugger-hurler. Babe Ruth was not thrilled with the salary he was drawing of $7,000. He informed Frazee that at the end of the 1918 season he wanted to be paid at least $12,000 a season. Ruth also made it clear that he wanted a two-year contract. Frazee refused to meet the Babe's demands.

The Babe told reporters that if he was not to be given what he thought was his financial due, he would retire from baseball and spend his time on his farm in suburban Massachusetts and lavish his attention on his 20 head of cattle, his three dozen pigs, his scores of hens, his three horses and his Collie dog "Dixie."

Harry Frazee thought that Ruth was just "whistling Dixie," and announced that he would not give in to "the absurd salary demands." That winter of 1919 Ruth escalated his salary demands and claimed that he was fed up being platooned as a pitcher and outfielder.

"I want to be a regular player," snapped Ruth. "I'll win more games playing in the outfield that I will pitching every fourth day. And everybody knows that."

The 1919 schedule was reduced to 140 games because of the demands and repercussions of World War I. The Red Sox were scheduled to begin spring training Florida in mid-March. They had abandoned their usual Hot Springs, Arkansas site in order to play a series of exhibition games with the Giants of John McGraw and then barnstorm their way north. Babe Ruth was still holding out for more money. He knew that without him on the scene much of the glitter of the Red Sox would be missing from the tour.

On March 21, Babe Ruth and Harry Frazee were scheduled for a get together in the Sox owner's office in Manhattan. All over the walls were posters and photographs related to the shows he had produced. There were autographed pictures of Eddie Foy, George M. Cohan, the Barrymores, George Gershwin, Irving Berlin—Frazee's show business friends. Ruth was in a jovial mood, after kidding with secretaries and signing autographs before entering the private office for the meeting. When he came face to face with Frazee, his mood quickly changed.

"I want $10,000 a year for three years," Ruth demanded of Frazee, "and I want to play the outfield full time."

The Broadway impresario grabbed at his chest, almost dropping the pen he held in his hand in anticipation of the Babe's signing a contract.

"You've gotta be nuts," he screamed at Ruth. "I don't even pay my stage fellows that kind of money."

"What the fuck do I care about actors?" Ruth was livid. "I'll be a bigger star one day than every goddamned one of them. All I want is my goddamned money, and I tell you, Frazee, I'll hold out for the entire season if I don't get it! I want what I'm telling you, or I don't play for you."

Ruth got what he wanted. Frazee was disgusted with the Babe and the situation but realized the star status of his young and gifted player. "Besides," Frazee quipped later, "how the hell could you argue with someone like Ruth who had no respect for the acting profession?"

In 1919, Frazee and baseball fans all over got their money's worth. Babe Ruth batted .322 and set a new major league record for

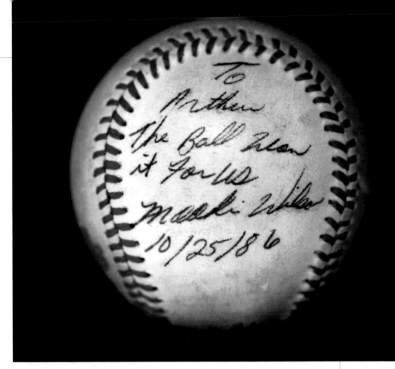

The seth swirsky collection/SETH.com

home runs in a season—29. It was a mark many thought would last forever. The Babe also had 139 hits—75 of them for extra bases. He also won nine games as a pitcher, finishing the year with a 2.97 ERA. But even with the man players called "Jidge" doing what he did best—hitting a baseball—the drab Boston Red Sox finished in sixth place, drawing just 417,291 paying customers into Fenway Park.

On January 9, 1920, what would be known as "Harry Frazee's crime" happened. It was a cold morning. At a news conference Yankee owner Jacob Ruppert announced: "Gentlemen, we have just bought Babe Ruth from Harry Frazee of the Boston Red Sox. I can't give exact figures, but it was a pretty check—six figures. No players are involved. It was strictly a cash deal."

Sox general manager Ed Barrow had told Frazee: "You ought to know that you're making a mistake."

For Frazee, it was apparently the only way for him to retain control of the Red Sox. He received $100,000 in cash, a guaranteed $350,000 mortgage on Fenway Park and the promise of more money for more players if needed.

News of the sale of Babe Ruth to the New York Yankees sent shock waves throughout New England. Frazee was hung in effigy. "Hairbreadth Harry" was just one of the phrases of disgust used to describe him.

In defense, Frazee said: "Ruth's 29 home runs were more spectacular than useful. They didn't help the Red Sox get out of sixth place." To intimates, Frazee was more honest. "I can't help it. I am up against the wall. Joe Lannin was starting to call in his mortgage on Fenway

Park. I needed money desperately."

Ruth was at first shaken and annoyed that he was going to the Yankees. "My heart is in Boston," he told reporters. "I have a farm in Sudbury. I like New England."

In New York City, manager John J. McGraw of the Giants gritted his teeth and prepared for the attendance battle he knew was in the future. The peppery pilot knew full well the gate potential of George Herman Ruth.

The dark age of Boston baseball can be traced directly to the sale of Babe Ruth to the Yankees. Beginning in 1919 the BoSox began a 15-year streak of losing campaigns, dropping at least 100 games in a season five times, and at least 90 games five more times. Last-place finishers in that era nine times, they were a sad excuse for a baseball franchise.

The golden age of Yankee baseball can be traced directly to their acquisition of the George Herman Ruth. The Yankees have won 26 world titles since the Red Sox won their last.

Boston has appeared in only four World Series since 1918, losing each one in seven games. Some say it also explains the ball dribbling through Bill Buckner's legs in Game 6 of the 1986 World Series, Aaron Boone's pennant-winning home run in the 11th inning of the 2003 Championship Series, and every other piece of misfortune that has attached itself to the sad "Sawks" since the Babe went to New York.

"I've never believed in the curse until 2003," said former New York City Mayor Rudy Giuliani.

And the animosity, the ill feelings, the combative atmosphere that still characterize Red Sox-Yankees competition has much to do with the Harry Frazee shuttle of players to New York. Up until the sale of Ruth, the Red Sox were one of the most successful of franchises. With the coming of Ruth, the Yankees became baseball's most successful franchise.

The seth swirsky collection/SETH.com

Comfortably clothed in pinstripes, with a guaranteed salary of $20,000 a year for his first two seasons, Ruth did not miss Boston much. And Harry Frazee even less.

"That Frazee," Ruth announced to all who listen, "was a cheap son of a bitch. They had a Babe Ruth day for me last year [1919] and I had to buy my wife tickets to the game. Fifteen thousand fans showed up and all I got was a cigar."

George Herman Ruth got much more than a cigar from the New York Yankees. He got money—lots of it. But it was all money very well spent.

In 1920, Babe Ruth slammed 54 home runs—more than any other team total except the Phillies. His .847 slugging percentage stood as the all-time best until Barry Bonds and 2001 came along. He batted .376, drove in 137 runs, led the league in runs scored and stolen bases, too.

Everything about the Babe was excessive: his bat—44 ounces, his frame—top playing weight of 254 pounds, his appetites—food and drink consumed in abundance.

The Yankee gain was the Red Sox loss. The name and face of Babe Ruth became known to more people in the United States than any other player in baseball. Writers competed with each other, straining to characterize the phenomenal slugger.

He was called "Sultan of Swat," "The Bambino," "the Wali of Wallop," "the Rajah of Rap," "the Caliph of Clout," "the Wazir of Wham," "The Colossus of Clout," "Maharajah of Mash," "The Behemoth of Bust," and "The King of Clout." Opponents called him "The Big Monk" and "Monkey" and a lot of unmentionables.

The 1920 Yankees finished in third place, two notches ahead of the struggling Red Sox. In 1919, without Ruth, the Yanks drew 619,614. With Ruth acting like a magnet at

OPPOSITE: *Babe Ruth, having his cake and eating it, too. (Photofest/Icon)*

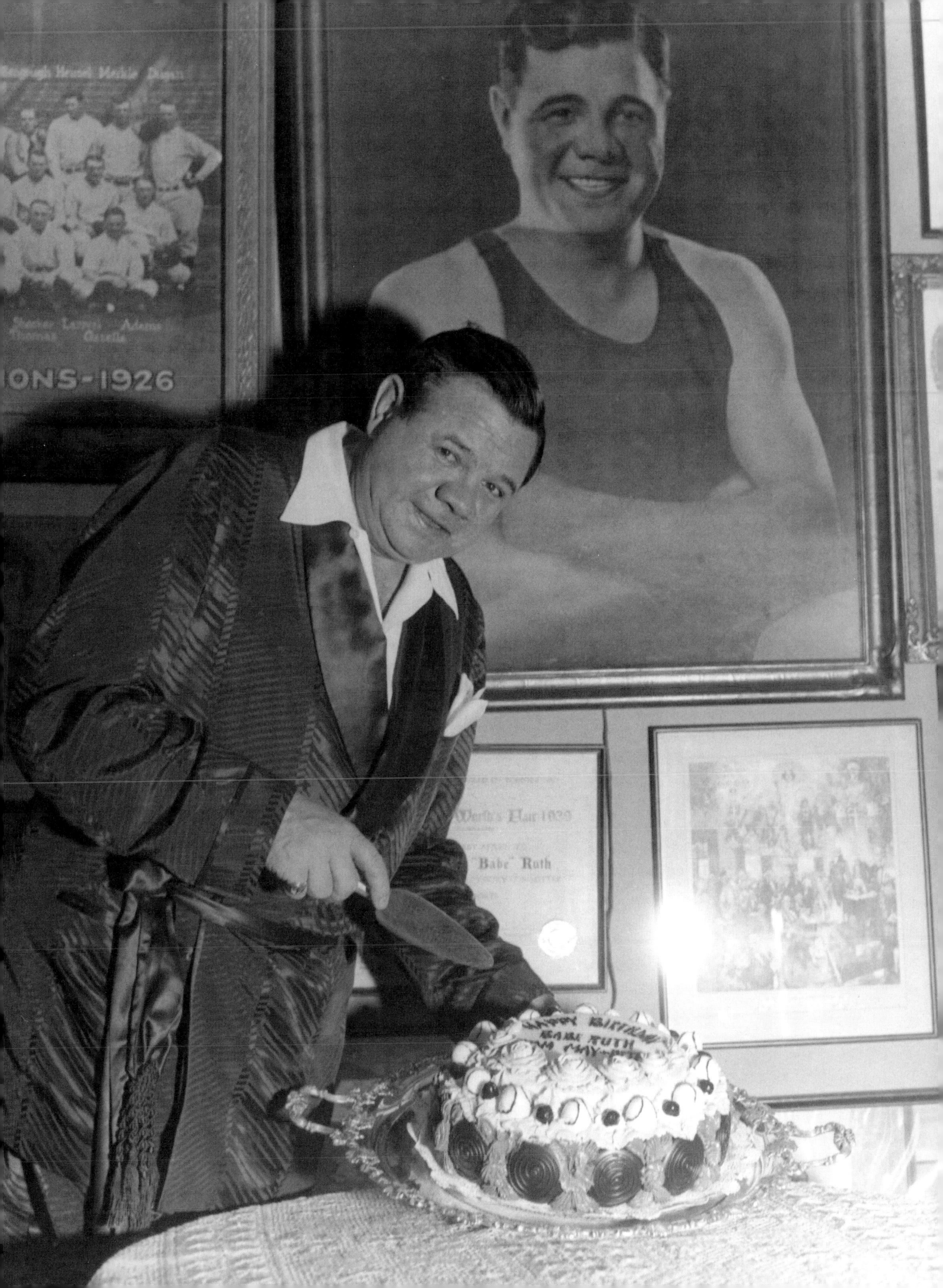
IONS-1926
"Babe" Ruth

the turnstiles, the 1920 Yankees attracted 1,289,444—an attendance record that stood until 1946.

Boston general manager Ed Barrow, who had believed that Ruth's best position was as a pitcher but was proven wrong—followed the path of so many others—from the Red Sox to the Yankees. He parted company with Harry Frazee on October 19, 1920, a year after Ruth had joined the Bronx Bombers. Barrow would now be on the receiving end of the New York-Boston shuttle instead of on the sending end.

Old school, quick to use his fists, quick to anger, Barrow ran the affairs of the Yankees from the Stadium and his office on 42nd street. A two-time Major League Executive of the Year, Barrow was respected but also feared by his peers.

On December 15, Barrow made his first trade with his former team. The Yankees received pitchers Waite Hoyt and Harry Harper, infielder Mike McNally and catcher Wally Schang. The Sox obtained outfielder Sam Vick, third baseman Derrill Pratt, pitcher Herb Thormahlen, catcher Muddy Ruel and cash. Cash was always the supremely important factor for Boston.

Key in the trade was hurler Waite Hoyt. Just 6-6 with Boston in 1919, he won 19 games in each of the next two seasons for the Yankees and was on his way to the Baseball Hall of Fame. It was Hoyt who coined the expression: "It's great to be young and a Yankee." He might have added, "And to no longer play for the Red Sox."

Hoyt supplemented his income in unusual ways. An artist, writer and singer, in the late 1920s he appeared in vaudeville, dancing and singing, even performing a few times at the Palace Theater in New York City. He also was a mortician and once said of his two off-season careers, "I'm knocking 'em dead on Seventh Avenue while my partner is laying 'em out up in Westchester."

The Yankees were knocking 'em dead at the Stadium while the Sox were growing weaker and weaker at Fenway. And Boston fans grew fewer, more vociferous, testier as the seasons moved on and the one-sided trades kept happening.

"Who did Frazz sell today?" was the question asked throughout New England. Telegrams were sent and phone calls were made to baseball commissioner Landis objecting to "the rape of the Red Sox."

The man most responsible for "the rape of the Red Sox" was colonel Jacob Ruppert, one of the richest men in the United States with a personal fortune of about $50 million, most it coming from his beer business and real estate investments. The Ruppert New York City brewery occupied 35 red brick buildings that stood like fortresses on four blocks from East 90th Street to East 94th Street in Yorkville between Second and Third Avenue.

Born in New York City on August 5, 1867, he was the son and grandson of beer tycoons who founded the Ruppert Breweries. In his youth he tried out for the New York Giants but couldn't make the club.

His was a life of luxury filled with all that money could buy, including the New York Yankees. Heir to the family millions, Jake Ruppert used his money to get elected and serve as a four-time member of the House of Representatives from 1899 to 1906, representing the "Silk Stocking" district of Manhattan.

Aristocratic, arrogant, he lived in a fashionable 12-room apartment on Fifth Avenue; five full-time servants catered to his every whim. As a bachelor, he seemed to always have one desirable woman or another with him as he made the rounds of New York's high society. His hobbies included collecting fine art and bric-a-brac. He had a passion for raising thoroughbred horses and pedigreed dogs.

Everyone called him "Colonel," but the title was an honorary one. It came from a stint served in the National Guard in the 1890s. He was an aide to camp to the governor of New York State.

Jake Ruppert (Photofest/Icon)

When Jake Ruppert had purchased 50 percent of the Yankees on January 11, 1915, he was convinced that the team would be a good vehicle to aid his beer company sales. He was rebuffed by the 13 managing editors of New York City newspapers who voted against his proposal to change the name of his baseball team to Knickerbockers, after the name of his best-selling beer. Ruppert vowed that he'd find another way to make the franchise pay for itself—by winning on the field. By tapping the Harry Frazee pipeline of BoSox stars, Jake Ruppert kept his vow.

The 1921 Yankees won 98 games and lost 55 and won their first American League pennant by four and a half games over the Cleveland Indians who had seven regulars who batted .310 or more. Boston finished in fifth place, 23 and a half games off the pace.

The Yankees had a decided Red Sox flavor. Babe Ruth was very close to peak form. He slashed 59 home runs, drove in 171 runs and batted .378. Catcher Wally Schang chipped in with a .316 batting average. Mike McNally was the regular third baseman. Carl Mays, who had not wanted to pitch for the Red Sox, was the workhorse of the Yankee staff. He appeared in more games, pitched more innings and won more games than any other pitcher in the league. And Waite Hoyt, a six-game winner for Boston in 1920, won 19 games for New York in 1921.

The World Series was all New York—the Giants against the Yankees. Despite the Herculean efforts of Waite Hoyt (27 innings and no earned runs allowed) the Yankees lost the series to the Giants.

Downcast, Yankee manager Miller Huggins told Ruppert: "We could have won if we had more pitching."

Huggins wanted more pitching. Ruppert went about getting more. On December 20, Boston shipped pitchers Joe Bush and Sam Jones and shortstop Everett Scott to the Yankees for two pitchers, shortstop Roger Peckinpaugh and cash.

Peckinpaugh was a valuable player acquired by the Red Sox in that trade. But the shortstop was a member of the Red Sox for a day. For cash and "Jumping Joe" Dugan, Frazee peddled Peckinpaugh to the Washington Senators.

But the story did not end there. In midsummer of 1922, Dugan playing his usual steady game and batting .287 for Boston. The Yankees were involved in a tough pennant race and had a gap at third base. Once again, Jake Ruppert turned to his "Boston farm team." Dugan and outfielder Elmer Smith were dispatched to the Yankees for pitcher Lefty O'Doul, a couple of no-name players. And, yes, cash. There was always cash, even though all the Boston-New York trades were announced with the tag line: "There were no other considerations."

It was just another of the deals that did in Boston and created the Yankee dynasty. The controversial trade made in the heat of a pennant race caused an uproar and helped bring about the creation of the June 15 trading deadline the following year. In seven Yankee seasons Dugan would field flawlessly, bat .286, and perform admirably in five World Series.

In 1922, with Dugan contributing and with ex-Boston pitchers Hoyt, Jones, Bush and Mays combining to win 77 games—the Yankees won their second straight pennant. Boston finished in last place—33 games out.

Once again the Yankees were pitted against the New York Giants in the World Series. And once again the Giants were the victors, sweeping the Yankees in four straight. The Yanks had strong pitching arms—Mays, Bush, Jones, etc. But they were all right-handers.

Huggins once again approached Ruppert with a request to strengthen the Yankees. "We could win the whole thing," he said, "if we could only pick up a strong left-handed pitcher." The Colonel told his little manager: "I'll see what I can do."

When the 1922 season ended, *Reach's Baseball Guide* for 1923 commented that "Boston last season reached the fruits of four years' despoliation by the New York club, and for the second time in American League baseball history, this once great Boston team, now utterly discredited, fell into last place, with every prospect of remaining in that undesirable position indefinitely."

It was that "discredited" club that colonel Jake Ruppert surveyed, looking for a southpaw pitcher. Like a vulture, the Yankees had picked the Boston roster clean over the years. There was not much left, but there was a left-hander named Herb Pennock, the "Squire of Kennett Square," one of the classiest individuals in the baseball of his time. He had attended the finest prep schools, was a horticulturist and bred red silver foxes at his country home near Kennett Square, Pennsylvania. Pennock had won just 10 games in 1922 against 17 losses, but most baseball experts agreed that with a good team behind him, Pennock would be an effective pitcher.

Ruppert made his deal with Frazee for Pennock on January 30, 1923, and George Pipgras, a player with promise. Boston received pitcher Norman McMillan, pitcher George Murray, outfielder Camp Skinner and cash.

When the 1923 season opened, Babe Ruth already had 197 career home runs—25 percent of which would be his lifetime total of 747. He and Pennock were old friends from their days together on the Red Sox. And with Ruth pounding away, the stylish pitcher was re-born in pinstripes; Pennock's first season saw him lead the league in winning percentage (.760) the first of four over-.700 seasons.

In 1917, when Harry Frazee purchased the Boston Red Sox, the team was the best franchise in the American League. Out of the 13 World Series played, the Red Sox had won four. Within five years Frazee turned a great team into mush, selling 15 players, most of them to the Yankees.

In July of that 1923 season, after seven and a half years of diminishing returns, Harry Frazee sold out his last-place team for $1.5 million to a group of Ohio businessmen. Veteran front office man Bob Quinn from St. Louis was brought in to run the club. The main moneyman was millionaire Winslow Palmer. Boston fans were thrilled at the news and hopeful of a turnaround in the fortunes of the Sox.

Maybe it was the "Curse of the Bambino," maybe it was bad breaks—the turnaround didn't really happen. Palmer passed away less than two years after Frazee sold out. The years of the Great Depression eroded extra cash that Boston fans would have spent on the team. And there was also the phenomenon known as "Quinn's Weather." Inclement atmospheric conditions always seemed to be plaguing and affecting attendance at Fenway Park. "Every time we got set for a big crowd," sighed Quinn, "it seemed to rain."

While Quinn struggled with the weather and other issues, Jake Ruppert's Yankees just sailed along. On May 6, 1930, the financial stresses that seemed to have always afflicted Frazee were front and center for Quinn, who followed the former Sox owner's path going after cash. He traded pitcher Red Ruffing to the New York Yankees for outfielder Cedric Durst and cash—$50,000 of it.

Durst was 34 years old, and in six previous seasons had never performed in more than 92 games a campaign. That 1930 season was his last—he batted .240, four points below his lifetime average. With Boston, Ruffing twice led the league in losses. A 22-game winner in his first New York season, Ruffling was just another BoSox reject who came to the Yankees and started shining. Utilizing a moving fastball with a sharp breaking curve, the powerful Ruffing went 231-124 in 15 Yankee seasons. He had four consecutive 20-victory seasons and won seven of nine World Series decisions for the Yankees.

On February 25,1933, ownership changed again for the Red Sox. A 30-year-old multimillionaire sportsman paid Bob Quinn $1.5 million for the Red Sox. Thomas Austin Yawkey would spend 44 years as the sole owner of the team, many times spending grandly while pursuing a winner.

A nephew of the late Bill Yawkey, onetime owner of the Detroit Tigers, he had come into the bulk of a huge financial estate trust fund and vowed to spend as much of it as it took to make the Bostons winners. In the dozen years before the coming of Yawkey, the Red Sox had become the street urchins of the American League. There had been nine lastplace finishes in that time period. And Fenway Park had become a dilapidated, downtrodden slum. In that same time period, the Yankees in their brand-new, glittering Stadium had copped seven pennants.

Frommer Archives

Tom Yawkey shelled out $750,000 to reconstruct Fenway Park in 1934 and another $250,000 to acquire player-manager Joe Cronin from Washington in what was the second biggest deal in baseball history to that point in time.

Cronin, the 28-year-old son-in-law of Washington Senators owner Clark Griffith, was installed as Sox shortstop and manager in 1935. And for the first time since 1918 and the days of Ed Barrow, Boston played over .500 ball, finishing in fourth place, 16 games out of first.

Yawkey even paid off the mortgage on Fenway Park ahead of schedule as a result of the unexpected Red Sox success on the playing field. When the sportsman Yawkey had acquired the Sox, he made arrangements with Yankee ownership to carry the Harry Frazee demand mortgage through the 1934 season.

But when the BoSox swept the Yankees in 1933 in five games at Fenway, Ruppert was furious. "It was a costly sweep," recalled Yawkey. "Ruppert demanded immediate payment on the mortgage." The payoff to the Yankee owner was immediate, and it severed forever any financial linkage or leverage between the two archrival franchises.

Through the years Colonel Ruppert always had the quick pen and ready checkbook to improve the Yankees. Now he had a worthy rival. Tom Yawkey was intent on spending whatever it took to make the Red Sox into winners. He picked up stars from other teams—Lefty Grove, Max Bishop, Heinie Manush, Rube Walberg, Jimmie Foxx.

Boston finished in sixth place in 1936, and in fifth place in 1937. There were back-to-back second-place finishes in 1938-39 behind the Yankees.

The BoSox improvement in the late 1930s was due in large part to the leadership of shortstop/manager Joe Cronin and the stabilizing influence of veterans like Jimmie Foxx and Lefty Grove. The addition of Ted Williams and Bobby Doerr gave the Sox the wherewithal to challenge the Yankees and Tigers for dominance in the 1940s.

And in July 1939, in one of the most satisfying moments in rivalry history for Boston fans, the Sox swept the Yanks in five straight games at Yankee Stadium chopping the 11 and a half New York lead to six and a half games.

A furious Yankee manager Joe McCarthy bellowed: "Just who the hell are supposed to be the world champions? Us or the damned Red Sox? We're a whole lot better than Boston."

Agonizing as it was for fans of the Fenway team to hear—Marse Joe was correct. The Yankees were the better team.

In 1942, Boston finished in second place—the fourth time in five seasons that the Sox were in that position—behind New York.

From 1938 through 1951, Boston wound up third or higher 10 times. However,

OPPOSITE: *Hall of Fame catcher Bill Dickey in a familiar pose. (Photofest/Icon)*

there was but one pennant during that time period—in 1946. Boston lost the World Series that year in seven games to the Cardinals. It was a painful defeat, the only chance at a world championship that was ever there for the taking for Ted Williams, Bobby Doerr, Dom DiMaggio.

But Tom Yawkey kept pursuing his dream (some would say obsession) of beating out the hated foe—the New York Yankees. "Ruppert bought some pennants when he was able to reach out to the Red Sox for players," said Yawkey. "But it doesn't seem to work for us when we buy old champions. So, we've got to do something else and raise our own. We've got to build up a farm system such as Branch Rickey has built in St. Louis and Barrow and Weiss in New York. That's the only way we can catch the Yankees."

Yawkey and the Red Sox attempted to catch up. But the Yankees with general manager and master builder George Weiss on the scene, always forging ahead—it was tough.

The buzz was that Weiss not only emulated Branch Rickey's farm system concept, he improved on it. Yankee farm teams were located all over the place: Kansas City, Butler, Pennsylvania; Norfolk, Virginia; Springfield, Massachusetts; Augusta, Georgia; Akron, Ohio; Bassett, Virginia; Beaumont, Texas.

The glittering jewel of the Yankee organization was at Newark, New Jersey where from 1932 to 1938 the Bears racked up five straight first-place finishes. In 1937, the club posted a 109-43 record; 16 of its 17 regulars went on to become players in the major leagues.

A short, dour man, George Weiss pursued excellence with frugality and passion. "There is no such thing as second place," he said. "You're first or you're nothing." From the 1930s through the 1960s, the drab and detail-oriented George Weiss was the main man responsible for Yankee success. There were those who called him the Yankee inspector-general because he held sway over everything— the positions players were slotted for, the quality of toilet paper, the look of the players and their uniforms.

From 1932 to 1943, Weiss Yankee teams won eight pennants with players mainly produced from the farm system. Just $100,000 was spent for player purchases. One of those purchases cost $25,000. His name was Joe DiMaggio.

Throughout the decade of the 1950s, the team from Fenway was generally a fourth-place finisher. It was a down time for the Fenway faithful, for some it was teary eye time—seeing the Yankees finish first eight times.

By the early 1960s "Teddy Ballgame" had retired, but left field was ably manned by Carl Yastrzemski who signed as a shortstop off the campus of Notre Dame in February 1959. Yaz played 23 seasons for the Sox—winning three batting titles and a triple crown. Then Jim Rice took over in left field, and then Mike Greenwell in the 1980s. The Boston Red Sox have always seemed to have a thumper.

But thump away as they did (11 batting championships from 1962 to 1988), there was the "Curse" always in the air, always seemingly affecting Boston's destiny. Big games somehow could not be won.

In 1967, Yaz won the Triple Crown and led the team to the Series, where they were vanquished in seven games by St. Louis. In 1972, Detroit nipped Boston on the last day

OPPOSITE: *Vic Raschi: The man they called the "Springfield Rifle." (Photofest/Icon)*

Vic Raschi

Red Sox slugging outfielder Jim Rice. (Photofest)

stead, Lynn, Fisk, and Lansford were all let go and the team aged slowly, but not like fine wine.

In 1986, a young flamethrower named Roger Clemens carried the club to victory after victory. There was an exciting come-from-behind win in the ALCS over the Angels. It seemed the time was right for a Red Sox title. But in the World Series, just one strike from their first championship since 1918, the Sox were victimized by a New York Mets rally that enabled them to win Game 6. Of course Boston also lost Game 7.

Boston made two playoff stops in 1988 and 1990, with batting champion Wade Boggs and Clemens torquing the team. By the 1990s, disarray was the operative factor. There was a last-place finishing 1992 (73-89 .451). There was a parade of pilots—Joe Morgan, Butch Hobson, Kevin Kennedy, Jimmy Williams. The team and its fans watched in anguish as Jeff Bagwell blossomed into a superstar for Houston after the Red Sox had dealt him in a late-season trade.

The arrival of Pedro Martinez in 1998 did wonders for the pitching staff and brought two immediate payoffs—wild card berths in '98 and '99. But once again the Sox failed to capitalize, falling short due to a weak bench and inconsistent defense. In addition, beyond Martinez the Boston pitching was slim.

Mo Vaughn jumped off the Red Sox listing ship and signed with Anaheim after the 1998 season. Boston went after Yankee star outfielder Bernie Williams. It seemed they had him signed and delivered. What seemed was not reality—he stayed in the Bronx. Two years later pitcher Mike Mussina was the apple of Boston's eye. But he said "yes" to a contract to the team from the Big Apple. He agreed to

of the regular season, denying the Sox an AL East title. In 1975, Boston rode rookie sensations Rice and Fred Lynn to the pennant only to lose to Cincinnati in a thrilling seven-game World Series.

The ultimate slap in the face came in 1978 when that same Red Sox team built around Rice, Lynn, Yaz, Carlton Fisk, and Luis Tiant squandered a huge lead and allowed the hated Yankees to catch them in the division race. In a one-game playoff, Bucky Dent did more than dent the Sox season—he ended it with an unlikely three-run homer. The Red Sox curse was firmly in place.

The Sox should have gone into the 1980s with Rice, Lynn, Fisk, Dwight Evans, and Carney Lansford solidifying their lineup. In-

Wade Boggs as a Red Sox player. (Photofest)

Burly Mo Vaughn, once a BoSox favorite. (Photofest)

2000, the BoSox were unable to catch the Yankees despite a late-season collapse by New York. In 2001, Boston imploded—firing Williams as manager, suspending could-have-been-a-star outfielder Carl Everett for several embarrassing incidents. In 2002, there was some early joy in Boston, but once again there was the famous Red Sox fade.

Going into the 2004 season, Boston had finished six straight times in second place in the American League East. The team that wound up ahead of them was the Yankees.

The 2003 Yankees had a $180 million-plus payroll—the largest in the history of sports. The Yankees had never lost a division race when leading by six or more games at any point during the season, and the team from the Bronx was 35-for-35 when taking a lead into September. In the last 100 years the Yankees have been in first place on the first day of September 35 times, and they have finished first those 35 times.

Enter, for the Red Sox of Boston, a new kid on the block in 2003—Yale-educated Theo Epstein, the youngest general manager in the major leagues. He grew up just a 10-minute walk from Fenway in Brookline. "On certain nights from our home you can hear the roar of the crowd," his father Leslie Epstein, the head of the creative writing program at Boston University, noted. "And on certain nights you could certainly see the lights of the stadium.

"I felt a mixture of pride and horror that Theo became the general manager of the Red Sox at age 28. It was his dream to accomplish

continue with the Yankees even before the Red Sox made their offer to him.

Boston's 1999 team deserves some credit—they were the first Red Sox team to face the New York Yankees in postseason play. But the New Yorkers knocked them out of the postseason in five games.

From 1998 through 2000, the Yankees were never out of first place after July 7. In

Theo Epstein (Frommer Archives)

that by age 50. The horror—because I knew what was in store for him."

But Theo Epstein has seemingly turned all the doubters in New England into believers. He takes the New York Yankees for what they are—the challenge.

"We know that to get to the World Series we have to go through the Yankees at some point or another," Epstein acknowledges.

"They are a great team and a great franchise, and we have to beat the Yankees on the field. They raise the bar, the level of competitiveness for us.

"The rivalry is one of the cities as well as the teams. I don't like to wax poetic about it. The curse of the Bambino gets more attention in literary, media, popular culture circles than it does in the clubhouse. We don't think of the curse. We have quite a few new players this year of 2003 and we are trying to win as many games as we can. We don't buy into curses. It is not significant to us what happened 84 years ago—we are concerned with putting the best team on the field."

So is George Steinbrenner. And he is now, as he has always been, obsessed with the Boston Red Sox. "George has definitely heightened the rivalry," notes veteran *New York Daily News* baseball writer Bill Madden. "George singled out the Red Sox many years ago. Now you have both teams going at each owner especially with the 'Evil Empire' comment of Boston president Larry Lucchino."

The Christmas Day 2002 headline in the *New York Daily News* read: "An ace under Yankees' tree." The headline referred to the signing of 31-year-old Cuban defector pitcher Jose Contreras to a four-year $26 million deal that made the Red Sox fume in the process. Boston had been in hot pursuit of Contreras and allegedly was willing to pay "significantly higher" than the Yankees for the services of the Cuban hurler.

Boston principal owner John Henry hosted Contreras at his south Florida home while former pitching great Luis Tiant, a Cuban idol, hyped both the city of Boston and the Red Sox franchise. But Contreras chose New York saying, "For me it's an honor to play for the Yankees."

In the end, the Yankees had too much to counter—history, tradition, resources and New York.

"It's very difficult to bid against a team that has an unlimited budget," said John Henry. "It doesn't matter how many outfielders or how many [starting pitchers] they have. With an unlimited budget you can buy anyone you think you need."

Red Sox team president Larry Lucchino was not nearly as diplomatic. When the Contreras signing was announced he said: "No comment." Then he switched gears: "No, I'll make a comment. The evil empire extends its tentacles even into Latin America," Lucchino said. He went on to call the signing of Contreras ludicrous.

Ludicrous or not, it was just another chapter in the historic second-fiddle-to-the-New York Yankees life of the Boston Red Sox. Even in December.

In 2003, the Red Sox could not ease off the "Star Wars" theme. When the Yankees took batting practice at Fenway, the organist played a theme from the movie.

And Leslie Epstein, long-time Yankees hater who has compared rooting for the Yankees to voting Republican, also got into the act with his "Star Wars" analogy to George Steinbrenner: "If Darth Vader the convicted felon should be discomforted, well, it pleases me to no end."

In 2003, the Red Sox again finished second to the Yankees, for the sixth straight time. And Boston, despite a late lead in the seventh and deciding game of the American League Championship Series, finished a runner-up in that series as well, losing on an 11th-inning home run by Aaron Boone.

OPPOSITE: "Mr. October," Reggie Jackson, and George Steinbrenner. (Photofest)

V

THE MOOD,
THE CULTURE

It is perhaps the oldest and strongest rivalry in American sports history—the Yankees of New York vs. the Red Sox of Boston. Part of the rivalry is the stark contrasts in the images of the two teams. The Red Sox are Avis. The Yankees are Hertz.

In Boston, they scream: "Yankees suck! Yankees suck! " And even when the Yankees are not playing in Boston, you can hear those words at Fenway during a Tampa Bay, Mets or a Baltimore game.

In New York, they chant: "1918! 1918!"

The New York Yankees are the most successful of all franchises in baseball history, in sports history. A club of leaders and legends: Babe Ruth, Lou Gehrig, Lefty Gomez, Bill Dickey, Earle Combs, Joe McCarthy, Joe DiMaggio, Whitey Ford, Yogi Berra, Thurman Munson, Allie Reynolds, Vic Raschi, Casey Stengel, Billy Martin, Mickey Mantle, Roger Maris, Reggie Jackson, Ron Guidry, Goose Gossage, Don Mattingly, Bernie Williams, Derek Jeter.

Through the years winning has been as much a part of the ethos of the Yankees as the pinstriped uniforms, the monuments and plaques in deep centerfield. It was once said: "Rooting for the New York Yankees is like rooting for General Motors." Unlike General Motors, the Yankees roll over teams, especially the Red Sox. The Yanks are the champions, the front runners, the crème de la crème of Major League Baseball.

The Boston Red Sox, less successful, more human, more vulnerable, have seemed like the rest of us. For the team and its fans, winning at times has not seemed as important as beating the Yankees and then winning. For through the years, the success of the Sox has been measured against Yankee success.

Item: In 1925, the Yanks sought to trade a first baseman even up to the Red Sox for Phil Todt. Boston passed on the trade. The first baseman, Lou Gehrig, became one of the great players of all time. Todt batted .258 lifetime with 57 home runs.

Item: Since shipping Babe Ruth to the Big Apple, the Sawks have lost the flag in a playoff in 1948 and 1978, and lost Game 7 of the World Series four times: 1946, 1967, 1975 and 1986.

Pregame inside the Red Sox dugout. (Frommer Archives)

Item: There have been 13 years of Boston runner-up finishes to Bronx Bombers—1938, 1939, 1941, 1942, 1949,1977, 1978, 1998, 1999, 2000, 2001, 2002, and 2003. The second-place blues have frustrated the Red Sox Nation and further stoked the coals of the Boston-New York rivalry.

Item: During a time of Yankee glory from 1919 to 1945, the Red Sox never placed first in the eight-team American League, finishing an average of 30 games behind in the standings. They came in last nine times, and had five 100-plus-loss seasons.

For the fans of the old Brooklyn Dodgers, the slogan used to be this hopeful refrain: "Wait 'til Next Year." For Boston fans, it has been this sarcastic snipe: "When are they going to fold this year?"

The Yankee-Red Sox competition involves much more than a baseball team representing Boston against a baseball team representing New York. It is, in reality, a competition between the provincial capital of New England and the mega-municipality that is New York City: the different lifestyles of the residents of those areas, the different accents they speak in. The contrasting symbols are like guideposts to their cities. It's the Charles River vs. the East River, Boston Common compared with Central Park.

History, style, culture, pace, dreams, self-images, bragging rights—all are mixed in, mixed up with the rivalry in one way or another. And the fact that both teams have been in the American League since the beginning of the last century doesn't hurt the competition either.

The late Bill Crowley, former Boston public relations director, said: "Red Sox fans hate the Yankees desperately. The pinstripes, the hoopla, the glamour—it is something that is very deeply resented. And when they win—especially over us—you can cast a pall over the entire area."

Red Sox territory comprises five and a half states—Massachusetts, Vermont, Maine, New Hampshire, Rhode Island and half of Connecticut.

"The Sox give away western Connecticut to the Mets and the Yankees," noted Crowley, "and there are pockets of resistance in Providence, Rhode Island and Worcester, Massachusetts. Most of the pockets are Italian. The people there were fans of Yankee stars like Crosetti, Lazzeri, DiMaggio, Berra, Rizzuto. And they passed their feeling on to their sons and grandsons."

Crowley had the unusual experience of being a Boston kid "who grew up to work for the Yankees, first." Working with Mel Allen and broadcasting Yankee games, Crowley was the third-string announcer. "Ralph Houk," Crowley pointed out, "was the third-string catcher. It was back in those days that Crowley was made acutely and passionately aware of the Sox-Yankee Connecticut dividing line.

"Mel Allen was supersensitive," Crowley recalled. He worried that his third-string announcer had a wife who was rabidly pro-Sox who might say something negative about the Yankees at a dinner party or gathering and be overheard by New York general manager George Weiss, a man who was passionately anti-Red Sox.

"We'd sit there at the Stadium," Crowley remembered, "for a Sunday doubleheader with the Sox. Fifty, sixty thousand people would show up and some of them would carry placards:

OPPOSITE: *The great Mel Allen, always enjoying his justly deserved awards. (Frommer Archives)*

JFK and Mel Allen—two icons. (Frommer Archives)

"EAST WATERBURY SAYS MEL ALLEN STINKS."

"Mel would get very upset," continued Crowley. "I'd say, 'Wait just a few minutes, Mel. West Waterbury will come by and everything will be all right.' A little while later West Waterbury did come by and their placards bragged: 'WEST WATERBURY THINKS MEL ALLEN IS GREAT.'"

Through the decades Yankee fans have been sated and satisfied with the greatness and the spectacular dominance of the Bronx Bombers over their baseball competition. The Yankees have piled up 39 American League pennants and 26 world championships. Boston has managed just 10 pennants and five world championships, the last one in that long ago year of 1918.

These statistics have contributed in part to Boston's bittersweet romance with its fans and its writers. Dubbed "the Olde Towne Teame," romanticized by authors like John Updike and John Cheever, the Red Sox have been likened to a "bad broad." Summer ro-

mance usually turns into a jilting in the fall, but by spring the fans fall in love again, seemingly more deeply than ever before.

The unfortunate and sexist metaphor of the "bad broad" and the repeated and heartbreaking losses to the New York Yankees has elicited some sharp rebukes and big boos from Boston writers.

On June 1, 1950, one of them wrote about that season's Red Sox entry: "Look at them all out there—nice fellows, all well paid, all good players, but Birdie Tebbets excepted, there isn't enough spirit in the whole lot of them to provide a enough flickering flame for one cigarette lighter."

An even more vituperative commentary was delivered by Mike Barnicle in the September 9, 1979 *Boston Globe*. "What has 18 legs and no arm?" he asked. "What folds easier than toilet paper? What baseball team can impersonate the main course of a Thanksgiving dinner? The Sox could qualify for a group rate on a heart transplant...They have looked like accordions or folding chairs...They're an embar-

Ted Williams, Bobby Doerr, Dom DiMaggio and Vern Stephens. (Frommer Archives)

rassment, a very collection of dressing room fighters. They are a pathetic team without character."

Writers such as these have earned the reputation and the appellation as "the vicious Boston press," according to Crowley. "They are never satisfied. They are like a combination of fan writers. They go to the winter baseball meetings and are impressed by a couple of trades and things they hear about the team. They go to spring training and again are impressed. 'This is going to be it.' And if it doesn't

happen—like the disappointed bridegroom, they become extremely negative."

In 1946, 1967 and 1975 there was no negativism, no disappointed bridegroom. The atmosphere throughout New England in those seasons was unrestrained and widespread euphoria.

When the 1946 season began, some experts wisecracked that "the Red Sox will win in their league and the Yankees will win in the American League." Seventh-place finishers in 1945, Boston had last won a pennant in 1918.

The Yankees had reeled off six pennants in the nine years prior to the 1946 season.

On Opening Day of the 1946 season, it looked like the same old story. The Bronx Bombers pounded Sox hurler Tex Hughson and crushed Boston, 12-5. The next day, however, the BoSox swamped the Yankees by the same score and were off and running on a 15-game winning streak. In May, Boston won 21 of 27 games.

By the All-Star break, the Red Sox had a 54-23 record. It was a team stocked and led by farm products and fashioned to fit the strange and friendly contours of Fenway Park: Ted Williams, Bobby Doerr, Dom DiMaggio, Mickey Harris, Earl Johnson.

More than 600,000 fans came out to see the season series between the Yankees and Red Sox. Thousands more were turned away. Posting a 60-17 record at home, the Sox won 104 games, the most in their history. They finished the season with a .675 percentage, the highest in their history. Boston also recorded its first million attendance for a season as 1,416,944 crowded into tiny Fenway spurring on the home team.

Bitter and disappointed Yankee fans blamed their team's disappointing third-place finish (17 games out) on slumps by Joe DiMaggio, Charlie Keller, Joe Gordon and Tommy Henrich. Jubilant Sox zealots simply made the point that Boston was the better team. Indeed, Boston did win 15 of the 22 games they played against the Yankees.

The 1946 Red Sox were an exciting and talented club. Ted Williams batted .342 and led the league in walks, runs scored, slugging percentage and total bases. He also hit 38 home runs and drove in 123 runs. Dom DiMaggio batted .316 and was a master center fielder.

Johnny Pesky steadied the infield, batted .335, led the league in hits and was second in runs scored. Rudy York, acquired in a key trade, drove in 119 runs. The four starters solidified the team. "Boo" Ferriss was 25-6. Tex Hughson went 20-11. Mickey Harris was 17-9. Joe Dobson was 13-7. And their task was made much simpler because of the potent Boston lineup that paced the league in batting average, slugging percentage and runs scored.

If rooting for the Red Sox in 1946 was like eating a bowl of cherries, in the words of one Boston fan, "For long years after that, it was the pits," in the phrase of another Sox follower.

The 1948 BoSox defeated the New York Yankees twice in the final two days of the season, doing what they had to do. The first victory denied the pennant to the Yankees. The second win set up the first single-game playoff in the history of the American League. Some of the fans of the BoSox were more thrilled by the first win than the second. But Cleveland defeated Boston in the playoff game, and the Sox had to be content with a second-place American League finish—a game off the pace.

In 1949, Boston came to Yankee Stadium with a one-game lead, needing a split in their two-game series to clinch the pennant. The Sox succumbed to the Yankees, 4-0 in the first game. And the Bronx Bombers, with a four-run eighth inning, won the second game, 5-3. It was the second straight second-place finish for the men from Fenway. That was bad news, bad times. But worse times were ahead—long, long years of mediocrity.

From 1949 to 1965, the Red Sox finished behind the Yankees in the standings. From 1960 to 1966, Boston was twice last, twice

Phil Rizzuto, Casey Stengel, Billy Martin, and Yogi Berra. (Photofest/Icon)

eighth, twice seventh, once sixth. Only in 1966 did the Red Sox finish ahead of the Yankees—in ninth place, a half game ahead of the 10th-place New Yorkers.

Dick Williams assumed command of the 1967 Red Sox. A rookie pilot, he had his work cut out for him. "There had been tremendous teams at Boston," Williams recalled, "but they had won just one pennant in 21 years. At home they were excellent, but they just could not win on the road because it was a team manufactured to play at Fenway Park."

Williams made up his mind not to allow the dimensions of Fenway to influence his managing style and the play of his ball players. "I made it clear," Williams explained, "that the Green Monster was not going to be a fac-tor. I had seen too many players ruining themselves taking shots at the wall. I made my pitchers concentrate on pitching to right-handed batters who always came up there looking for the ball away thinking we'd get them to avoid pulling. I knew that the way to pitch at Fenway is to get the ball inside and gradually back the batter up a little."

They are still debating whether Williams's theory had anything to with what happened or not—but he worked a miracle. The Sox, a 100-1 shot to win the pennant proved the experts and the oddsmakers wrong. Behind the pitching of Jim Lonborg, who won 22 games, and the Triple Crown batting of Carl Yastrzemski (.326, 44 homers, 121 RBIs) the Sox leaped from ninth place to first place in one season.

They were dubbed the "Cinderella Sox." Their accomplishment was called the "Impossible Dream." And Elston Howard, who came over from the hated enemy New York Yankees, exclaimed: "I never saw anything like this, and we won a lot of pennants when I was in New York."

There was another pennant for the Sox in 1975. And there was more rejoicing, for not only did Boston finish two notches higher than New York, the Hub team playing in a much smaller ballpark out-drew the Yankees in attendance, too.

In 1986, behind the pitching of Roger Clemens, Boston won another pennant. It was especially sweet for Sox fans, because this time

LEFT: *Elston Howard, the first black Yankee catcher who went on to play for the Red Sox. (Photofest)*

OPPOSITE: *Roger Clemens as a Red Sox pitcher. (Photofest)*

Phil Rizzuto, Casey Stengel, Billy Martin, and Yogi Berra. (Photofest/Icon)

eighth, twice seventh, once sixth. Only in 1966 did the Red Sox finish ahead of the Yankees—in ninth place, a half game ahead of the 10th-place New Yorkers.

Dick Williams assumed command of the 1967 Red Sox. A rookie pilot, he had his work cut out for him. "There had been tremendous teams at Boston," Williams recalled, "but they had won just one pennant in 21 years. At home they were excellent, but they just could not win on the road because it was a team manufactured to play at Fenway Park."

Williams made up his mind not to allow the dimensions of Fenway to influence his managing style and the play of his ball players. "I made it clear," Williams explained, "that the Green Monster was not going to be a fac-

tor. I had seen too many players ruining themselves taking shots at the wall. I made my pitchers concentrate on pitching to right-handed batters who always came up there looking for the ball away thinking we'd get them to avoid pulling. I knew that the way to pitch at Fenway is to get the ball inside and gradually back the batter up a little."

They are still debating whether Williams's theory had anything to with what happened or not—but he worked a miracle. The Sox, a 100-1 shot to win the pennant proved the experts and the oddsmakers wrong. Behind the pitching of Jim Lonborg, who won 22 games, and the Triple Crown batting of Carl Yastrzemski (.326, 44 homers, 121 RBIs) the Sox leaped from ninth place to first place in one season.

They were dubbed the "Cinderella Sox." Their accomplishment was called the "Impossible Dream." And Elston Howard, who came over from the hated enemy New York Yankees, exclaimed: "I never saw anything like this, and we won a lot of pennants when I was in New York."

There was another pennant for the Sox in 1975. And there was more rejoicing, for not only did Boston finish two notches higher than New York, the Hub team playing in a much smaller ballpark out-drew the Yankees in attendance, too.

In 1986, behind the pitching of Roger Clemens, Boston won another pennant. It was especially sweet for Sox fans, because this time

LEFT: *Elston Howard, the first black Yankee catcher who went on to play for the Red Sox. (Photofest)*

OPPOSITE: *Roger Clemens as a Red Sox pitcher. (Photofest)*

it was the Yankees that came in second place to the Red Sox. But Boston could not quite escape from New York's shadow, losing a dramatic seven-game World Series to the New York Mets that fall. A crucial ground ball through Boston first baseman Bill Buckner's legs led many Sox fans to once again wonder if their team was truly cursed.

"The curse exists only if you think it does," observes *Boston Globe* sports columnist Dan Shaughnessy. " It's like if you think you are going to pitch better in patent leather shoes, then maybe you do."

The seth swirsky collection/SETH.com

Despite some banner seasons—1946, 1967, 1975, 1986—historically the negative cycle of Boston Red Sox baseball seems to repeat itself. Just as Labor Day approaches and Boston children prepare for school, and the zinnias and the marigolds in the public gardens bloom in all their glory, a down mood takes over. Throughout these Indian summers, fans keep coming to Fenway. Some fans come to boo. Others come to cry. And still others come to pray.

Historically, the fans of the Red Sox rank among the most loyal as well as the most excitable in all of baseball. The Sox, for example, drew more people into the tiny ballpark in the decade of the '70s than any other American League team. And when the competition for the BoSox is the New York Yankees—it's one of the toughest tickets in all of sports, especially if both teams are battling to be top dog in the standings.

Boston attendance figures have ballooned through Yankee-Sox encounters. Historically, on given days, up to 10,000 fans have taken flights between Boston and New York. Some have made the flight to witness a single game; others have stayed for an entire series. There have been times when the national television networks have been outdrawn in the ratings by local stations broadcasting the games between the ancient rivals.

One who doesn't watch is Ted Spencer, Baseball's Hall of Fame curator, who was born in 1943 in Quincy, Massachusetts. "My folks named me for Ted Williams—they were and are such Red Sox zealots. But I don't watch the Yankees-Red Sox on TV. I can't, it'll kill me. I kind of walk in and out—I can't take it."

At diners, gas stations, roadside rests, zealots have congregated, contesting and censoring each other's opinions as they stop off on their drives to the Stadium and Fenway from Connecticut, Vermont, New Hampshire, Rhode Island, western Massachusetts, New Jersey, New York, North Carolina, Georgia and other places.

Behind the scenes, the late Bob Fishel, first as a Yankee publicist and later performing some of the same duties with the American League office, saw the rivalry up close.

"When I was with the Yankees," said Fishel, "we never had to promote the competition between the two teams. It didn't need promotion. People buy tickets months in advance for Yankees-Red Sox games. From a scheduling point of view in the American League office, a conscious effort is made to capitalize and schedule weekend games [and] late-season match-ups to maximize the rivalry."

On the field, inside the white lines, the rivalry has been characterized by some of baseball's wildest moments.

In all my years of covering the New York Yankees," notes *New York Daily News* sportswriter Bill Madden, "I can hardly remember a game at Fenway Park that was a normal game. I'm sure there were some, but it seems like they have been low scoring, tension filled, white-knuckle games or these 10-9 barnburners where no lead was safe. Players will never admit it, but the intensity level is up whenever the Yankees and Red Sox meet."

In the first game ever played at Fenway Park, on April 12, 1912, the Sox trimmed the Yankees, 7-6 in 11 innings. The game was finally played after it had been rained out for two straight days.

On August 12, 1934, what was then the largest crowd in Fenway Park history, assembled to see Red Sox vs. Yankees up close, going at each other. They split a doubleheader and Babe Ruth played his last game in a Yankee uniform in the Boston ballpark where he had begun his professional career.

On August 7, 1956, 36,350 watched as the Sox defeated the Yankees, 1-0, in 11 innings. Ted Williams walked with the bases loaded to drive in the winning run. "Terrible

Ted" was so infuriated at not being given a chance to swing his bat that he sprayed Fenway Park with saliva.

Odd, awesome and unpredictable rallies have contributed to the zany and wild mood. It's just part of the atmosphere in meetings between the Yanks and Sox. New York had a six-run 11th inning in 1970, a seven-run ninth inning in 1940, an eight-run ninth inning in 1937, a 10-run fourth inning in 1915, an 11-run seventh inning in 1952, and a 13-run fifth inning in 1945.

In 1954, the Red Sox had a 5-1 lead over the Yankees in the first game of a doubleheader and lost. They were trailing 7-0 in the second game and won. The big Boston blow was a Jimmy Piersall home run off Johnny Sain.

On August 29, 1967, both clubs struggled through 19 innings until Boston went down to defeat in the 20th inning. The Yankees won the game, 4-3.

On September 19, 1981, Boston was able to pull out an 8-5 triumph with a seven-run eighth-inning rally.

Many still talk about the long summer of 1949 when the Yankees and the Red Sox battled for the pennant, playing out their drama in jammed stadiums before rabid and enraptured fans. Each day was another chance for the tension, the drama and the excitement to be recharged.

Those who witnessed and those who were the principal characters never tired of replaying the time Cliff Mapes of the Yankees threw Johnny Pesky of Boston out at home plate on the Fourth of July at Yankee Stadium. Pesky was the runner at third base. Al Zarilla hit the ball to right field. "All of a sudden," Phil Rizzuto recalled, "this big cloud of something covered the sun. Holy Cow! Cliff Mapes loses

Pitchers Whitey Ford, Ed Lopat, Allie Reynolds, and Vic Raschi. (Photofest)

the ball in the sun. It drops in. Pesky, bewildered, confused, finally heads for home. And the throw by Mapes," Rizzuto smiled, "beat him."

With but two weeks left in the 1949 American League season, as fate would have it, Johnny Pesky was once again positioned on third base in a game against the Yankees. Both teams were tied in the standings and were battling, clawing and scratching at each other attempting to pull out a victory.

Darkness was starting to rapidly descend. Bobby Doerr dropped down a surprise bunt, attempting to squeeze Pesky home. Tommy Henrich, playing out of position at first base and corseted to cushion the stress and strain of back injury pains, picked up the bunt. He threw the ball to Yankee catcher Ralph Houk. The throw appeared to have beaten Pesky. But plate umpire Bill Grieve ruled the Boston runner safe. Pandemonium prevailed. The Yankees protested long and loudly. It was useless.

Casey Stengel drew a $150 fine. Houk and Mapes, both highly agitated, paid for their emotional state—they were each fined $200. Boston won the game, 5-4.

And Johnny Pesky insists: "I was safe. Ralph left a bit of the plate unblocked. I slid into that little part of the plate under his tag."

With the perspective of all the long years behind him, Johnny Pesky, still a part of the Red Sox scene, talks about the mood and the culture of the Yankees-Red Sox rivalry back in his playing days.

"Allie Reynolds was a peach of a guy. Eddie Lopat, Vic Raschi—they were decent people. If they pitched you close you didn't bother to look out there, because they'd say: 'If you didn't like that one, how about this one?' And the next one would be even closer. They didn't want to hurt you. They always thought that if they couldn't get you out with their ability as pitchers they didn't belong out there. Truthfully, I think there was affection.

"There was tough, hard competition, but there was respect. If you didn't love Yogi Berra or Phil Rizzuto, there was something wrong with you. And playing back then, there was real awe of the guys who would be double superstars today, DiMag, Williams, people like that.

"The rivalry has been great for the teams and the cities, but it has gotten a lot of people

Former Boston manager Joe Cronin in a relaxed mood. (Frommer Archives)

in Boston upset, especially when it's gotten out of hand. When you go into Yankee Stadium today, you see so many people getting into jams in the stands there. That was unheard of when I played. The profanity, the physical violence—they'll wear the "Red Sox Suck" tee shirts today, and then they'll come over and ask for your autograph."

The rivalry intermittently has flared into rage, sometimes into violence. Sometimes it has been triggered by personality clashes—other times the trigger has simply been the "bad blood" and frenzy that has been part of the mood and culture when the ancient rivals go at it.

In 1938, players from both teams stormed the mound at Yankee Stadium when Jake Powell of the Yankees and Boston's Joe Cronin started throwing punches at each other. The flash point for the battle royal was Powell's rushing out to the mound to throttle Sox southpaw Archie McKain. Cronin was ejected from the game. Moments later, he was assaulted by several Yankee players under the stands.

The following year at Fenway the Sox and

Boston infielder Bobby Doerr. (Photofest / Icon)

Yanks were immersed in an on-field demonstration of stalling and slow-motion tactics. Lots of nasty language was tossed in for good measure by some of the less refined members of both teams. Ultimately, the game was forfeited in favor of the Yankees by American League president Will Harridge. Later on, the Red Sox came to play at Yankee Stadium and were unceremoniously greeted with batches of dumped debris by irate New York fans.

In 1947, a year in which the Yanks had 19 straight wins, New York fireballer Joe Page pitched fast and close to many Boston batters during a night game at Fenway. Bobby Doerr received an especially thorough dusting. Later in the game, Doerr had apparently stolen third

base but was called out. Echoing their 1939 Yankee counterparts, the Fenway faithful showered any Yankee they could get at and their little ballpark with garbage and debris.

Jimmy Piersall of Boston was a rookie in 1952. He would later go on to write a book, *The Truth Hurts*. He wrote: "Probably the best thing that ever happened to me was going nuts. Whoever heard of Jimmy Piersall, until that happened?" But he was "heard of" as a result of what happened that season.

The Red Sox outfielder had the audacity—or the ignorance—to shout out during a game to Billy Martin of the Yankees: "Hey, Pinocchio!" It was an overt and obnoxious reference to the size and contours of the Yankee second baseman's nose. "Too damn yellow to fight?" "Put up," snarled Martin, "or shut up your damn ass. Let's settle this under the stands right now!"

Martin entered the Yankee dugout. Piersall sped into the Sox dugout, and then circled under the stands lusting for the violent rendezvous. Martin was trailed after by Yankee coach Bill Dickey. Ellis Kinder, a Boston hurler, ran after Piersall. The two hot-headed athletes faced off, both full of fury. There were some more unprintable words that spewed forth from Martin and Piersall. Then Martin jabbed two powerful shots to Piersall's face. Bleeding profusely from the nose, the Boston outfielder dropped quickly to the ground. The one-sided battle ended as Dickey and Kinder moved between the two combatants.

A relaxed Casey Stengel in the Yankee dugout, was informed as to what had taken place. "That was all right, all right," said the sagacious pilot who regarded Martin as a son. "I'm happy as long as he starts with the other

OPPOSITE: *Bill Dickey (left) and Casey Stengel. (Frommer Archives)*

teams and doesn't start with any players on the Yankees."

That moment in Yankee-Red Sox history underscored the "bad blood" that existed. But it was not the most famous of the on-the-field altercations. Not by a long shot. The one that qualifies for that title took place on August 1, 1973.

Both teams were battling for the lead in the American League East. Two nights before in the opening game of a series, the Yankees had scored twice in the ninth inning to tie the game. But the Sox scored once in the home half of the ninth to win. New York scored three times in the ninth inning of the second game of the series to notch its first Fenway park victory in a year. What happened the next day epitomized the frenzy of the rivalry and underscored the raging debate over the relative abilities of Boston catcher Carlton Fisk and Yankee backstop Thurman Munson. The bickering brought back memories of New York City baseball's 1950s contentious conflict among fans that centered on who was the best centerfielder: Willie Mays of the New York Giants, Duke Snider of the Brooklyn Dodgers or Mickey Mantle of the Yankees. Fisk, that summer of 1973, had led in the American

Yankee second baseman Billy Martin. (Photofest)

League All-Star balloting for catcher. Munson was voted runner-up. "That was part of the conflict," explained the late Yankee broadcaster of that era, Frank Messer. "And there was even some personality conflict between the two of them."

"Fisk hated Munson," said Don Zimmer. "Munson hated Fisk, and everyone hated Bill Lee." The August 1 game was tied, 2-2, as the ninth inning began. Sparky Lyle was the Yankee pitcher. John Curtis was on the mound for Boston. Munson opened the New York ninth with a double down the left-field line. An infield groundout by Nettles moved him to third base. Gene Michael missed a squeeze bunt, but the solidly built Munson came tearing down the line attempting to score. He slammed into Fisk who had the baseball and was blocking the plate. The two catchers collided, but Fisk held onto the ball. Munson was out. Fisk shoved the Yankee catcher off his body and Munson punched the Sox catcher in the face, bruising his left eye.

Then the two got into a clinching, clawing encounter. Michael, who was Munson's roommate, managed to get in a few punches of his own. The next thing that happened was that 61-year-old Fenway Park was swarming

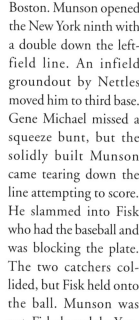

OPPOSITE: *Taking care of baseball business, Carton Fisk and Butch Hobson. (Photofest)*

★ ★ ★ ★ ★ ★ ★ ★ ★ ★ ★ ★ ★ ★ ★ ★
MOST GAMES, PURE RELIEF, LIFETIME

'77 RECORD BREAKER ★ ★ ★ ★ ★ ★ ★ ★
SPARKY LYLE

Sparky Lyle, another who pitched for the Red Sox and Yankees. (The Topps Company, Inc.)

with players pushing, shoving, and cursing. The playing field erupted with anger. More than 60 players and coaches, even those from the bullpen 350 feet away, were full of fury and out on the field. When order was finally restored, Carlton Fisk and Thurman Munson were ejected from the game. "There's no question," Munson said later, "I threw the first punch, but he started it and then my roomie got into it. Fisk was lucky that he didn't get into a fight the night before the way he blocked the plate on Roy White."

"Munson and I were just bumping chests," Fisk explained later. "I flipped him off, but the big thing started when Michael got into it."

Oddly enough, Michael was allowed to remain in the game, and this triggered another lengthy delay as the Red Sox protested loudly and their partisan fans screamed out their rage. When Boston finally came to bat in the bottom of the ninth inning, Mario Guerrero singled in Bob Montgomery who had replaced Fisk as the Sox catcher. The home team calculated a 3-2 triumph, and the Yankees dropped out of first place. Ironically, Guerrero was the player-named-later in the 1972 Sparky Lyle for first baseman Danny Cater deal.

A typical '70s type, a wisecracking lefthander with a sizable paunch quite visible beneath his uniform, Albert Walter Lyle lost for the fifth consecutive time, his second time in three games to his former BoSox teammates. For Boston, the victory over New York was especially sweet. Lyle had openly antagonized his former teammates through the many negative comments he had made about them after he was traded to the Yankees.

The crossover of Sparky Lyle to the New York Yankees on March 22, 1972 was unusual. Perhaps the memory of Babe Ruth moving from Boston to New York and becoming one of the greatest players in history, one who changed the destinies of both franchises, put somewhat of a damper on significant trades between the two rivals. But Lyle's movement to New York ranks as one of the worst trades Boston ever made. "When I was with Boston," Lyle said, "the Red Sox fans and players treated me well. I was made to feel part of the team and there was never any animosity. But after the trade, sometimes people came up to me at banquets and said, 'I can't root for you anymore because you're with the damn Yankees now.' I thought that was good. At least they were rooting."

Lyle was fond of observing: "Some people say you have to be nuts to be a relief pitcher. But the truth is I was nuts before I ever became one," he said. "Why pitch nine innings when you can get just as famous pitching two?" was another Lyle-ism.

He would do anything to get a laugh—exiting from a coffin, sitting around nude, showing up at spring training with his limbs in casts.

The image of his entering games at Yankee Stadium in that pin-striped Toyota to the accompaniment of "Pomp and Circumstance" intensified the wacky image of the man they called "The Count" who, like George Steinbrenner, was born on the Fourth of July. On the mound, though, he was pure business. In seven Yankee seasons Lyle pitched in more games than any other Yankee, posting a 57-40 record with 141 saves and a 2.41 ERA. Those stats earned Lyle three All-Star selections and helped move the Yankees into three World Series.

Ironically, the trade for Lyle was engineered by Ralph Houk, the Yankee manager and general manager. Houk, known as "the Major," went from the Yankees to Detroit to retirement, and then was named skipper of the Red Sox on October 27, 1980.

At the winter baseball meetings in 1980, the late Bill Crowley noted: "Houk was asked to recall what was the best trade he was ever involved in. Sparky Lyle was Ralph's answer.

Ralph Houk managed both the Yankees and Red Sox. (The Topps Company, Inc.)

"'Hey, Ralph,' I said, 'You're on our side now.'

"So what, Bill? It was still the best trade I ever made."

The major who battled the Red Sox for many years while in a Yankee uniform admitted it was strange at first to be wearing a Boston Red Sox uniform. "But it was not as bad as when I first left the Yankees and went to Detroit. The fact that I didn't come directly from New York to Boston softened things. When you are away from an organization for a while, many of the players are not the same anymore. It made it easier for me not competing against that many players I had known personally."

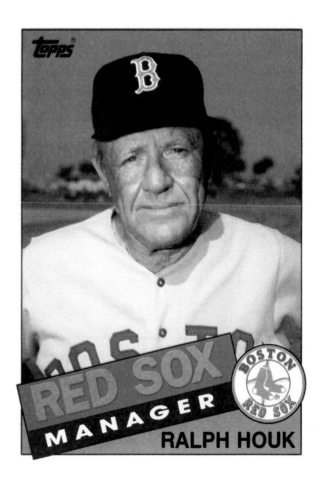

Joe McCarthy, one of the most famous crossovers, didn't have the same options as Houk. He was deeply involved with both teams. Yankee manager from 1931 to 1946, he piloted the Bronx Bombers to seven pennants, including four in a row (1936 to 1939). He won titles with such apparent ease and regularity that he was dubbed the "Push Button Manager." He even had his own "Ten Commandments for Success in the Major Leagues:"

1. Nobody can become a ballplayer by walking after a ball.

2. You will never become a .300 hitter unless you take the bat off your shoulder.

3. An outfielder who throws in back of a runner is locking the barn door after the horse is stolen.

4. Keep your head up, and you may not have to keep it down.

5. When you start to slide, slide. He who changes his mind may have to change a good leg for a bad one.

6. Do not alibi on bad hops. Anybody can field the good ones.

7. Always run them out. You can never tell.

8. Do not quit.

9. Do not fight too much with the umpires. You cannot expect them to be as perfect as you.

10. A pitcher who hasn't control, hasn't anything.

Joe McCarthy as Red Sox manager.
(Photofest)

A minor leaguer player for 15 seasons, McCarthy never played in the major leagues, but he is the winningest manager of all time. "Never a day went by," Joe DiMaggio said, "when you didn't learn something from McCarthy."

He permitted himself no diversions, no hobbies. Then on May 24, 1946, 35 games into the season, Joseph Vincent McCarthy announced he was quitting as manager of the Yankees. "He was drinking too much," Joe DiMaggio told reporters. "He wasn't eating right, and he was worried about the team because it was playing so lousy."

In his 16 years in pinstripes, Joe McCarthy's teams recorded 1,460 wins, 867 losses and an astounding .627 winning percentage.

In 1948, Marse Joe returned to the baseball wars—as manager of the Boston Red Sox. Appearing at a winter banquet, he was introduced to Johnny Pesky. "I remember your first home run in 1942," snapped McCarthy. "It beat my Yankees."

"It's all right," Pesky quipped. "I will be more than happy to return the favor."

Joe McCarthy brought the Red Sox excruciatingly close to winning the 1948 pennant and the 1949 pennant. In 1950, after 24 years as a major league manager, McCarthy,

OPPOSITE: *Joe McCarthy (Photofest/Icon)*

who had once said: "Sometimes I think I'm in the greatest business in the world and then you lose four straight and you want to change places with the farmer, and call it a career," did just that. Boston was in third place at the mid-point of the season.

One of the questions that was always asked of McCarthy was his opinion as to who was the greatest player—Joe DiMaggio or Ted Williams.

"When I was with the Yankees," McCarthy smiled, "I was crazy about DiMag. Now that I'm with the Red Sox, I'm crazy about Williams."

And the most famous rumored trade of all time was one that allegedly involved the Red Sox and the Yankees and Ted Williams and Joe DiMaggio. As the story goes, Sox owner Tom Yawkey and Yankee boss Dan Topping were talking and drinking, drinking and talking. The banter finally got around to just how much better Ted Williams would bat at Yankee Stadium and how much better Joe DiMaggio would hit at Fenway Park. The banter, as the story goes on, concluded with the two owners exchanging a handshake and agreeing to make a DiMaggio-Williams trade.

It was reported that when Topping arrived home and realized what he had agreed to, he picked up the phone and called Yawkey. The time allegedly was 4 a.m. Topping's tone was one of excitement, but some would say panic.

"Tom," he began, "I'm sorry, but I can't go through with the deal."

"Thank God," it was reported, was Yawkey's reply.

Another version of the purported DiMaggio-Williams deal has Tom Yawkey being the one who made the phone call. "Dan, I know it's 5 a.m., and it's very, very late, and I still want to make that trade we discussed. However, if you still want to make it, you'll have to throw in that left-handed hitting out-fielder, the odd-looking rookie."

"I can't," Topping was reported to have been very nervous at the turn of events. "We have very big plans for him. We want to make him a catcher. I am afraid we will have to call off the deal."

As everyone knows, there was no deal. Joe DiMaggio and Ted Williams played out their careers with the New York Yankees and the Boston Red Sox, respectively.

The little, left-handed hitting outfielder remained a Yankee. He became a catcher, a pretty good one. His name? Lawrence Peter Berra.

Although "The Great Rivalry" has triggered very few trades of consequence over the past decades, it has probably spawned more hate mail, obscene letters and assassination threats than any other rivalry in baseball.

In August 1953, a letter addressed to Mickey Mantle arrived at Yankee Stadium. "Hello…Mickey…Tom Umphlette got you 50 to 1. Don't show your face in Boston again or you're [sic] baseball career will come to an end with a 32…. Remember, I make every RED SOX and cheater Yankees game and I'll be sure to be there September 7. I've got a good gang that dont [sic] like the Yankees and you'll find out if you play the series starting September 7.

"This ain't no joke if you think it is.
"yours untruly,
"A loyal RED SOX fan
"P.S. You may think this is a joke or not think anything of it but you'll wish you had

OPPOSITE: *Mickey Mantle and Whitey Ford (with bats) in a relaxed moment at the Stadium. (Photofest)*

Yankee skipper Casey Stengel has his say. (Frommer Archives)

thought of it you better tell casey to keep you out of the game it would be better if you didn't bring your damn team to boston."

The New York Yankees did come to Boston, and Mickey Mantle was there, too. The series was played with the Red Sox. Extra security personnel diligently watched from patrol posts all over Fenway. There were no incidents.

Another assassination threat leveled at another Yankee superstar had almost comic overtones. Phil Rizzuto recalled what happened: "It was the year I won the MVP award. Some crank letter I had gotten was turned over to the FBI. They said if I set foot in Fenway Park somebody was going to shoot me with a high-powered rifle.

"Casey Stengel said: 'We do not want Rizzuto shot.' So they switched uniforms with Billy Martin and me. It was a very exciting game for me, but it was even more exciting for Billy. I felt much more relaxed but Billy never sat still for one single second. I never saw him move about so much in my life. He didn't want them to have a standing-still target."

The context for the Phil Rizzuto assassination threat was when the Yankees went into Boston for the final three games of the 1950 season. Rizzuto was one hit shy of 200 for the year. The Scooter, who claims he always hit well at Fenway ("At least one of my four homers each year was there,") singled in the first game for his 200th hit of 1950. And then old Casey took his little shortstop out of the game, claiming it was always better to be safe than sorry.

OPPOSITE: *Both GM George Weiss and Casey Stengel are fired after the 1960 season by the Yankees, to the delight of Boston fans. (Photofest/Icon)*

Charles Dillon Stengel was born on July 30, 1890, in Kansas City, Missouri. He died on September 29, 1975 in Glendale, California. "There comes a time in every man's life," Casey said, "and I've had plenty of them."

Under his leadership from 1949 to 1960, the Yankees won 10 pennants and seven World Series, and a record five straight world championships, from 1949 to 1953. Only once in his dozen seasons did his teams win fewer than 90 games; his Yankee career managing record was 1,149-696, a winning percentage of .623.

Ted Williams was a very staunch admirer of Casey. "He was a great manager," the Splendid Splinter said, "and had a great sense of character. He is right up there with Judge Landis, Babe Ruth and Ty Cobb when it comes to baseball greatness. He was the real leadership—not the players. When guys like Gil McDougald or Jerry Coleman decided to take charge and calm down a pitcher, it was because Casey picked his nose or rubbed his ear telling them to get in there and slow down the pitcher to stall for time to give another guy a chance to warm up."

"They loved Casey Stengel in Boston," Bill Crowley pointed out. "And they hated him for winning so much against the Sox. Tom Yawkey had a high regard for Stengel, and whenever the Yankees came to Fenway, Mr. Yawkey used to always place a bottle of good booze in Casey's locker."

Caught in the media's eye, framed in memory, the stark image contrasts of the New York Yankees and the Boston Red Sox produce a special type of mood, a culture, a feeling. It seems everyone claims an insight, a different perspective.

"I didn't even know there was a big rivalry until I came to the Red Sox," said Don Zimmer, "but I found out soon enough. I was coaching at third base in 1974 at Yankee Stadium, and the fans were throwing so much crap on the field that I had to put on a helmet for protection. The players don't really hate each other. It's a rivalry of fans."

Goose Gossage, who was a star Yankee relief pitcher, recalled: "When I first came to the Yankees, the guys said, 'You won't believe this series. You won't believe the people, the way the two teams go at each other.' In late June of 1978, I made my first appearance against the Red Sox. I was all psyched up. The first game of that series was like the World Series. I wanted to go out there and kick the hell out of them."

Chico Walker, an infielder, joined Boston in 1980. The rivalry was an important part of his professional life. "It goes back to when I broke in in rookie ball," said Walker. "Every time we played the Yankee teams, the manager would try to get us up for them. From rookie ball to double A to triple A, I felt it. Everyone in the Red Sox organization is pumped up playing against the New York Yankees."

Mike Torrez moved as a free agent from the Yankees to the Red Sox. Bob Watson moved as a free agent from the Red Sox to the Yankees. Both have special feelings about the rivalry.

"I actually became aware of the rivalry when I played for Baltimore," said Torrez, "but you had to put on the uniform to really feel it. When I was with the Yankees, the players on that team really hated the Boston players. When I was on Boston, we tried to beat their asses. We wanted to beat the Yankees bad, and I'm sure they wanted to beat us bad. And both teams talked about it. Fans talked about it, and they anticipated something bad happening because of all the history of violence."

Bob Watson wanted to stay on with the Red Sox for a longer time than he did, but said: "The management at that time did not have me in their plans." The powerful first baseman played a half season for the Sox. "Even though I was there for just a short time, I got to see that Boston fans are probably per capita the most knowledgeable fans in all of baseball. The rivalry is something that I can really appreciate having been on both teams, Yankees and Red Sox. When the two clubs meet, it gives the players and their fans a chance to talk about the old times…when the Yankees came in and did that…when the Red Sox were able to do this and that. It's a good thing for all of baseball."

Torrez agreed. "There's all those past memories," he said, "that players talk about and feel. That's good, but there's also the violence that is part of the past and who's to say those things cannot flare up again? The 'Boston Sucks' signs don't bother me as long as they don't get physical. However, some things have been thrown from the upper deck at Yankee Stadium, and everyone is aware of that. You kind of hid your head in the dugout when you came in there. It's good that you've got the concrete above you in case something does come flying down."

The late Frank Messer joined the Yankees as an announcer in 1968. "I became really impressed by the intensity of the rivalry," he said, "It's the two teams going at each other making for the excitement. People get worn out with excitement watching them play. I hated to think of doing a bad job broadcasting a Yankee-Red Sox game, for all those games are something special."

A New Englander all his life, Wynn Bates hailed from Braintree, Massachusetts and worked for a long time at the *Brockton Enterprise* as a sportswriter. He studied "The Great Rivalry" for years as a New Englander and as a reporter.

"Baseball is the king of all sports out here in Boston," Bates said. "And the Yankee-Red Sox competition is always the big story. No matter where the teams are in the standings, Fenway Park is always crowded for games between the rivals. If there's a tight pennant race, you can't get a ticket. People here really want to beat the Yankees. Maybe it's the animosity some in New England feel toward the city of New York. There's an uptight attitude. Sometimes Sox fans get a little out of hand. The atmosphere can be scary, especially when Yankee fans stand up and root at Fenway, and that gets some violence going."

The late Ron Luciano was a neutral among all the partisans. He watched the rivalry play out for 11 seasons from within his American League umpire's uniform. Then he went on to call them as he saw them as an NBC-TV baseball announcer. Luciano had a double perspective.

"As an umpire," Luciano said, "you play on the crowd. If you're at Fenway Park with 35,000 or at the stadium, with 45,000, 50,000, your adrenaline is up. You're always looking for strange things to happen.

"Notoriously, over the years there have been throwing incidents, there've been fights, there've been runners running into catchers at home plate. The time Reggie was pulled off the field by Billy Martin was during a Red Sox series. Some might say the rivalry did not have anything to do with it, but I think it did. The rivalry got to be so much that Martin was upset that everyone wasn't pulling 200 percent. The rivalry is so intense that everyone plays just a bit harder. It's a bigger letdown for the Yankees to lose to Boston, and umpires feel that before they walk out there and this is passed along among umpires.

"Fans," continued Luciano, "react more to the umpires in a Boston-New York series. The umpire has to watch his life afterwards walking out of the ballpark. Boston-New York is a do-harder thing. You want to do your best in those games. It's a bargaining point. Umpires going in to talk next year's contract use it as a bargaining point. 'Hey,' they say, 'I had the Yankees and the Red Sox. You wanted your best up there in that crucial series. Reward me. I worked The Great Rivalry.'"

As an announcer, Luciano viewed the rivalry from another vantage point. "You know that every player down there is going to try a little harder because of the rivalry and the crowd reaction. Even if they are both in last place, the rivalry is still there. Everybody builds it up: the newspapers, the camera, the players themselves, but it should be that way. It's a whole regional competition between two great cities and two great organizations."

The rivalry is Boo and Bucky and Butch. It is Carl Yastrzemski trotting out to left field at Fenway with cotton sticking out of his ears to muffle the boos of disheartened and disgusted Red Sox rooters. It is the Scooter, the Monster and the Hawk. It is Rich McKinney on April 22, 1972, making four errors on ground balls to third base that figured in Boston's scoring nine runs to defeat the Yankees, 11-7.

It is the Yankee Clipper and the Thumper, Yaz and the Commerce Comet, Mombo and King Kong. The rivalry is Mickey Mantle slugging a 440-foot double at Yankee Stadium in 1958 and tipping his cap to the Red Sox bench. It's George Herman Ruth. It's Williams spitting. It's all the headaches Carlton Fisk had from tension coming into Yankee Stadium. It's Mickey Rivers jumping out of the way of an exploding firecracker thrown into the visitors' dugout at the Fens.

It's Ted Spencer, chief curator at the Baseball Hall of Fame recalling the 1950s: "In those days the American League played to see who was going to finish second to the Yankees, and the National League played to see who was going to lose to the Yankees in the World Series."

It's Roger Clemens maintaining that he wants to go into the Hall of Fame wearing a Yankees cap. And it's Jeff Idelson, vice president of communications and education for the Hall explaining: "We're a history museum, so the logo on a player's cap is important to us from a historical representation standpoint. We want the logo to be emblematic of where this player made his most indelible mark. What we don't want to end up with is a decision that doesn't make sense 50 years from now when someone walks into the Hall of Fame. If you make the wrong decision, it would be like walking into the Hall now and seeing Ty Cobb in a Philadelphia A's cap...or Babe Ruth in a Brooklyn Dodgers cap."

The Great Rivalry is Nomar Garciaparra vs. Derek Jeter. Take your pick. Who is better? It's Luis Tiant vs. Reggie Jackson, Allie Reynolds squaring off against Ted Williams.

The rivalry is Pedro Martinez against Roger Clemens.

Sometimes the rivalry is even a factor in presidential elections. In the 2004 Democratic presidential primary, Massachusetts senator John Kerry claimed his opponent, former Vermont governor Howard Dean, was not a liberal or conservative, but something far worse in New England: "A Yankees fan."

Dean, who was born in New York City, said he stopped rooting for the Yankees after pitcher Roger Clemens beaned Mets catcher Mike Piazza in the 2000 season. But Kerry's campaign spokeswoman, Kelley Benander, retorted: "Of all the flip flops, this is the most inexplicable and indefensible. It's like switching from the Redskins to the Cowboys or from Carolina to Duke."

It's The Wall vs. The Monuments, Red Sox Rule and Yankees Suck vs. We'll See Who's Standing in October, WFAN vs. WEEI.

The rivalry is signs:

"I LOVE NEW YORK, TOO.

IT'S THE YANKEES I HATE."

"BOSTON CHOKES, BOSTON SUCKS. BOSTON DOES IT IN STYLE."

BALLPARKS: YANKEE STADIUM AND FENWAY PARK

"Very few buildings managed to meld their history literally with the present. Yankee Stadium does. There is something glorious about knowing that the physical form of the structure (never mind how badly it has been altered) ties Derek Jeter to Joe DiMaggio."

—Paul Goldberger,
The New York Times, architecture critic

Fenway Park and Yankee Stadium, symbols of the Boston Red Sox and the New York Yankees, are more than just home fields. Their sizes, shapes, locations and histories have influenced the rivalry and the personalities and makeups of their teams.

Boston first began playing at Fenway Park in 1912 on the property of the Fenway Realty Company. New York's initial season at Yankee Stadium in the Bronx was in 1923 on the site of a former lumberyard.

Ironically, the first game at Fenway Park pitted the Sox against New York, and the initial contest at Yankee Stadium was a match between the Yankees and Red Sox.

That first Fenway Park game took place on April 20, 1912—the final score was Bos-

ton Red Sox 7, New York Highlanders 6. There were 27,000 on hand and New York's Harry Wolter recorded the first hit in the new park.

The first Yankee Stadium game was played on April 18, 1923, and saw the Yanks best the Sox, 4-1. The reported attendance was 74,200, and Boston's George Burns managed the first hit, a single, in the new home of the Yankees.

YANKEE STADIUM

Yankee Stadium is the third oldest Major League ballpark. Only Wrigley Field and Fenway Park have more years on it. The stadium was the site of All-Star games in 1939, 1960 and 1977—seasons in which the Yankees also were in the World Series. The Sta-

Lou Gehrig Farewell Speech. (Photofest)

Yankee Stadium Souvenirs. (Photofest/Icon)

dium is where Notre Dame coach Knute Rockne made his "Win One for the Gipper" speech, where Johnny Unitas won the 1958 NFL championship in the so-called "Greatest Game Ever Played," where Muhammad Ali talked the good talk and fought even better. It's where Casey Stengel slammed the first World Series home run for the old New York Giants—an inside-the-parker in Game 1 of the 1923 World Series, where Mickey Mantle (whose 266 homers in Yankee Stadium from 1951 to 68 are the most in history) slugged a fly ball off the third-deck facade. It's where Thurman Munson's locker with his No. 15 jersey and catching gear is as it was the day he was killed in a 1979 airplane crash.

It seems that everyone has an opinion about Yankee Stadium.

"Most guys won't admit it," pitcher Al Leiter said, "but it can be an intimidating thing your first few times there. All the lore of the stadium and the mystique can be difficult to deal with."

"It is the most magical ballpark ever built," former Yankee Phil Linz said. "Playing there as a Yankee was like being in the Marines, the feeling that you were in a special ballpark, special town, special uniform, special history."

"When I went to the American League as an umpire, I had never been to a major league ballpark," said Bill Valentine. "This was 1963. You went out of the umpire's dressing room and down the hallway and up the ramp and stepped out onto the field. Here's this kid from Little Rock, Arkansas standing in New

York City in Yankee Stadium. It was a pretty incredible thing."

"Being from New York," Phil Rizzuto said, "It meant a lot for me to play in my hometown. I knew every nook and cranny there, and we had the fans behind us."

From 1903 until April 11, 1913, the New York Highlanders played all their home games at Hilltop Park. Then they became tenants of the New York Giants at the Polo Grounds. In 1920, Yankee attendance, pumped up by the drawing power of the new slugger Babe Ruth, doubled to 1,289,422, almost 100,000 more than the Giants.

The relationship between the two franchises, never especially friendly, turned very, very cold. The next season, the Giants served walking papers on the Yankees.

Yankee co-owner Jake Ruppert had dreamed of tearing down the Polo Grounds and creating a 100,000-seat stadium to be shared by the Giants and Yankees.

Now, however, he and co-owner colonel Tillinghast l'Hommedieu Huston announced a plan to create a new ballpark for the Yankees alone. It would be, Ruppert said, shaped along the lines of the Roman Coliseum.

The Yankees' new home was built on ten acres on a lumberyard in the Bronx. The exact location was at the mouth of a small body of water called Crowell's Creek. Identified as City Plot 2106, Lot 100, the land had been a farm owned by John Lion Gardiner prior to the Revolutionary War.

Osborne Engineering Co. of Cleveland, the architectural firm, was under mandate to create the greatest and grandest ballpark of its day. Original plans called for the action to be visible only by fans inside; but when the sta-dium was complete, outsiders could look in from the elevated trains and from surrounding buildings.

Throughout baseball history, many teams have built their teams to fit their stadiums. The Red Sox, for example, have stocked up on right-handed power hitters, hoping to take advantage of the Green Monster in left field. In more recent years, teams playing on artificial turf have tailored their team for the playing surface, loading up on speedy contact batters and fleet-footed outfielders. But the Yankees actually inverted this logic, building a stadium to match the team's strengths. The House That Ruth Built was, more precisely, built for Ruth.

Yankee Stadium's dimensions favored left-handed power: read Babe Ruth. A fly ball down the right field line had to travel only 295 feet to clear the fence. The stadium would be stingy to right-handed pull hitters and straightaway swingers—460 feet to left center field and 490 to center.

Yankee Stadium's inaugural game took place April 18, 1923. Babe Ruth had said: "I'd give a year of my life if I can hit a home run in this first game in this new park." He got his wish and so did all those in attendance. The Babe's homer highlighted the Yankees' 4-1 triumph over the Red Sox.

"Governors, general colonels, politicians, and baseball officials," A *New York Times* account reported, "gathered solemnly yesterday to dedicate the biggest stadium, in baseball…in the third inning with two teammates on the base lines, Babe Ruth smashed a savage home run into the right field bleachers, and that was the real baptism of Yankee Stadium."

Summertime fun at Yankee Stadium. (Photofest / Icon)

With the opening of Yankee Stadium, property values all around the area skyrocketed. New parking lots, a small theater, restaurants and bars opened. The nearby Concourse Plaza Hotel catered to visiting players.

Right off the bat, the cathedral of a ballpark was a place where pigeons, fat from peanuts and popcorn, lodged in the rafters and beams. Whenever crowds crowed over Yankee heroics, the pigeons flew up and about.

Yankee owner Jacob Ruppert presided over his team and Yankee Stadium. He was fond of saying: "Yankee Stadium was a mistake—not mine, but the Giants."

In 1932, the Yankees began honoring their legends with a monument for Miller Huggins. Monuments for Lou Gehrig and Babe Ruth followed. Located in straightaway centerfield as part of the playing field 10 feet in front of the wall, the monuments were part of the background for hitters in front of the flagpole.

Outfielders were wary of the monuments as they ran back to track down long fly

OPPOSITE: *Babe Ruth batting. (Photofest / Icon)*

balls. There were times when long drives managed to roll behind the monuments. Retrieving the ball was sometimes an odd and "ghoulish" task for an outfielder as he jockeyed around the "gravestones."

On one occasion Casey Stengel watched in dismay as one of those long drives skipped past his centerfielder and bounced around the monuments. Frustrated, Casey yelled: "Ruth, Gehrig, Huggins, someone throw that darned ball in here NOW!"

"Death Valley" in deep left and center fields was a place of heartbreak as many a right-handed slugger would watch in frustration as towering fly balls that seemed fated to be homers died there. Death to straightaway hitters, in 1923 Yankee Stadium's straightaway centerfield was 490 feet from home plate.

By 1937, the distance was still a considerable 461 feet. A green curtain was installed in left-center. Raised and lowered like a window shade, the curtain forced visiting batters to face a background of white-shirted bleacher fans while allowing Yankees hitters to face a dark green background.

In 1937, the right field stands were enlarged. Triple decks were extended past the foul pole in right field. Homers were now possible into the upper decks in right and left field. In 1937-38, an enlarged grandstand replaced "Ruthville," the original old wooden bleachers where Babe Ruth hit so many homers.

As the outfield bench seats were gradually replaced with chair seats in the 1930s and 1940s, Yankee Stadium's seating capacity gradually dropped from more than 70,000 to about 67,000.

In 1946, $600,000 worth of renovations were made, including the installation of arc lights which equaled the illumination of 5,000 full moons, as the Yankee press release claimed. Irish turf was brought in by Larry MacPhail so the grass became greener. A new paint job made the Stadium greener and bluer. Dugout locations were switched: visiting teams were located on the third base side and Yankees on the first base side of the infield. Another new feature was the creation of the Stadium Club for box holders, a place where the high and mighty—and others who wanted to be—congregated and ate and drank at what was for quite some time the largest bar in the state of New York.

The adding of lights in 1946 was about the only major change in Yankee Stadium until the winter of 1966-67 when the team's new owner, CBS, spent $1.5 million to modernize the park with 90 tons of paint. The brown concrete exterior and the greenish copper facade were painted white while the green grandstand seats were painted blue.

Yankee Stadium has been owned by the City of New York since 1971. On September 30, 1973, the final game was played at the old Yankee Stadium. In the audience of 32,238 fans were the widows of Babe Ruth and Lou Gehrig. The Yankees played their final season at the old Stadium in 1973. A half-century after it had been built, Yankee Stadium was completely renovated in 1974 and 1975, while the Yankees shared Shea Stadium with the Mets in Queens. The Yanks drew more than 1.2 million fans each season at Shea and posted a total record of 90-69.

When "The House that Ruth Built" reopened on April 15, 1976, the stadium had undergone a $100 million facelift. Gone were many of the obstructions from the old

Jimmie Foxx, Babe Ruth, Lou Gehrig, Al Simmons. (Photofest/Icon)

Babe Ruth, bigger than life. (Photofest/Icon)

ballpark, such as steel columns. The new park allowed for a more comfortable experience, as old 18-inch wooden seats were replaced with 22-inch plastic ones. There were now approximately 11,600 fewer seats, bringing the capacity down to 54,200. And the Yankees offered fans baseball's first "telescreen."

The new scoreboard cost 30 times what Colonel Jacob Ruppert paid to purchase Babe Ruth from the Red Sox. And the scoreboard's girth and size eliminated the special views many once had from the 161st Street station of the IRT subway and the rooftops of adjacent apartment houses.

The leftfield and centerfield fences had been drawn in considerably, but were still pokes of 430 feet and 417 feet, respectively. In 1988, they were pulled in further still, to 399 in left-center and 408 in center field.

In 1976, Monument Park was re-located between the Yankee and visitor bullpens. It would be moved to the left field corner in 1985 and opened for public touring up to 45 minutes before game time. Miller Huggins, Jake Ruppert, Lou Gehrig, Babe Ruth, Casey Stengel, Edward Barrow, Joe DiMaggio, Mickey Mantle, Joe McCarthy, Lefty Gomez, Whitey Ford, Elston Howard, Phil Rizzuto, Don Mattingly, Billy Martin, Bill Dickey, Yogi Berra, Allie Reynolds, Pope Paul VI (who said mass at Yankee Stadium in 1965) and Pope Paul II (who said mass at Yankee Stadium in 1979) are among those honored in Monument Park. Plaques also exist for Yankees who have had their numbers retired.

OPPOSITE: *Babe Ruth's farewell. (Photofest/Icon)*

Yankee Stadium panorama. (Photofest/Icon)

When the new Yankee Stadium opened on April 15, 1976, it was before the largest Opening Day crowd since 1946. Among the 52,613 present were legends Yogi Berra, Mickey Mantle, and Joe DiMaggio as well as the widows of Babe Ruth and Lou Gehrig. Bobby Richardson delivered the pregame prayer. Ceremonies honored the 1923 team. Bob Shawkey, 85, who had won the 1923 Stadium opener, threw out the first ball. The Yanks slammed the Twins, 11-4.

"When I first came to Yankee Stadium I used to feel like the ghosts of Babe Ruth and Lou Gehrig were walking around in there," Mickey Mantle noted. "After they remodeled Yankee Stadium I didn't feel that the ghosts were there anymore. It just wasn't the same."

"It had a sort of plastic look," veteran sportswriter Red Foley said. "When they took the frieze down they found out that it was made of galvanized steel. The dugouts before were different, a little bigger, more intimidating."

"The American League Baseball Grounds," "The House That Ruth Built" may have lost some character through the long seasons. Still it has remained the home of baseball's most fabled franchise, the site of some marker moments and frenzied battles between the Yankees and the Red Sox. It has also remained a playing field that has elicited all kinds of opinions.

"Yankee Stadium was made for rabbits and giants," was a point made with emphasis by Boston catcher Carlton Fisk. "You have to be a rabbit to catch a ball out there in the outfield and you have to be a giant to hit the ball out."

Fisk might have added that it didn't hurt to be a left-handed hitter. That's something that Joe DiMaggio, who hit right, picked up on.

"In the late '40s," recalled the Yankee Clipper, "I hit a ball about 400 feet to left center. We were playing the Red Sox, and my brother Dom had no trouble making the catch. Joe Gordon followed and hit one about 420 feet to the same area. Dom caught it. Then Yogi Berra cracked a line drive into the right-field seats near the foul line. If you remember, there was a low railing out there about three feet high. The ball barely cleared it. Yogi couldn't have hit the ball more than 300 feet. Joe Gordon and I watched him trot around the bases with a big grin on his face. We looked at each other and shrugged our shoulders. If we were born left-handed, our shots would've landed in the bleachers. They didn't name that area in left-center field Death Valley for nothing."

While the special dimensions of Yankee Stadium have posed problems for teams such as the Red Sox, especially when they built their teams around right-handed power, the same obstacles exist for Yankee right-handed hitters.

"I cried for days," said premier batting coach Charley Lau, "when a right-handed batter hit a ball 430 feet and it is an out. I think when you hit a ball that far, you should be rewarded for it. However, that's the way the park is. And Yankee left-handers have trouble in Fenway, so it evens out."

Whitey Ford Day at Yankee Stadium. (Photofest / Icon)

"I loved Yankee Stadium because I was left-handed," noted former superstar hurler Whitey Ford. "I usually faced mostly right-handed hitting teams there. The fence in centerfield was 461 feet away, and left centerfield was 457 feet. As long as you kept the hitters from hitting the ball down the line, it was a great park to pitch in."

Mickey Mantle, who starred for so many seasons at Yankee Stadium and Fenway Park, had special memories of both. "I loved to play at Fenway Park. But center field there was kinda tough. There were all those angles and the short center field fence. Down here at the Stadium you could run for two days in the outfield. There you had to watch it. You'd turn around and smash into the fence."

At every game at Yankee Stadium, almost as a taunt to cities such as Boston, the huge electronic sound system pipes out the voice of Frank Sinatra singing: "If I can make it here, I'll make it anywhere/It's up to you, New York, New York." Another phrase in the song refers to "those little-town blues" underscoring the differences between the Yankees and the Red Sox and the parks they play in.

Although Boston is by no means a "little town," it's not New York. "When the Yankees sell out on any given date," explained Bill Crowley, "their gross income is much higher than that of the Red Sox because of the disparity in seats between the two ballparks for one thing. With the gap in income, it's imperative that Boston has large numbers of fans coming to the ballpark to stay competitive."

If the contrasting sizes of the cities and the parks help shape the rivalry, the mix of fans helps to shape the mood.

"The crowd at Yankee Stadium is definitely pro-Yankee," said Frank Messer, the late Yankee broadcaster, "and pro-Boston at Fenway. However, crowds are never that one-sided because of the geography."

The geography involves many New Yorkers attending college in the Boston area who come to Fenway and sit in the bleachers, sometimes out-numbering Red Sox fans. These exiles come to root the Yankees on. The "geography" is also an intermingling of New Englanders at the Stadium, some cheering on Boston, others rooting for New York. In the Big Apple there is still a small faction of former Brooklyn Dodger and New York Giant fans, as well as a large contingent of Mets fans, attached to the Red Sox. They come to the Stadium and demonstrate an almost fanatical devotion to the visiting team.

"I was always aware of the mix at Fenway Park," said Lou Piniella, who managed and played for the Yankees. "There was always a lot of excitement in that small park that made it special. You might have 20,000 Red Sox fans at Fenway and 15,000 Yankee fans. Their rivalry helped our rivalry. It excited the players who had to respond to it."

Former Red Sox batting star Dwight Evans was not nearly as enamored with the atmosphere at Yankee Stadium as Piniella was with Fenway Park. Evans made his first of many appearances at the Stadium in 1972.

"When you have coke bottles go by your head from the third deck," he said, "and they miss you by six inches, you wonder what kind of people these are. When you have cherry bombs thrown at you or thrown into crowds, that's not fun and that's not fans. Don't get me wrong—but I think the people that are crazy in New York are more crazy than the ones in Boston and you have crazy people, there, too. When they say it was the Bronx Zoo, I agreed. I think the majority of the people that come to the Stadium are great, knowledgeable baseball fans. But they know what I mean when I talk about the crazy ones that are there. I've had to wear helmets out there in the outfield many times. It's a great ballpark to play in, yet you have to watch out for things. When they throw a penny or a dime from the third deck and it hits you, it's going to put a knot on your head.

"They used to throw glass balls at me, broken glass wrapped in masking tape. And when it hit you, it punctured. Think about trying to play in the outfield and having things thrown at you all game long. I like people who like baseball, but not the nuts."

"**Fenway Park** in Boston is a lyric little bandbox of a ballpark. Everything is painted green and seems in curiously sharp focus, like the inside of an old-fashioned peeping type Easter egg."

—John Updike,
"Hub Fans Bid Kid Adieu"

The Dwight Evans perspective is from many decades back. But a view from former Yankee infielder Alex Arias expressed in 2002 is not much different: "I grew up in New York City a big Yankees fan, no doubt. I went to a lot of Red Sox games at the Stadium. One time I was sitting down the left field line, and this guy had a Boston jersey on, and they just ripped it off his body. The Yankees were losing that day. They ripped his hat and his shirt right off his body. That's one thing I'll always remember. He was drunk, you know, he was kind of loud, and they just took his clothes and just ripped them to shreds. I was scared. I mean, I thought those people were crazy. I wouldn't get caught dead in that place now."

The smallest and oldest park in the major leagues, Fenway is a place where the stories about great players of the past and the performance of modern day icons come together—Cy Young, Babe Ruth, Jimmy Collins, Duffy Lewis, Tris Speaker, Harry Hooper, Joe Cronin, Mel Parnell, Bobby Doerr, Johnny Pesky, Ted Williams, Jimmie Foxx, Carlton Fisk, Jim Rice, Fred Lynn, Carl Yastrzemski, Carlton Fisk, George Scott, Wade Boggs, Roger Clemens, Manny Ramirez, Nomar Garciaparra, Pedro Martinez and on and on.

Besides its cozy, backyard feel, nothing marks Fenway Park more than its asymmetry. A world-class jumper with a trampoline couldn't scale the 37-foot high Green Mon-ster in left field, yet a kid could hop over the right field fence, only three feet high in some spots. Fenway is a famously friendly hitters' ballpark, yet there's plenty of room for out-fielders to run down fly balls in centerfield, 420 feet from home plate. One of the sport's few centerfield corners is formed at the junction of a 17-foot-tall mini-monster in left-center and a five-foot-high wall in front of the right-field bullpen.

The Green Monster has always been the most inviting target for hitters. Only 310 feet down the line, it can turn pop flies into home runs, most famously for Bucky Dent in the Yankees' 1978 playoff game victory over Boston on an unseasonably warm fall day in New England. The shortest distance in the park is actually the right field line, just 302 feet away from home plate. It's called "Pesky's Pole" in honor of Johnny Pesky, a Red Sox shortstop in the 1940s and '50s who went on to become a Boston coach and manager. One of Pesky's six lifetime homers at Fenway snuck just past the right field foul pole, winning the game for pitcher Mel Parnell, who gratefully coined the term.

Despite the short launch, right field is not the best place to shoot for home runs, because the right field wall quickly juts out from the foul pole.

The Green Monster offers a more steady mark for hitters as well as a tougher challenge

FOLLOWING PAGE: *Crowd celebrating at Fenway. (Frommer Archives)*

Left to right: Sam Nede, Ted Williams, Stan Spinee, Dom DiMaggio. (Photofest/Icon)

for fielders. A skilled left fielder can look as comfortable as a 10-year-old stickball player catching tennis balls off his elementary school wall.

The Monster, although long linked with offense, can be turned into a potent defensive force. Carl Yastrzemski was famous for holding hitters to long singles by routinely catching balls off the wall on a fly and firing to second base. Less graceful fielders, however, can find the Monster's ricochets and caroms frightening.

Two-hundred-and-forty feet wide, the Green Monster is anchored by a steel and concrete foundation that goes 22 feet below the field. In 2003, the team installed seats on top of the Green Monster, which quickly became one of the most popular vantage points to watch the action. A manual scoreboard in the wall still keeps the score and updates out-of-town American League games. The Monster wasn't actually green until 1947, when the team decided to paint over the advertising billboards that had adorned it. That was how the

Boston outfielder Jim Rice poised to make the outfield play. (Photofest)

nickname "The Green Monster" came to be. There were no more Calvert owl ("Be wise"), Gem Blades ("Avoid 5 o'clock shadow"), Lifebuoy ("The Red Sox use it") and Vimms ("Get that Vimms feeling") signs.

The Red Sox generally build their teams around the contours of Fenway Park, which means stocking up on right-handed power hitters at the expense of speedy players. That often gives the Sox a big home-field advantage but can backfire on the road.

In 1949, the team lost a one-game lead and the American League pennant by dropping the final two games of the season at Yankee Stadium. That year Boston went 61-16 at home (a torrid .792 pace) but only 35-42 on the road (.455).

"The result was inevitable—Boston goes ahead, Yankees catch up and win. Tied. Same outcome the next day and New York wins the pennant," recalled Walter Mears, a Pulitzer-prize winning retired political reporter for the Associated Press.

"There was no TV to watch then, and I sat listening to the radio in Lexington as the Red Sox blew it. At 14, it seemed like the end of more than just a season.

"I remember saying to my father, 'I think I'll just go for a walk,' which I did, so that he wouldn't see me cry. I think that's when I learned that there was no point in mourning the Red Sox. You just take it, knowing that they will come close and fall short."

"The Red Sox fans are tired, they're frustrated," said former Boston pitcher Willie Banks, who grew up a Yankees fan. "But they have the right to be that way, because they haven't won in a long time. Yankees fans are so spoiled, they're just used to going to the World Series and winning it every year."

Fenway Park was not the original home of the Red Sox. Until 1912, the team played at the all-wooden, 9,000-seat Huntington Avenue Baseball Grounds, now part of Northeastern University. Home games in the first World Series in 1903 were played there.

On April 9, 1912, Harvard University and the Red Sox christened Fenway Park in a spring snowstorm exhibition game, won by the Red Sox.

A veteran bought the team for his son John I. Taylor in 1904. In 1907, owner Taylor changed the club's name from the Pilgrims to the Red Sox.

On April 20, the Red Sox played their first official major league game at Fenway (so named because of its location in the Fenway section of Boston). Fittingly enough, that first game was against the New York Highlanders (who changed their name to the Yankees a few years later).

Boston mayor John "Honey Fitz" Fitzgerald, the grandfather-to-be of John F. Kennedy, threw out the first ball. The Red Sox won, 7-6 in 11 innings, on Tris Speaker's RBI. But news of the sinking of the Titanic overshadowed Fenway's opener.

Two years later, on June 21, 1916, the first no-hitter was thrown at Fenway. Boston pitcher George "Rube" Foster no-hit New York in a 2-0 win and was rewarded with a $100 bonus. His teammates were each given gold-handled pocketknives with the no-hitter date engraved.

Bars and restaurants, vendors and scalpers still make a trip to Fenway a truly urban sporting experience. The stadium is two miles away from the bar used in the TV program *Cheers,* whose main character, Sam Malone, pitched for the Sox in the 1970s. His main

Red Sox fans begin to gather outside Fenway Park before a big game. (Frommer Archives)

claim to fame: the sport's only switch-hitting pitcher.

Fenway is one of the most traditional settings in baseball, yet it has gone through some makeovers and modernizing through the years. In 1947, the stadium was fitted with lights, and the Red Sox played their first night home game on June 13, 1947. By contrast, Chicago's Wrigley Field, the stadium most often compared to Fenway Park, didn't install lights until 1988.

Fenway also debuted a rule change that still rankles baseball purists. On April 6, 1973, the first designated hitter ever came to bat in a Yankees-Red Sox game at Fenway Park. In the first inning of that game, New York DH Ron Blomberg walked with the bases loaded, and finished one-for-three with a run scored and an RBI. Boston DH Orlando Cepeda went 0-for-six, but the Red Sox won, 15-5.

Through much of the 20th century, the Red Sox have shared Fenway Park with several Boston football teams. The Boston Redskins played there until 1937, when they moved to Washington, D.C. The Boston Patriots (now the New England Patriots) played at Fenway from 1963 to 1968. And the Boston Yanks (the Yanks!) called Fenway home from 1944 to '48 before moving to New York, Dallas, Baltimore, and finally, Indianapolis, where they are now the Colts.

Day and night at Fenway Park. (Frommer Archives)

Some of the stadium's rough edges have been evened out over the years. From 1912 to 1933, there was a 10-foot-high hill in front of the left-field wall where fans were allowed to sit. It became known as Duffy's Cliff, in honor of skilled Boston left fielder Duffy Lewis. But the ground was flattened in 1934, as part of a renovation following a fire that damaged much of the stadium. An earlier fire in 1926 destroyed the bleachers along the left-field line. Because the owner at the time of the first fire, John Quinn, didn't have the money to replace the seats, fielders routinely ranged out to catch balls behind the stands.

Some changes were made to help the team. In 1940, new bullpens were built in right field, so the fence could be moved in 23 feet to take advantage of the dead-pull hitting skills of young slugger Ted Williams. The new bullpens were dubbed "Williamsburg."

But a few years later, Williams hit a ball that looked like it might make it to Williamsburg, Brooklyn. His 502-foot home run into the right field bleachers, the longest ever inside Fenway Park, is now marked by a red-painted seat—Section 42, Row 37, Seat 21. Williams's blast bounced off the head of fan Joseph A. Boucher, visiting from Albany, New York.

"The sun was right in our eyes," recalled Boucher. "All we could do was duck. I'm glad I didn't stand up. They say it bounced a dozen rows higher, but after it hit my head, I was no longer interested."

Fans weren't the only ones who had to watch out for Williams. He once went out before a game and shot about 40 pigeons, joining owner Tom Yawkey on the hunt. Reporters tipped off the Humane Society, and Williams promised not to do it again.

Pigeons have been a mainstay at Fenway Park for decades, and they occasionally affect the outcome of a play. One even got an assist. In 1945, an outfielder's throw deflected off a pigeon and the ball landed in the mitt of the second baseman, who tagged out Boston's Skeeter Newsome trying for a double. The pigeon flew away unharmed.

A rat, meanwhile, may have led to the most dramatic television sports shot ever. NBC had put a cameraman inside the Green Monster for the 1975 World Series between the Red Sox and the Cincinnati Reds. With the Reds leading three games to two, Game 6 at Fenway Park was delayed three straight days because of rain. The teams finally got to play on October 21.

The Reds, up 6-3 in the eighth-inning, were four outs away from a world championship when Boston's Bernie Carbo tied the game with a three-run, two-out pinch-hit homer. Then the Red Sox loaded the bases in the bottom of the ninth, but came away with nothing after Reds left fielder George Foster threw out Denny Doyle trying to score on a Fred Lynn fly ball.

The game went into extra innings. Cincinnati third baseman Pete Rose went up to Boston catcher Carlton Fisk in the 10th inning and said, "Some kind of game, isn't it?"

"Some kind of game," Fisk replied.

When Fisk came up in the bottom of the 12th inning, at 12:30 in the morning, the rat inside the Green Monster froze the cameraman, leaving the camera frozen on Fisk. That let viewers see Fisk waving his arms frantically, trying to will his fly ball fair and off the left field foul pole for a game-winning home run and a 3-3 series tie.

Alas, the Sox lost Game 7 the next day.

Critters and all, a ticket to Fenway is one of the hottest in Boston, and it's never hotter than when the Yankees visit.

"When the Yankees were coming to town, those dates were circled on everybody's calendar," said Red Sox infielder Lou Merloni, who grew up in Framingham, Massachusetts. "The city is different; they're just different games. I remember my dad trying to get tickets every time the Yankees played, and we'd go to those games, and they were just so much fun. Then I'd watch them play the Twins, and it would just totally be a different game, a different crowd, a different energy in the stands."

The largest crowd in Fenway history, in fact, came out for a New York-Boston showdown at the height of the Great Depression. More than 47,000 fans jammed into the tiny park to see a doubleheader between the two rivals on September 22, 1935. The Yankees swept, driving seven ground-rule doubles into the roped-off crowd in the second game alone.

The year before, just less than 47,000 fans had jammed the park to see Babe Ruth's farewell at Fenway Park, in which he singled and doubled. After World War II, more stringent fire laws and league rules prevented overcrowding of this sort, and such crowds have never been repeated.

In 1977, Fenway Park drew its two millionth fan of the season for the first time ever—and became just the fourth stadium in the American League to do so. The Red Sox finished with a home attendance of 2.08 million.

Boston shattered that attendance record the next season, drawing 2.3 million, but Fenway Park was the sight of much heartbreak that year. After shrinking Boston's 14-game summer lead to four games, the Yankees came to Boston for a crucial four-game series in September. The result: a four-game New York sweep dubbed the "Boston Massacre," in

A panoramic view of a Fenway Park sellout. (Frommer Archives)

Yankee members stretch before a game against the Red Sox at Fenway Park. (Frommer Archives)

which New York outscored Boston, 42-9. Three weeks later, Bucky Dent hit his famous pop fly three-run homer over the Green Monster, giving the Yankees a 5-4 win in their one-game playoff, and the American League East title.

Fenway's current capacity is about 34,000. The Red Sox have considered replacing Fenway Park with a new ballpark, arguing the team needed more seats and luxury boxes to make enough money to be competitive. But the passion for Fenway led fans in 1998 to form a group called "Save Fenway Park," which has fought such efforts.

The group has found a more sympathetic ear under the team's new owners, led by financier John Henry, who have said they would prefer to preserve Fenway Park. Possible renovations include an upper deck with luxury boxes.

In 1999, Major League Baseball held its 70th All-Star game at Fenway Park, showcasing the sport's All-Century Team. The star at-

traction was 80-year-old Ted Williams, who threw out the first ball. The famed Sox slugger was moved to tears as current All Stars surrounded and paid homage to him. In 1960, he had finished his career with a home run in his final at-bat at Fenway Park.

Boston's Pedro Martinez continued to make history in the game, becoming the first pitcher in All-Star history to strike out the game's first three batters. In just two innings, Pedro struck out five batters—Barry Larkin, Larry Walker, Sammy Sosa, Mark McGwire and Jeff Bagwell. Martinez's performance won him the Most Valuable Player award in the American League's 4-1 victory.

Later that year, the Red Sox and Yankees met in the playoffs for the first time since 1978—this time in a best-of-seven American League Championship Series. New York took the first two games at Yankee Stadium, and then the series switched to Fenway. Former Boston stopper Roger Clemens took the mound for the Yankees against Martinez, who

The Green Monster. (Frommer Archives)

THE YANKEE CLIPPER
AND TEDDY BALLGAME

"Ted Williams was what John Wayne would have liked us to think he was. Williams was so big, and handsome, and laconic, and direct, and unafraid in that uniquely American cowboy way."
—Robert Lipsyte

PEN SKETCH OF JOE DIMAGGIO

No greater effort than a breeze that blows
Across the field when some fly ball is struck.
A drifting phantom where the long smash goes,
That has no helping teammate known as luck.
No desperate stab—no wild one-handed catch,
Few ringing cheers that churn the summer air
A shift—a turn—a movement none can match,
The ball drifts down—DiMaggio is there.
Ty Cobb has ruled—and Ruth has sung his tune—

Tris Speaker was a melody in rime—
DiMaggio—you won't forget him soon—
Here is the master artist of our time.
—Grantland Rice

"They can talk about Babe Ruth and Ty Cobb and Rogers Hornsby and Lou Gehrig and Joe DiMaggio and Stan Musial and all the rest, but I'm sure not one of them could hold cards and spades to [Ted] Williams in his sheer knowledge of hitting. He studied hitting the way a broker studies the stock market, and could spot at a glance mistakes that others couldn't see in a week." —Carl Yastrzemski

"MRS. ROBINSON"

Heaven holds a place for those who pray.
Joltin' Joe has left and gone away.
Where have you gone, Joe DiMaggio?
A nation turns its lonely eyes to you.
—Paul Simon

Perhaps no two players have symbolized the Yankee-Red Sox rivalry as much as Joe DiMaggio and Ted Williams. Both Califor-

OPPOSITE: *Joe DiMaggio—The Yankee Clipper. (Frommer Archives)*

nians, they found stardom in the East. Both bigger than life, they seemed sculpted into their respective superstar roles. One was an outspoken iconoclast, the other a soft-spoken team man.

Born November 25, 1914, in Martinez, California, Joseph Paul DiMaggio was one of nine children of a fisherman father who had emigrated from Sicily. The 11-member DiMaggio family included Giuseppe and Rosalie, five brothers (Mike, Tom, Vince, Joe, and Dom), and four sisters (Marie, Mae, Nelly, and Frances). Their home was on Taylor Street in the North Beach-Telegraph Hill section of San Francisco. Rosalie would cover for the DiMaggio boys when they arrived home with torn pants and encourage them to play. It was planned for Joe to become a fisherman like his father. His real passion was playing baseball.

"I began playing baseball on a vacant lot in San Francisco with the other kids in my neighborhood when I was about 10 years old," the man they would call the Yankee Clipper recalled. "In those days, I preferred almost anything to working on my father's fishing boat or cleaning it up when the fishing day was over. I hated the smell. My father looked on baseball in much the same way as I did on fishing."

In 1934, the Yankees purchased the contract of Joe DiMaggio from the San Francisco Seals of the Pacific Coast League, which at that time was the closest thing the West Coast had to major league baseball. "Getting him," general manager George Weiss was fond of saying, "was the greatest thing I ever did for the Yankees." The price for DiMaggio was $25,000 and five players. The deal also contained the condition that the graceful out-fielder be permitted to play one more season for San Francisco. DiMaggio gave the city of San Francisco something to remember, batting .398 with 270 hits and 154 RBIs.

Permission was granted in 1936 for DiMaggio to drive cross-country with fellow San Franciscans Tony Lazzeri and Frank Crosetti to the Yankee spring training camp in St. Petersburg, Florida.

Reportedly, Lazzeri turned to DiMaggio after the trio had concluded one day of driving and said: "You take over, Joe."

"I don't drive," DiMaggio supposedly answered, the only words he uttered during the three-day California-to-Florida journey. "Joe DiMaggio was a guy who didn't graduate from high school," noted Yankee teammate Jerry Coleman. "He went to about the 10th grade. He was totally insecure, and consequently his quietness came from his saying nothing rather than saying something that would make him look bad."

On March 2, 1936, DiMaggio finally reported to spring training. Red Ruffing greeted him with, "So you're the great DiMaggio?"

Joe's father sent him a telegram during that first spring training with the Yankees: "Come home, Joe. The fish are running. Give up this game of baseball. It is for loafers."

He played in his first major league game on May 3, 1936 at Yankee Stadium against the St. Louis Browns. In his first time at bat, he hit the second pitch into left field for a single. He had another single and then a triple to left field. Joe DiMaggio played 138 games in his rookie season, hit .323, with 29 home runs and 125 runs batted in.

Ted Williams was born on August 30, 1918, in San Diego. In 1935, as a pitcher-out-fielder at Herbert Hoover High School in his hometown, he hit .586. His mother, an ardent Salvation Army worker, thought he was worth a $1,000 bonus for signing with a major league team. Bill Essick, a scout for the Yankees, listened, thought, and finally decided that Williams was not worth that much money.

"I don't know whether $1,000 stood between me being a Yank or not," Williams recalled. "There were those who said years later, 'You will regret not having been a Yankee. You would be a great hero in New York. Yankee Stadium was built for a left-handed hitter.'"

Williams signed with the San Diego Padres of the Pacific Coast League. He played in 42 games in 1936, and then hit .291 with 23 home runs and 98 RBIs the following season. The manager of the National League's Boston Bees, a humorous but baseball-wise gent named Casey Stengel, observed Williams playing for San Diego. He recommended that Boston sign the youngster. The Bees' management decided that the asking price was too high. The other Boston team, the Red Sox, thought the price was right and signed Williams.

When the six-foot-three, curly-haired Williams arrived at the Red Sox spring training camp in 1938, he noticed that all the team's stars were from someplace else: Joe Cronin and Ben Chapman were from Washington; Doc Cramer hailed from Philadelphia; and Joe Vosmik came from St. Louis. Jimmy Foxx, who had starred for many years with the A's, was winding up his Hall of Fame career with the Red Sox.

"Ted," said Bobby Doerr, a friend of Williams from their PCL days, "wait 'til you see this guy Foxx hit."

"Bobby," snapped Williams, "wait till Foxx sees me hit."

Williams did not hit that well in spring training for 1938, and to the delight of some of the Red Sox stars he had alienated, he was sent down to Minneapolis of the American Association for more seasoning. "I'll be back," he snarled at some of the Boston stars, "and I'll be greater than you guys." At Minneapolis, he led the American Association in homers (43), RBIs (142) and batting average (.366) and was poised to batter American League pitching.

Ted Williams's first year with the Red Sox, 1939, was Joe DiMaggio's fourth season with the New York Yankees. In his first three seasons, the Yankee Clipper had batted .323, .346, and .324, and glided about the center field pastureland of Yankee Stadium with a quiet ease and grace.

The Boston Red Sox and New York Yankees went head to head for the pennant in 1939. And Williams and DiMaggio went head to head in the first of many seasons during which they would vie for the attention and admiration of fans.

Williams was to begin his rookie season in New York to play at Yankee Stadium against the Yankees of Lou Gehrig, Tommy Henrich, Frank Crosetti, Bill Dickey, Charlie Keller and Joe DiMaggio. But it rained for two days before he was able to play in his first game. Red Ruffing, one of Boston owner Harry Frazee's "gifts," was the Yankee pitcher.

Perhaps a bit over-anxious, Williams struck out in his first two at-bats. His third time up he smashed the ball to deep right-center field. It missed the bleachers by inches, and Williams wound up at second base with a double, the first of 2,654 major league hits—and it came against the Yankees.

Williams batted .327 in his rookie season, with 31 home runs and 145 RBIs. He formed a potent partnership with Foxx, who batted .360 and lashed 35 home runs. But the great DiMag prevailed over both of them. Hitting a league-leading and career-best .381, the quiet Yankee drove in 126 runs and rapped 30 homers. Both Williams and DiMaggio were named to the All-Star team—the first of six times they played together. The Yankee Clipper earned the first of his three Most Valuable Player awards. That was how the Williams-DiMaggio competition began.

Joe DiMaggio would step into the batter's box and stub his right toe into the dirt in back of his left heel. It was almost a dance step. His feet were spaced approximately four feet apart, with the weight of his frame on his left leg. Erect, almost in a military position, Joe D would hold his bat at the end and poise it on his right shoulder—a rifle at the ready. He would look out at the pitcher from deep in the batter's box and assume a stance that almost crowded the plate. Without a bat and with his left arm extended straight out, "standing in the batter's box," observed sportswriter Tom Meany, "Joe DiMaggio with his hand cocked close to the breast looked like an old boxing print of John L. Sullivan."

Ted Williams was a contrasting image. Left-handed, "loose as a goose," in the phrase of same fans, he stood at the plate wiggling and waggling his bat. His eyes were everywhere, checking the pitchers, the fielders, the wind, the plate. He seemed to be possessed by a nervous twitch, driven to hit the ball if it was a strike.

"Ted Williams looked like the hitter on the cover of an old *Spaulding Guide*," said Casey Stengel, "but when they pitched to him

everything happened in just the right way. I bet there wasn't more than a dozen times in his life when he was really fooled by pitchers."

"You could shut your eyes behind home plate when Williams was hitting," said the late umpire Ron Luciano. "If it was a strike, Ted would swing at it. If it was a ball, he would let it go. He was an umpire at bat. Williams trained himself to swing at good pitches, although the opposition complained that he got four strikes."

"Joe was the complete player in everything he did," said Joe McCarthy, who managed both Williams and DiMaggio. "They'd hit the ball to center field, and Joe would stretch out those long legs of his and run the ball down. He never made a mistake on the bases and in a tough park for a right-hander, he was a great hitter, one of the best. But of course, there wasn't anything Williams couldn't do with a bat."

In 1941, the United States was poised on the brink of World War II. The interest of the nation was dominated by war news. The interest of baseball fans was riveted on the deeds of the Red Sox star and the Yankee hero as they went head to head, setting records that still stand.

Joe DiMaggio hit safely in 56 consecutive games. Ted Williams became the first player to bat over .400 since Bill Terry hit .401 in 1930.

DiMaggio's streak began on May 15 and ended on July 17. During that incredible stretch that had fans—especially Yankee fans—agog with admiration, he hit 15 home runs, four triples and 16 doubles, drove in 55 runs, scored 56 times, and batted .408—all while striking out only five times. The scoreboard

OPPOSITE: *Ted Williams (Photofest)*

operator in left field at Fenway Park would pass on the news of DiMaggio's progress to Ted Williams. And Williams would yell to Joe's brother, Dom, who played center field for the Red Sox, "Joe's just got another hit."

There was a rivalry between the Sox and Yankee fans, but Williams rooted all the while for DiMag to keep the streak going. As a hitter, he could appreciate the magnitude of the accomplishment. Referring to two other single-season records, Williams said, "You can talk all you want about Hornsby's .424 average, and Hack Wilson's 190 RBIs, but when DiMag hit in those 56 consecutive games, he put a line in the record book. It's the one that will never be changed."

Day after day throughout 1941, Williams pursued a .400 batting average—another line that will probably never be duplicated. He leaned into pitches with that bull-whipping, elastic grace. Those pitches that were not strikes, he let go. At one point he had a string of 36 walks in 19 straight games.

There were those who said that Williams had super-human vision. Williams did have extraordinary vision, 20-10, but his excellence came from his dedication. "I was a guy who practiced until the blisters bled," Williams said. "And then I practiced some more. I lived by a book on pitchers. I honestly believe that I can recall everything there was to know about my first 300 home runs—who the pitcher was, where I hit the ball, what the score was, where I hit the pitch."

With a week left in the 1941 season, Boston manager Joe Cronin suggested that Williams sit out the remaining games to protect his average. The Thumper was batting .406. "If I'm a .400 hitter," snapped Williams, "I'm a .400 hitter for the entire season, not a part of one. I'll play out the year." As the Sox prepared to play their final 1941 weekend series with the Philadelphia Athletics, Williams's average had dropped to .39955, which would have been rounded up to .400 had he chosen to sit out.

Saturday was dreary and cold, and the game was rescheduled as part of a season finale doubleheader the following day. Sunday was another nasty day, and only 10,000 showed up at the Philadelphia ballpark. Frankie Hayes, the A's catcher, told Williams as he came up for his first turn at bat, "If we let up on you, Mr. Mack (the A's owner-manager) said he would run us out of baseball. I wish you all the luck in the world, but we're not going to give you a damn thing."

Plate umpire Bill McGowan dusted off home plate and avoided looking at Williams. "To hit .400 a batter has got to be loose," McGowan said. "Are you loose, Ted?"

In the first game, Williams came to bat five times and stroked four hits. In the second game, he went two for three. It was an awesome hitting demonstration. In the doubleheader, he had six hits in eight tries, including his 37th home run. His final batting average was .406, making him the last player in baseball history to hit .400 in a season. Hardly anyone noticed that his slugging average was an amazing .735. Williams not only led the league in batting and slugging, he was also first in home runs, walks, runs scored and home run percentage.

The Yankee Clipper, meanwhile, batted .357 and paced the American League in RBIs. When it came time for the Most Valuable Player award, it was Joe DiMaggio who was selected, with 291 votes to Ted Williams's 254 votes. The Yankees had won the pennant by

17 games over the second-place Red Sox, and DiMaggio had set the hitting streak record—that was the rationale. The Yankee-Red Sox rivalry had become not just one of teams, but an individual showdown between two of the game's best players.

That season of accomplishment accentuated the skills and the differences that made Williams and DiMaggio such contrasting personalities, such different types of ball players.

DiMag was cooperative; Williams was controversial. The Boston slugger did not care about fielding. DiMaggio's outfield skills made him the complete player. Ted hurt his team by walking too much. The Yankee Clipper was at his best in the clutch but he didn't have the natural hitting power of Williams. So the debate raged.

Ted was tempestuous; Joe was dignified. Williams did not wear a tie and favored casual sports clothes. DiMaggio was always well-groomed, and in 1936 was voted one of the 10 best-dressed men in America. Williams was red-necked, rabbit-eared, outspoken and opinionated; a physical man, he did 50 push-ups a day, and then 50 more on his fingertips. DiMag rarely smiled, sipped his half-cup of coffee, kept his feelings inside. His exterior was placid; some said it was cold and sullen and unfeeling. No. 5 was the ultimate perfectionist, who took it very personally when the Yankees lost.

Williams was the main man of the BoSox, but DiMaggio was the Yankee Clipper. With Williams, Boston was a top half of the standings team, a frequent contender. Without him, Boston was a bottom half of the standings club, out of the money. In Ted's first two decades with the Red Sox, they finished out of the top half of the standings just

three times—all while Williams was in the Armed Services.

In the 12 years before DiMaggio arrived on the scene, the Yankees won the pennant four times. In his 13 seasons with the Bronx Bombers, they won 10 pennants. The Red Sox, meanwhile, won just one pennant in Williams's 19 seasons.

Many viewed Boston's shortcomings and New York's success as directly attributable to Williams and DiMaggio. Sportswriter Dan Parker summed up this view when he wrote:

"The Yankees take their cue from Joe DiMaggio. He is a true team player obsessed with winning…After paying tribute to Ted's gift of meeting the ball and sending it squarely on a line, some of us have come to the conclusion that despite his tremendous batting ability, Williams is what is wrong with the Red Sox…a team with such an outstanding star usually takes its cue from him. No one can say that Williams is a team player. His chief interest seems to be in fattening Ted Williams's batting average."

Other comparisons were drawn. Williams played at Fenway Park, a southpaw slugger handicapped by his home field, where many times the wind was blowing in. Yet he hit .360 at Fenway, including 248 home runs and 978 RBIs. At Yankee Stadium, he hit 309 with 30 home runs in 476 trips to the plate.

There were many who thought he could have done more, who were not happy with his attitude, his outspokenness, aspects of his play. Williams was criticized for failing to run full-tilt after fly balls, for seemingly leaning against an invisible fence in left field in a lazy fixed position. "They'll never get me out of a game running into a wall," said the man some called Terrible Ted. "I'll make a damned good

try, but you can bet your sweet life I won't get killed. They don't pay off on fielding."

"I saw guys who were .220 hitters who did the same thing," recalled Ted's longtime teammate Johnny Pesky, "but it was never magnified to the same extent. When you're a player of the stature that Williams was, they want you to do everything perfectly. Ted was a loafer. DiMag was a different type of person."

Ted Williams's lapses were grist for gossipy headlines. He was criticized because he didn't visit his mother often enough and because he was not present at the birth of his first child. What was overlooked was that he gave much financial aid to his mother, and that the birth of his first daughter was a premature one.

In his second season with the Sox, Williams decided he would not tip his cap to the fans. It was not his way. He refused to sign autographs when he wasn't in the mood. He lingered in the clubhouse hours after a game to safeguard his privacy—as did DiMag. Perhaps it was because the Yankee Clipper avoided controversy and Williams seemed to go looking for it that DiMaggio was able get away with doing things that the Boston slugger was criticized for.

In the first game of the 1942 season, Williams was booed at Fenway Park. Headlines and stories about his draft deferment stoked the "boo-birds." The Sox outfielder answered back with a three-run homer his first time at bat. DiMaggio, who had also received a draft deferment, drew cheers at the Stadium. Both players wound up missing the 1943, '44 and '45 seasons for military service.

A letter written to (and printed by) a Boston newspaper typified the controversy that swirled around Williams:

"Ted Williams is the all-time, all-American adolescent. He never wears a necktie unless he wears it to bed. He'll never tip his cap to the guys who pay his over-stuffed salary. He'll never bunt, steal, hustle or take a sign…unless it suits his convenience. In short, he'll continue to be just what he has always been—the prize heel that ever wore a Boston uniform."

In 1942, the Red Sox again finished second to the Yankees, and once again Williams finished second to a Yankee for the Most Valuable Player award. The moody Red Sox slugger won the Triple Crown with a .365 average, 36 home runs and 137 RBIs, but Joe Gordon won the MVP. Williams had eclipsed the Yankee outfielder in every offensive category—including press relations. There were many who said that was the reason he lost out to Gordon. Ted's troubles with the draft board also contributed to negative feelings about him.

But even the Sox fans who booed and criticized Williams were incensed at the MVP balloting, especially since the award went to a Yankee. In 1941, Williams maintained that DiMaggio deserved the MVP award. But now, the Boston outfielder was livid. He took out his feelings on the press; many reporters remembered and they worked their typewriters with a fury to get back at him.

"If his ego swells another inch, Master Ted Williams will not be able to get his hat on with a shoehorn," wrote Jack Miley in the *New York Post*. "When it comes to arrogant and ungrateful athletes, this one leads the league."

OPPOSITE: *In a classic pose—Joe DiMaggio. (Photofest)*

Criticism ticked Williams off. Fans cursed him. He cursed back. "Damn New England buzzards," was his expression for those who attacked him. When words failed him, he sometimes answered with obscene gestures, stroking more controversy. Williams's baiters throughout his career used to line up in the left field grandstand at Fenway Park where the corner runs close to the playing field. Fans armed with containers of beer would dare the thumper to chase a fly ball within their pouring range. To protect Williams, the Boston management withheld selling seats in that area until all other grandstand seats were sold out.

They called him "the kid," and he acted like one. He fired a shiny new pistol from the box seats behind home plate at the left field scoreboard at Fenway Park and shattered some $400 worth of light bulbs. On another occasion, his fondness for firing a weapon landed him in a new controversy.

There were many pigeons at Fenway Park. It was reported that each time the population became too large, the groundskeeper would shoot the birds. One day Williams went out with his 20-gauge shotgun and destroyed about 40 pigeons. Owner Tom Yawkey came out and joined Williams in the pigeon shoot. "By the time we were done," Williams said, "we knocked off 70 or 80 pigeons. We had a hell of a time." Reporters tipped off the Humane Society.

"So I apologized and promised I wouldn't shoot any more pigeons," Williams wrote in his autobiography, *My Turn At Bat*.

But it was not the end of his continuing feud with the press.

Approached by a reporter who had attacked him in print, Williams lashed out. "You

Ted Williams (right) and two of his friends Bobby Doerr (left) and Johnny Pesky (middle). (Frommer Archives)

write crap stuff about me, and you want to get an interview. Get the hell away from me."

Two of Ted's severest critics were Boston writers. "No grown man in full possession of his faculties would make the vile gestures that Williams made," wrote Dave Egan in the *Boston Record*. And Harold Kaese wrote in the *Boston Globe* that "Ted Williams should do himself a favor. He should quit baseball before baseball quits him."

Theodore Samuel Williams was many things, but he was not a quitter. In 1946 he hit 38 home runs, batted .342, and led the league in runs scored, walks and slugging percentage. The Red Sox won the pennant, and Williams won his first MVP award. It was a season in which he let his bat do his talking.

OPPOSITE: *A very young Ted Williams. (Photofest)*

A winter operation had severely handicapped Joe DiMaggio after the '46 season, and he saw very limited action the following spring training. Driven to make up for lost time, he spent many hours taking extra batting practice. Asked by Yankee management to pose for some Army recruiting posters, Joe D refused. He claimed he could not spare the time. He was fined $100—the first and only fine of his career.

"What are you trying to do, Joe," Williams said supposedly, "steal my act?"

Before a Yankee-Sox game at the Stadium there was a home-run-hitting contest. Williams easily won the left-handed hitting one, powering deep drives into the right field seats. No winner was announced for the right-handed hitters. In the actual game, Joe D, unable to do anything in the pregame contest, slugged a three-run homer into the stands. When it mattered, DiMag was there.

Fans of Boston and New York passionately debated the merits of the Thumper and the Yankee Clipper. Others joined in the banter and helped the rivalry along.

Joe Page, Yankee relief pitcher and DiMaggio's roommate, was as much anti-Williams as he was pro-DiMaggio. Page delighted in putting a little extra on his fastball when he faced Ted. In Page's view, "Williams couldn't hold a candle to DiMag as a ballplayer."

Another who was part of the legion of loyalists was sportswriter Jimmy Cannon. "There was nothing they could teach Joe D. When he came to the big leagues, it was all there. Other guys hit for higher average, struck more home runs. But this is the whole ballplayer, complete and great. There are no defects to discuss."

After batting a career-low .263 in 1951, DiMaggio retired. He was 36. The Yankee management tried to coax him into performing in pinstripes for one more season, but he had too much pride and too many defects. "He can't stop quickly," read a scouting report prepared by the Brooklyn Dodgers for the 1951 World Series, published in *Life* magazine. "He can't throw real hard. You can take an extra base on him if he's in motion away from the line of the throw. He won't throw on questionable plays. He can't run and he can't pull the ball at all."

DiMag was content that he had done his best, thankful in his phrase to "the good Lord for making me a Yankee." The Yankee Clipper left behind the memory of a man who moved about in the vast center field of Yankee Stadium with an almost poetical grace. He had played when he was fatigued, when he was hurt, when it mattered a great deal, when it didn't matter at all. DiMaggio won three MVP awards, two batting titles, was named to the All-Star team every season he played, slammed 361 career homers, was struck out just 369 times, averaged 118 RBIs and had a .325 lifetime batting average. The Yankee Clipper homered once every 18.9 at bats, his homer-to-hit ratio was one to six. He won home run titles 11 years apart, in 1937 and 1948, slugging percentage titles 13 years apart, in 1937 and 1950.

"Those statistics don't even tell the story," said pitcher Eddie Lopat, DiMaggio's former teammate. "What he meant to the Yankees, you'll never find in the statistics. He was the real leader of that club. DiMag was the best."

Even Ted Williams agreed. "I learned from DiMag," he said. "I was able to see that

you could get an edge on the toughest pitcher by waiting on the pitch. Joe was one of the few hitters around who waited so long he seemed to hit the ball right out of the catcher's mitt. He was the best right-handed pull hitter I ever saw. DiMaggio was the greatest."

But there are many who cite Ted as the greatest hitter ever. "Anytime anyone mentions the Boston Red Sox," said Mickey Mantle, who was signed for a $1,150 bonus in the back seat of a 1947 Oldsmobile, "the first thing that comes to my mind is Ted Williams. I don't think he was the greatest all-around player, but he could hit." In 1951, Mantle replaced DiMaggio as the Yankee superstar, just as the Yankee Clipper had succeeded Babe Ruth.

With Joe DiMaggio gone, Ted Williams played on "with the best combination of power and average," in hitting coach Charlie Lau's phrase, "that I ever saw. He more or less used half the field to hit in." Teams would use a shift on Williams because he was a dead-pull hitter.

They called him "Teddy Ballgame," a nickname that according to Leslie Epstein, father of Boston GM Theo, originated in the family. "Freddy Kaplan, a very well known sports photographer, knew Ted Williams, and sometimes he would take his son Lee and other kids to the game. One day Lee, who was my nephew, announced, 'We are going to see Teddy Ballgame,' mixing up Ted and going to the ballgame. And it all stuck from that point on."

In 1956, Williams battled Mickey Mantle for the batting crown, just as he had in earlier years gone head to head with Joe D. Closing out the season against the Red Sox, Yankee pitchers held Williams to two hits in 11 at-bats. Mantle went six-for-nine, and won the batting crown with a .353 average, to Williams's .345.

In 1957, Williams batted .388, his highest batting average since hitting .406 in 1941. Even at 39 years old, the Thumper was just five hits away from another .400 average, and was the oldest player to win a batting title. "What's five hits?" he wrote in his autobiography. "I was 39 years old, aging and aching. There had to be among a season's collection of groundballs at least five leg hits for a younger Ted Williams."

But the Yankees won the pennant, and Mickey Mantle won the MVP award. All over New England a roar of disapproval was unleashed. Tom Yawkey was livid. "The voting was done by some incompetent and prejudiced people," he charged. Two Chicago writers voted Williams ninth and 10th, respectively, in the MVP balloting.

In 1958, Williams again heard the boobirds. After taking a called strike three at Fenway Park, he threw his bat in rage and disgust at the umpire's decision. It hit the housekeeper of former Red Sox manager Joe Cronin, who was sitting 70 feet from home plate in the stands. On her way out of the park, headed to the hospital, the housekeeper asked, "Why are they booing Ted?" They cheered him, too when he won his sixth batting title that year. He was 40 years old.

In 1959, Williams hit just .254, the only sub-.300 season of his career. But he found vindication in 1960, his last season, hitting .316 with 29 home runs in just 310 at-bats. On September 28, 1960, at Fenway Park, before 10,454 fans, Ted Williams engaged in his last hurrah. There was a weekend series still to be played against the Yankees, but for Williams, this was the final game.

Ted Williams batting at Fenway. (Photofest)

In the pregame ceremonies, Williams was given a silver bowl, a $4,000 check made out to the Jimmy Fund he had supported through all the years, and a standing ovation.

"If I were asked where I would have liked to have played," he said, his voice barely carrying over the crowd's roar, "I would have to say Boston…the greatest town in baseball and the greatest fans in America, despite the many disagreeable things said about me by the knights of the keyboard."

Then, in his last major league at-bat, in the eighth inning, Williams slammed home run number 521 into the bullpen in right-center field. Those who might have booed him in the past stood and cheered as he circled the bases at the Back Bay ballyard for the last time, trotting into history. He crossed home plate, and he didn't tip his cap.

As John Updike wrote, "Gods don't answer letters."

Theodore Samuel Williams had made his point. He had said at the start that he had wanted to be remembered as the greatest hitter who ever lived. And there were few who would have argued that he wasn't—even Joe DiMaggio, even the most rabid Yankee fan.

He ranks among the all-time leaders in home runs, RBIs, total bases, slugging and batting average—all this despite having lost the equivalent of six seasons to injuries and military service. He averaged almost a walk a game; one out of every 4.5 plate appearances was a walk. He led the league in walks eight times and finished with 2,019, second in baseball history. And he finished with a .344 lifetime batting average.

After their playing careers, the two men took very different paths. Joe DiMaggio went into semi-reclusion, prompting Simon and Garfunkel to ask, "Where have you gone, Joe DiMaggio? Our nation turns its lonely eyes to you," a plea from a 1960s America in need of a hero. Williams, meanwhile, went on to manage the Washington Senators and Texas Rangers in the late 1960s and early '70s.'

Joe DiMaggio died on March 8, 1999, at the age of 84 at home following a five-month bout with lung cancer and pneumonia. "He was to people all over the world what a baseball player was supposed to be like," said former Dodgers manager Tommy Lasorda. "If you said to God, 'Create someone who was what a baseball player should be,' God would have created Joe DiMaggio."

"Joe DiMaggio was always dignified—until the Marilyn Monroe period, and that's too bad," mused Mario Cuomo. "But for most of his career, he was just the dignified icon baseball player. He was just the hero. They sang songs about him. There was something special about Joe DiMaggio that made you write songs about him. It's not exactly inexplicable. There was the service, going off to the Army, at the height of his career. The immigrants' son. All of that put him at a level above the rest of us.

"I was Italian," Cuomo continued. "I had a name that was all vowels. He was an Italian. I was the son of immigrants. He was the son of immigrants. I was a backyard ballplayer, and a sandlot ballplayer who got lucky and signed a contract with Pittsburgh. But long before that, of course he's a hero for us. He made it. People respect him. People like him. His mother and father couldn't speak the language. Neither could mine. So you naturally say to yourself, isn't this wonderful? What you're really saying is, 'Lookit, if this guy could achieve all of that, who knows, who knows, maybe I can do something worthwhile.' Now you never dreamed of being a Joe DiMaggio, unless you were a really big dreamer. But it's encouraging and reassuring to you."

"Joe DiMaggio was my God, the God of all Italian-Americans," actor Ben Gazzara re-called. "First thing I'd ask when school got out—'What did Joe do today?' He wasn't hitting, I'd get depressed."

"The reverence for him was unsurpassed," noted Jeff Idelson, a vice president at the Hall of Fame. "American flags at Yankee Stadium were lowered to half-staff. So was the Hall of Fame flag in Cooperstown."

A few months later, in a very moving moment at Fenway Park, Ted Williams threw out the first ball at the All-Star game. Death came to Williams on July 5, 2002, just two months shy of his 84th birthday. In August of 2003, the ghoulish news was reported by *Sports Illustrated* that the body of Ted Williams was decapitated by surgeons at a cryonics company and that several samples of his DNA are missing. It was a macabre footnote to the life and death of the man who merged keen vision with quick wrists and a scientific approach to hitting.

"One of the greatest moments I had as baseball commissioner," recalled Fay Vincent, "was in 1991, when I hosted a breakfast for Williams and DiMaggio in Washington. We were going to go to an affair at the White House, and we had three hours to just talk baseball. Whenever the conversation lagged, I would ask stupid questions like: 'Could you guys hit the knuckleball?' Or 'What would you do if people threw at you?'

"They talked. DiMaggio was more reserved, Williams was much more animated. DiMaggio was always on, he always was aware that there was an audience, and that he was Joe DiMaggio. He never took the mask off. Whereas Williams was much more open and vulnerable, and bubbly. I wish I'd had a tape recorder."

THE MARKER GAMES

Through the decades there have been many games played between the Yankees and Red Sox that have not only been significant encounters in the history of the two franchises, but also memorable face-offs in baseball history. The first game at Fenway, the first game at Yankee Stadium, Babe Ruth's first home run, the Yankee Massacre, the Red Sox Massacre, the season record-setting 61st home run by Roger Maris, and the Bucky Dent homer all happened in Yankee-Red Sox games.

Herewith, a sampler of just a few of the marker games.

- THE FIRST MATCH UP: BOSTON-NEW YORK: May 7, 1903
- PENNANT LOST ON WILD PITCH: October 10, 1904
- FIRST MATCH UP AT FENWAY: April 20, 1912
- BABE RUTH'S FIRST HOME RUN: May 6, 1915
- THE MOGRIDGE NO-HITTER AT FENWAY: April 24, 1917

- YANKEE STADIUM OPENS: April 18, 1923
- BABE RUTH'S LAST PITCHING PERFORMANCE: October 1, 1933
- RECORD 45TH GAME OF JOE DiMAGGIO'S 56-GAME STREAK: July 2, 1941
- DiMAG: GRAND FINALE AT FENWAY: October 3, 1948
- JOE DiMAGGIO SHOW AT FENWAY PARK: June 28-30, 1949
- FINAL WEEKEND OF THE 1949 SEASON: October 1-2
- ALLIE REYNOLDS, SECOND NO-HITTER: September 28, 1951
- ROGER MARIS: THE 61ST HOME RUN: October 1, 1961
- BILLY ROHR'S NEAR-NO-HITTER: April 14, 1967
- THE FIRST DESIGNATED HITTER TO BAT: April 6, 1973
- YANKEE MASSACRE: June 17-19, 1977
- BOSTON MASSACRE: September 7-9, 1978

- BUCKY DENT'S HOME RUN: October 2, 1978
- SOX SEVEN-RUN EIGHTH TOPS YANKS: September 19, 1981
- DAVE RIGHETTI: THE NO-HITTER: July 4, 1983
- BOSTON'S SHORT-LIVED REDEMPTION: October 16, 1999
- MIKE MUSSINA: NEAR-PERFECT GAME: September 2, 2001
- ROCKET'S REVENGE: September 4, 2002
- THE SEVENTH GAME: October 17, 18, 2003

THE FIRST MATCH UP: BOSTON-NEW YORK: MAY 7, 1903

The New York and Boston Major League Baseball teams met for the first time at the Huntington Avenue Grounds in Boston, but they weren't yet known as the Yankees and Red Sox. Both franchises began with more geographically correct and appropriate names: the New York Highlanders, who played on the hilly terrain of upper Manhattan, and the Boston Pilgrims, a tribute to their New England roots and ancestors.

Cy Young was the ace of a superior Boston staff that included Bill Dineen and Tom Hughes. Both would be 20-game winners in 1903. The Bostons also featured third baseman-manager Jimmy Collins. Special bragging rights belonged to New York's Herman Long who returned home and received a diamond pin. But he also had two errors pinned on him for his work at shortstop.

The Pilgrims won 6-2, on a Hobe Ferris home run and Chick Stahl's two triples. Boston shelled Highlanders pitcher Snake Wiltse for 13 hits. "Until the seventh inning, clever fielding by the visitors had kept the Boston score to three runs," *The New York Times*, noted, adding that Wiltse "was batted even more freely than the score would indicate."

The Pilgrims went on to win baseball's inaugural World Series that year, while New York finished in fourth place, 17 games out.

PENNANT LOST ON WILD PITCH: OCTOBER 10, 1904

The New Yorkers and Bostons matched up in a season-finale doubleheader at Hilltop Park in upper Manhattan with the pennant on the line. Some of the overflow crowd of 25,584 stood 10 and 20 deep in the outfield.

New York, a game and a half behind Boston, needed a sweep. The Highlanders had occupied first place most of the season, but a late surge by Boston had enabled the Pilgrims to get on top.

In Game One, Highlanders spitballer "Happy Jack" Chesbro, a 41-game winner, and Boston's Bill Dineen, a 22-game winner, were locked in a scoreless duel until New York scored twice in the fifth. Boston tied the game with two unearned runs in the seventh on a pair of errors by New York second baseman Jimmy Williams.

In the top of the ninth, Boston catcher Lou Criger singled, moved to second on a sacrifice and took third on a ground ball. Chesbro got two strikes on the next batter, Freddy Parent, but then apparently left too much moisture on a spitter. The ball sailed over the head of catcher Jack "Red" Kleinow. Criger scored on the wild pitch. Holding the Highlanders scoreless in the bottom of the ninth, Boston clinched its second straight pennant.

But there was no World Series in 1904. The National League champion New York Giants, looking down on the upstart American League, refused to play the Pilgrims. It would take 90 years and a players' strike to cancel another World Series.

For the 1903 Highlanders and their fans there was some consolation. The team doubled its first season's attendance; the New Yorkers also won 20 more games than the season before. However, that 1904 season would be as close as the Highlanders would come in the first 18 years of their existence to winning a pennant.

FIRST MATCH UP AT FENWAY: APRIL 20, 1912

Former baseball commissioner A. Bartlett Giammati made the statement: "When I was seven years old, my father took me to Fenway Park for the first time, and as I grew up I knew that as a building it was on the level of Mount Olympus, the Pyramid at Giza, the nation's Capitol, the Czar's Winter Palace, and the Louvre—except, of course, that it was better than all those inconsequential places."

Contrary to some rumors probably spread by Yankee fans, the scholarly Giammati was not around for the start of play at Fenway, which was a very long time ago. Prior to 1912, the Red Sox played at Huntington Avenue Grounds, now part of Northeastern University. Fittingly, the first American League team to visit Fenway Park was New York—at that time known as the Highlanders, soon to become the Yankees. It was a damp and chilly New England spring that year. The Red Sox actually played their first game at Fenway 11 days earlier, defeating Harvard University in an exhibition game played in a snowstorm. Then the Red Sox and Highlanders had to sit out two rainouts before facing off on Saturday April 20, just a few days after the sinking of the Titanic.

The future grandfather of president John F. Kennedy, Boston mayor John "Honey Fitz" Fitzgerald was one of the 27,000 in attendance. He threw out the first ball in the park that was built at a cost of $350,000 that would come to be known as "Boston's Sistine Chapel."

They played on into extra innings. Boston prevailed, finally winning 7-6 on a Tris Speaker RBI in the bottom of the 11th inning. Red Sox spitballer Bucky O'Brien and Sea Lion Hall defeated New York's Jumbo Jim Vaughn.

Opening Day turned out to be a good predictor of the season's fortunes for both Boston and New York. The Red Sox took the American League pennant in 1912 with a 105-47 record, good for a winning percentage of .691, and went on to beat the New York Giants in the World Series. The Highlanders, suffering their sixth straight loss, went 50-102 (.329), finishing in last place, a whopping 55 games behind the Red Sox.

Even after the BoSox had Fenway as a home park, they didn't always play all their games there. From time to time, they scheduled "big games" at Braves Field to accommodate larger crowds than their little park could accommodate.

BABE RUTH'S FIRST HOME RUN: MAY 6, 1915

In the third inning at the Polo Grounds, 20-year-old pitcher Babe Ruth slammed the first pitch off Yankee right-hander Jack Warhop into the second tier of the right-field grandstand for a home run. It was the first home run for the youngster in his 18th time at-bat in the major leagues.

As Ruth trotted around the bases, the 8,000 in attendance, including Red Sox owner Joseph Lannin, American League president Ban Johnson and sportswriters Damon Runyan and Heywood Broun, cheered him on.

Runyan wrote in his account of the game: "Fanning this Ruth is not as easy as the name and the occupation might indicate. In the third inning, Ruth knocked the slant out of one of Jack Warhop's underhanded subterfuges, and put the baseball in the right field stands for a home run. Ruth was discovered by Jack Dunn in a Baltimore school a year ago where he had not attained his left-handed majority, and was adopted and adapted by Jack for use of the Orioles. He is now quite a demon pitcher and demon hitter when he connects."

Ironically, the momentous first of the Babe's 714 career home runs came against the team he would come to symbolize—the New York Yankees. The homer was his fifth major league hit. In 10 times at bat in 1914 and eight times at the plate in 1915, he had notched three doubles and a single.

"Mr. Warhop of the Yankees," wrote Wilmot Giffin in the *New York Evening Journal*, "looked reproachfully at the opposing pitcher who was so unclubby as to do a thing like that to one of his own trade. But Ruthless Ruth seemed to think that all was fair in the matter of fattening a batting average."

Ruth's singular shot and two other hits notwithstanding, the Yankees were able to eke out a 4-3 triumph in 13 innings over the Red Sox who committed four errors. The Babe was saddled with the loss.

THE MOGRIDGE NO-HITTER AT FENWAY: APRIL 24, 1917

George Anthony Mogridge out of Rochester, New York pitched for the Yankees from 1915 to 1920 and posted a 48-55 record. His ERA was 2.71, a sign that he had a lot on the ball including resin. When the American League banned the use of resin in 1920, Mogridge worked the powder into the underside of the bill of his cap. It worked for him as a convenient, efficient and never detected technique.

But the lean and long lefty is best remembered for what he achieved on April 24, 1917. He hurled the first no-hitter in Yankee history, beating the Red Sox, 2-1.

Traded off to Washington in 1921 as the Yankees were entering their first great years, Mogridge served with Walter Johnson to anchor the Senators' staff. When the career of the well-traveled southpaw finally ended in 1927 after 440 games, the one he talked about the most was the no-hitter he pitched that April day in 1917 as a member of the Yankees.

YANKEE STADIUM OPENS: APRIL 18, 1923

Fittingly enough, the Red Sox of Boston were the competition the day Yankee Stadium opened its gates. It was a cold April day in the Bronx. Wind whipped Yankee pennants as well as dust from the dirt road leading to the new ballpark.

The press release first announcing the new stadium indicated it would be shaped like

Yankee Manager Miller Huggins is dwarfed by Babe Ruth. (Photofest/Icon)

the Yale Bowl and that it would contain towering battlements enclosing the entire park so that those lacking tickets would not even be able to get a glimpse of the action.

Built at a cost of $2.5 million, "The Yankee Stadium," as it was originally named, had a brick-lined vault with electronic equipment under second base, making it possible to have a boxing ring and press area on the infield. Yankee Stadium was the first ballpark to be called a stadium, the last privately financed major league park. It was a gigantic horseshoe, shaped by triple-decked grandstands. Huge wooden bleachers circled the park. The 10,712 upper-grandstand seats and 14,543 lower grandstand seats were fixed in place by 135,000 individual steel castings on which 400,000 pieces of maple lumber were fastened by more than a million screws.

The announced crowd was 74,217, later revised to 60,000, while more than 25,000 were turned away as the fire department closed the gates. Many wore heavy sweaters, coats and hats. Some sported dinner jackets. Many lingered outside to listen to the roar of the crowd.

The Seventh Regiment Band, directed by John Phillip Sousa, escorted both teams to the centerfield flagpole, where the 1922 pennant and the American flag were hoisted. Governor Al Smith threw out the first ball to Yankee catcher Wally Schang; the game-time temperature was just 49 degrees.

Baseball commissioner Kenesaw Mountain Landis, mayor John Hylan, Yankee owner colonel Jacob Ruppert and governor Al Smith were seated in the celebrity box. At 3:25, Babe Ruth was given an oversized bat handsomely laid out in a glass case. At 3:30, Governor Smith tossed out the first ball to Yankee catcher Wally Schang. At 3:35, home plate umpire Tommy Connolly shouted: "Play ball!"

Joe Dugan's third-inning RBI single scored Yankee pitcher Bob Shawkey with the first run of the game. George Herman Ruth stepped into the batter's box. There were two Yankees on base, Whitey Witt and Dugan.

Babe Ruth remarked before the game: "I'd give a year of my life if I can hit a home run in the first game in this new park."

Red Sox pitcher Howard Ehmke tried to get an off-speed pitch past the Babe. He turned on it, sending a line drive into the right-field bleachers—the first home run in Yankee Stadium history. After crossing the plate, Ruth removed his cap, extended it at arm's length in front of him, and waved to the standing, roaring crowd.

Yankees pitcher "Sailor Bob" Shawkey, who wore a red sweatshirt under his jersey, pitched the home team to a 4-1 victory.

Babe Ruth as a Boston Red Sox pitcher. (Photofest/Icon)

BABE RUTH'S LAST PITCHING PERFORMANCE: OCTOBER 1, 1933

In 1933, the Yankees sent 38-year-old Babe Ruth to the mound for the season finale against the Red Sox at the Stadium, in an effort to draw fans for a meaningless game in the midst of the Great Depression. Both teams had already been eliminated from the pennant race, but Ruth's assignment was a magnet for the 20,000 fans who came out to see the game—up 8,000 from the day before.

Ruth had started his career as a pitcher for the Red Sox 19 years before, eventually splitting time between pitching and the outfield and first base. When the Yankees purchased him in 1920, the team turned him into a full-time outfielder, but Ruth made a hand-ful of pitching performances in 1920 and 1921. The Babe went nearly a decade before his next trip to the mound, beating Boston in the 1930 season finale, 9-3.

By 1933, Ruth's career was winding down. He hit .301 with 34 home runs and 103 RBIs in what turned out to be his second-to-last with the Yankees. (Ruth finished his career in 1935 with the Boston Braves of the National League.) Although outstanding by most standards, the numbers were far from Ruthian—they represented his lowest output since 1925. But in the season finale, Ruth's offense was top-flight. Forty years before the designated hitter, Ruth essentially DH'd for himself. Batting cleanup, he went one-for-three with a home run, scoring two runs.

Ruth's pitching performance was not as powerful, but it got the job done. Although he didn't strike out a batter and gave up 12 hits and five earned runs, he went the distance in a 6-5 win over his former teammates. Ruth held Boston scoreless for five innings before getting tagged for four runs in the sixth and one more in the eighth. The Red Sox left 10 more men on base.

With the win, Ruth's career won-lost record improved to 94-46, a .671 winning percentage. His lifetime ERA was a nifty 2.28. The numbers are a reminder that early in his career, Ruth was one of baseball's most dominant pitchers. In his first full season, 1915, he went 18-8 with a 2.44 ERA. The next year he improved to 23-12, with a 1.75 ERA; and in 1917, he was 24-13, with a 2.01 ERA.

The next two seasons, his last ones with Boston, Ruth was given more at-bats and began to establish himself as a dominant hitter, too. He led the league with 11 home runs in 1918, even as went 13-7 with a 2.22 ERA. And in 1919, he smashed the single-season home run record with 29, still getting enough pitching starts for a 9-5 record and 2.97 ERA.

The Yankees, however, ended the two-way arrangement. In 1920, his first in New York, Ruth made only one start. The change in emphasis paid off. The Babe hit .376 that year with 54 home runs and 137 RBIs.

RECORD 45TH GAME OF JOE DiMAGGIO'S 56-GAME STREAK: JULY 2, 1941

On the first day of July 1941, Joe DiMaggio tied the 43-year-old record of Wee Willie Keeler by hitting safely in both games of a doubleheader against the Red Sox. The Yankee Clipper had rapped out at least one hit in 44 straight games.

On July 2, the Yankees again faced the Red Sox. Joe DiMag was intent on getting a hit in his 45th straight game and setting a new major league record at Yankee Stadium. Dom DiMaggio, Joe's younger brother, was stationed in his normal position for the Red Sox, centerfield. Joe had invited him to dinner that evening at his home.

In his first at-bat against Boston pitcher Herbert Newsome, DiMaggio smashed a long drive that was flagged down by Stan Spence. Joe D swung a bit more forcefully his second time up and drove the ball to center field. Breaking at top speed as soon as he heard the crack of his older brother's bat against the ball, Dom ran it down and made a dramatic catch to rob his brother of an extra base hit. The two brothers rarely showed emotion on the baseball field, but looking at each other this time from inside their Yankee and Red Sox uniforms, they showed how they felt.

"It was a great catch," Joe recalled, "one of the best Dom had ever made. I was tempted at that point to withdraw the dinner invitation for the evening."

In his third turn at bat, with two teammates on bases, hungering for a hit, Joe took no chances. He belted the ball into the seats for what would be one of his 30 home runs he hit that historic 1941 season. He had the record, and it had come against archrival Boston.

The New York Yankees centerfielder and the Boston centerfielder dined that evening. "While Dom lapped up my steak and ate my spaghetti," Joe mused, "he had the audacity to tell me, 'You know, Joe, I couldn't have gone another inch for that ball.'"

OPPOSITE: *Dom DiMaggio showing off his swing. (Photofest/Icon)*

DiMAG: GRAND FINALE AT FENWAY: OCTOBER 3, 1948

There were 31,304 fans at Fenway, and in Joe DiMaggio's phrase, "They had come to see Yankee blood." Jack Kramer had pitched the Sox to a 5-1 victory over New York the day before, and on this final day of the season, the Indians led Boston by one game in the race for the American League pennant.

"We had nothing except satisfaction to play for," recalled DiMag. "You might say there must have been a letdown in our play. It is never fun to lose, and besides, the league standings did not convince us that there were two better teams in the league."

The DiMaggio family was in the stands rooting for Boston. Dom had a chance for the World Series. Joe and the Yankees did not. In the first inning, Joe D doubled for one Yankee run. The Sox scored five times in the third inning. The Fenway faithful screamed at the scoreboard news that after three innings Detroit was leading Cleveland, 5-0.

In the Yankee fifth, Joe Dobson began to falter for the Sox. DiMag came to the plate. Hurt and hobbled with a charley horse in both legs, the Yankee Clipper looked out at his teammates on the basepaths: Phil Rizzuto who had singled and Bobby Brown who had doubled. The honed-in DiMaggio slammed a Dobson pitch off the left field wall, cutting to the Sox lead to 5-4.

In the ninth inning, DiMag recorded his fourth hit of the game—a single. Yankee manager Bucky Harris, realizing that the game was virtually out of reach at this point—New York was trailing, 10-5, and knowing the pain that DiMaggio was feeling, sent in Steve Souchock to run for his center fielder.

"I turned and started for the dugout," recalled DiMaggio. "I guess I was limping pretty bad. Anyway, that's what they told me later. I'll never forget that crowd. It was standing and roaring like one man. I tipped my cap but it didn't stop. I looked up at the stands at this ovation they were giving to a guy who had tried to beat them."

JOE DiMAGGIO SHOW AT FENWAY PARK: JUNE 28-30, 1949

It was bitter rivalry time again, Yanks vs. Red Sox. The New Yorkers had a hold on first place; the Bostons had won four straight, 10 of their last 11. Joe DiMaggio was returning to the baseball wars after missing 65 games because of a bone spur in his foot. Fenway was jammed with 36,228 for the Friday night three-game series opener on June 28.

In his first American League at-bat in eight months, DiMag faced Mickey McDermott. "He could throw hard," DiMaggio said. "My timing was off. I kept fouling pitch after pitch to right field. Then I lined a hit over shortstop. It felt good."

It felt even better for the Yankee centerfielder his second time up. He hit a two-run home run. The rabidly partisan Red Sox fans gave DiMag a standing ovation. "I don't think I was ever booed at Fenway," he said. "The fans there always respected clean competition and good baseball."

With the Red Sox trailing 5-4 in the bottom of the ninth inning, Joe DiMaggio hauled in an extra-base bid by Ted Williams. That catch ended the Red Sox winning streak and broke the hearts of the Fenway faithful. The Yankee Clipper was back.

All admirers of Joe DiMaggio—Casey Stengel (center) and coaches (left to right) John Neun, Frank Crosetti, Jim Turner, Bill Dickey. (Photofest/Icon)

Game two on Saturday saw the Yanks down 7-1 after four innings. A DiMaggio three-run dinger sliced the Sox lead. Then in the eighth inning, it was that man DiMaggio again, with a two-run home run over the Green Monster. The Bronx Bombers had a 9-7 come-from-behind triumph.

"You can hate the Yankees," one sign read, "but you've got to love Joe DiMaggio!"

The third game on Sunday saw a standing-room-only crowd in attendance. After seven innings of a tight battle, it was Yankees 3 and Red Sox 2. A three-run smash by the Yankee centerfielder off the light tower gave the New Yorkers a 6-3 win and a sweep of the Sox.

It was truly the Joe DiMaggio show. He batted .455 in the three games, hit four home runs and a single, drove in nine runs.

"I think," Joe DiMaggio said later, "I was the most surprised guy in all of Boston."

FINAL WEEKEND OF THE 1949 SEASON: OCTOBER 1-2

"The first thing that comes to mind when I think of the rivalry is the '49 Red Sox and

Yankees and the weekend that DiMaggio had," said former major league hurler and current broadcaster Jim Kaat.

"The Red Sox Yankee rivalry was one of the most unique things in baseball history," said former Boston pitching great Mel Parnell. "In my era we were criticized as being a country club ball club being pampered by Mr. Yawkey, our owner. The differences in our ball clubs, Yankees and Red Sox, were that we were probably a step slower than the Yankees. They also had more depth.

"In 1949, I won 25 games and Ellis Kinder won 23. As the season came to its end we were either in the game or in the bullpen for 19 consecutive days. We were pretty well worn out."

It was Joe DiMaggio Day at Yankee Stadium on October 1, 1949, as the Yankees and Red Sox prepared to battle in the final two games of the season. A winner in 59 of its last 78 games, Boston needed just a victory to clinch the pennant. More than 140,000 would be on hand for the two games. Many without tickets would mill around outside of the Stadium, listening to the games on bulky portable radios.

Mel Parnell of the Sox was pitted against Allie Reynolds in the October 1 game. "We were behind 4-0," Phil Rizzuto recalled. "We were behind but not beaten. Casey had told Joe Page who came in for Allie 'Just hold them, Joe, just hold them.' I went up to hit and Boston catcher Birdie Tebbets who always talked to me this time got me angry.

"'Oh, Phil,' he said, 'we're gonna be drinking a lot of champagne tonight and we're gonna have a party because we're gonna clinch the pennant today and a kid from the minors will be pitching for us tomorrow.'

"Holy Cow, I was annoyed. I told Casey and some of the other guys when I got back to the bench and they were not too happy with what Birdie had said. I don't think that was the only factor in getting us back in the game, but it sure helped."

It sure helped. An eighth-inning home run by Johnny Lindell gave the Yanks the margin of their 5-4 victory. That set the stage for Sunday, October 2—the final day of the 1949 season, with the teams tied for first place.

The line for bleacher seats was more than a block long. Ellis Kinder was the Boston starter. Vic Raschi took the ball for the New Yorkers. As the shadows of autumn started to filter into and fill Yankee Stadium, the chances for Boston grew less and less. Kinder had surrendered only two hits but trailed 1-0.

Joe McCarthy, who had managed those many years for the Yankees, made a move as Boston pilot that would be questioned for years to come.

He sent up a pinch hitter for Kinder. It was to no avail. And then he brought in Mel Parnell, who had given his all the day before, to hurl the bottom of the eighth inning.

"I don't make excuses," Parnell recalled. "I was tired, but I was a professional and professionals are paid to pitch." The Yanks scored four times. The Sox fought back, scoring three times in their half of the eighth.

Ultimately, and sadly for the Boston Nation, it was the same old story—a Yankee victory over the Red Sox. "That was the first time I saw Ted Williams cry," remembered Mickey McDermott.

Casey Stengel, savoring the moment and the 5-3 pennant-clinching triumph, screamed out in the locker room: "Fellas, I want to thank

OPPOSITE: *Jerry Coleman was a Yankee rookie in 1949. (Photofest)*

Mel Parnell pitching pose. (Photofest/Icon)

you all for going to all the trouble to do this for me."

For the Pickering family of New England it was trouble. "1949 will live in infamy for all Red Sox Fans," songwriter Joe Pickering Jr. wrote. "That was the year I first saw my mother cry over the Red Sox and what the Yankees did to her!"

ALLIE REYNOLDS, SECOND NO-HITTER: SEPTEMBER 28, 1951

The Red Sox and the Yankees had each played 150 games in the 1951 American League season. Surging, charging, the Yankees played host to Boston at Yankee Stadium before 40,000 on September 28. The Red Sox

were the hottest-hitting team in the American League. The Yanks needed just two wins to wrap up their third straight pennant, one win to clinch a tie.

Allie Reynolds was tabbed by Casey Stengel to face the powerful Boston lineup. The big right-hander had recorded a no-hitter over Cleveland, a 1-0 beauty on July 12. Inning after inning on this September day Reynolds showed his mastery over Dom DiMaggio, Johnny Pesky, Ted Williams, Clyde Volmer, Billy Goodman, Lou Boudreau, Freddy Hatfield and Aaron Robinson.

The Yankees notched two runs in the first inning off stylish Mel Parnell, two more in the bottom of the third inning. By the time the game moved to the top of the ninth it was no contest. It was 8-0, New York on top.

Not only had the Yankees humbled Boston, the man they called the Super Chief had humbled the potent Sox lineup. He had not allowed a hit through eight innings.

"I was very much aware of the no-hitter and the ninth inning," Reynolds said. Pinch hitter Charlie Maxwell led off for the Sox and fouled out. Reynolds had gotten stronger as the game had gone on—Maxwell could not catch up to his heat.

Dom DiMaggio wiped his glasses, kicked a bit of dirt and stepped into the batter's box. Joe's brother was patient; Reynolds was impatient. Attempting to put too much on his fastball, attempting to overpower the little centerfielder, Reynolds wound up walking him.

The third batter of the ninth inning for the Red Sox came up, the combative Johnny Pesky. Reynolds fanned him for his ninth strikeout of the game.

OPPOSITE: *Allie Reynolds was one of the best Yankee right-handed hurlers ever. (Photofest/Icon)*

"All I had to get out was Ted Williams," Reynolds recalled. "Most times I tried to walk the damn guy. In my opinion it was just stupid to let an outstanding hitter like him beat you."

With two out in the ninth, Ted Williams was all that stood in the way of Reynolds's no-hitter and the Yankee clinching of the American League pennant.

Winding up his 10th straight .300 season, the gangly Williams looked disdainfully out at Reynolds on the pitcher's mound. It was a classic match-up: power right-handed pitcher vs. scientific southpaw slugger.

As Reynolds looked to catcher Yogi Berra for the signs and checked DiMaggio at first base, he heard the scream of fans: "Walk him. Walk him. Don't pitch to that guy."

But on this day, Allie Reynolds had made up his mind that he would pitch to that guy.

Reynolds got a fastball strike on Williams. The next pitch? Fastball again. Williams uncoiled. Ball popped up behind home plate. Yogi Berra under it, waiting. The ball bounced off the edge of his glove. Yogi bounced off Reynolds who was backing up the play.

Helping Berra to his feet, a tired and anxious Reynolds was kind: "Don't worry Yogi, we'll get him next time."

Berra, who recalls "that Williams was the greatest hitter I ever had to catch against—he used to take pitches I would swing against," returned to take up his catcher's position.

An exasperated and annoyed Williams told Berra: "You sons of bitches put me in a hell of a spot. You blew it, and now I've got to bear down even harder even though the game is decided and your man has a no-hitter going."

"I called for the same pitch, the same fastball," recalled Berra.

On the next Reynolds offering, Williams again popped up. Foul ball near the Yankee dugout. Berra raced back.

"Lotsa room, Yogi, lotsa room," screamed Tommy Henrich. "You can get it." This time Berra squeezed the ball good. "I just missed the first one and caught the second one," Berra said later.

Allie Reynolds had his second no-hitter of the 1951 season. The first American League hurler to accomplish that feat, he also had his seventh shutout of the year. The Yankees had an 8-0 triumph and their third straight American League flag.

A postscript to that memorable pennant-clinching game was recalled by Bill Crowley, who broadcasted the action as a Yankee announcer. "That winter I was in Toots Shor's in New York. A woman came over to me and said that she listened to the game and was keeping score for her son while he was away at school. At the same time, she was hosting her bridge club with her best china dishes. 'When you yelled out that Yogi had dropped the ball, I got so excited that I dropped the dishes. Bill Crowley, you owe me a set of dishes for scaring me like that.'"

ROGER MARIS: THE 61ST HOME RUN: OCTOBER 1, 1961

"When Roger Maris was going for the home run record he would eat only bologna and eggs for breakfast," his friend Julie Isaacson recalled. "Every morning we would have breakfast together at the Stage Deli in Manhattan. We had the same waitress, and I'd leave her

OPPOSITE: *Yogi Berra, striking a familiar pose. (Frommer Archives)*

the same five-dollar tip every time. After, I would drive Roger up to the Stadium."

In 1956, Mickey Mantle had smashed 52 home runs for the Bronx Bombers and there were many who viewed him as the man to break Babe Ruth's season record of 60. Mantle was the favorite, Maris had come to the Yankees in a trade with Kansas City; he was the outsider, the loner.

In 1961, Maris did not hit a home run in his first 10 games, but by the end of May he had a dozen. There were 27 by the end of June. By the end of July Maris had 40 home runs—and was six ahead of Ruth's record total that had stood since 1927.

"My going off after the record started off such a dream," the Yankee outfielder said. "I was living a fairy tale for a while. I never thought I'd get a chance to break such a record."

Reporters lined up by the Maris locker in ballparks all over the American League. "How does it feel to be hitting so many home runs? Do you ever think of what it means?"

"How the hell should I know," Maris, short-tempered, surly, shot back.

There were all kinds of commercial capitalizations. An enterprising stripper went by the name of Mickey Maris. The sales of M&M candy skyrocketed—a tip of the cash register to the "M &M Boys" who had not endorsed the confection.

Newspapers printed endless stories and charts comparing Mantle and Maris, Maris and Ruth, Ruth and Mantle, etc., ad nauseam.

There were stories that claimed animosity existed between Mantle who earned $75,000 that season and Maris who made $42,000. The stories were completely untrue.

"Roger," Mantle insisted, "was one of my best friends." The two shared a Queens apartment with Bob Cerv. The three young Yankee outfielders rode in Maris's open convertible back and forth from Yankee Stadium.

Media scrutiny was in Maris's face. Photographers insisted on pairing Mantle and Maris together in all kinds of posed shots. Maris was irked; Mantle was bemused. "We've taken so many pictures together," he smiled, "that I'm beginning to feel like a Siamese twin."

Against his former Kansas City teammates on August 26 in his 128th game of the 1961 season, Maris mashed home run number 51. That put him eight ahead of the Ruth pace. It was about that time that commissioner Ford Frick ruled that an asterisk would be placed next to Maris's name in the record books if he broke the Babe's record. Frick pointed out that Ruth set the record in a 154-game season. Maris was playing in a season with a 162-game schedule.

The "Mick" managed but one home run from September 10 on—Number 54. With Mantle a shell of himself and no longer a factor in the home run race, the pressure was now totally on Roger Maris.

Maris had 58 home runs on September 18 when the Yankees came to Baltimore for a four-game series. In a two-night doubleheader, games 152 and 153, Maris failed to hit a home run.

On September 20, a night game, Maris faced Milt Pappas of the Orioles. It was a media circus with reporters from all over the country converged on the scene. But there were only 21,000 or so in the stands.

The man they called "Rajah" lined solidly to right field his first time up. He was

OPPOSITE: *A very young Mickey Mantle. (Photofest)*

getting honed in. Then in the third inning, Maris caught hold of a Pappas pitch and blasted it almost 400 feet into the bleachers in right field—home run number 59! He had passed Jimmie Foxx and Hank Greenberg. Roger Maris had three more chances that night to tie the Babe Ruth record. But he struck out, flied out and grounded out.

Five days later at Yankee Stadium on September 26 in game number 158 for the Yankees, Jack Fisher of Baltimore threw a high curve ball in the third inning. "The minute I threw the ball," Fisher moaned, "I said to myself, that does it. That's number 60."

The record-tying home run pounded onto the concrete steps of the sixth row in the third deck in Yankee Stadium. The ball bounced back onto the field and was picked up by Earl Robinson, the Oriole right fielder who tossed the ball to umpire Ed Hurley who gave it to Yankee first base coach Wally Moses who rolled it into the Yankee dugout. The ball and Maris, running out the 60th home run, came into the dugout of the Bronx Bombers at about the same time.

Maris picked up the ball and barely looked at it; cheering fans kept calling for him to come out and take a bow. Finally, the Yankee slugger emerged. Standing sheepishly on the top step of the dugout, he waved his cap. An especially interested onlooker was Mrs. Claire Ruth, widow of the Babe.

It came down to the final three games of the 1961 season. It was Yankees-Red Sox. It was Maris-Ruth. Roger was shut out in the first two games by Boston pitchers who were determined not to be the ones to be linked with him in the record books.

It was October 1. A tired, bedraggled Maris faced 24-year-old Red Sox right-hander Tracy Stallard. In the Yankee bullpen in right field the pitchers and the catchers watched as the action played out. A $5,000 reward had been promised to the one who caught the ball.

"I told them," Maris said, "that if they got the ball not to give it to me. Take the $5,000 reward."

Stallard retired Maris in his first at-bat. The 23,154 roaring fans at Yankee Stadium were quieted. In the fourth inning, Maris came to bat again.

The voice of Phil Rizzuto vividly broadcast the moment: "They're standing, waiting to see if Maris is gonna hit number 61. We've only got a handful of people sitting out in left field, but in right field, man, it's hogged out there. And they're standing up. Here's the windup, the pitch to Roger. Way outside, ball one...And the fans are starting to boo. Low, ball two. That one was in the dirt. And the boos get louder...Two balls, no strikes on Roger Maris. Here's the windup. Fastball, hit deep to right! This could be it! Way back there! Holy Cow, he did it! Sixty-one for Maris!"

The ball traveled just 360 feet, went over outfielder Lu Clinton's head and slammed into box 163D of section 33 into the sixth row of the lower deck in right field. Scuffling, scrambling, fighting, fans went after the ball and the $5,000 reward.

On top of the world, Roger Maris trotted out the historic home run. A kid grabbed his hand as he turned and ran past first. The proud Yankee shook hands and then did the same thing with third base coach Frank Crosetti as he turned past third base and head home.

His Yankee teammates formed a human wall in front of the dugout, refusing to let him enter. Four times he tried—to no avail. Finally,

Maris waved his cap to the cheering crowd, and his teammates finally let him into the dugout.

"He threw me a pitch outside and I just went with it," Maris would say later. "If I never hit another home run—this is the one they can never take away from me."

"I hated to see the record broken," Phil Rizzuto said. "But it was another Yankee that did it. When he hit the 61st home run I screamed so loud I had a headache for about a week."

BILLY ROHR'S NEAR-NO-HITTER: APRIL 14, 1967

The Red Sox, coming off a ninth-place finish in 1966, were a 100-1 shot to win the American League pennant in 1967. Everyone agreed that they would need their share of miracles to accomplish anything that season.

Pitcher Billy Rohr got them started early.

Rohr, a 21-year-old southpaw, made his major league debut for the Red Sox at the Yankees 1967 home opener, squaring off against future Hall of Famer Whitey Ford.

Through five innings, the rookie had a no-hitter. In the sixth, Rohr injured his knee on a line drive, but kept going. He carried a no-hitter into the ninth inning. New York's Tom Tresh led off with a drive to deep left field, but Carl Yastrzemski made a diving catch to keep the no-hitter intact.

"I may have made better catches, but I don't recall any," Yaz said later.

After getting the second out, Rohr needed only to retire Yankee Elston Howard for a career-starting no-hitter. The count went to 3-2. Then Howard lined a ball to right-centerfield for a single. Yankee fans booed in disappointment.

Rohr had to settle for a 3-0, one-hit victory.

Congressman Ed Markey, a lifelong Red Sox fan, recalled the hope that Rohr brought to Boston fans in 1967.

"Billy Rohr in the early part of that season became the symbol of our renaissance—the lefthander we so needed over all those years," Markey said. Markey and thousands of other Red Sox fans were at Rohr's next start at Fenway Park, on April 21, when the Yankees had a chance at redemption against the slender rookie. Rohr vanquished the rivals a second time, this time beating Mel Stottlemyre, 6-1. Howard again had Rohr's number, hitting a seventh-inning homer for New York's only score.

Despite his promise, Rohr never won another game for the Red Sox. He finished the season with a 2-3 record and a 5.10 ERA, and finished the year in the minors. Ironically, Elston Howard would be traded to the Red Sox at the end of the season, helping to steady the Sox pitching staff.

Although Rohr wasn't in a Red Sox uniform for all of Boston's "Impossible Dream," he helped set the pace for it. The Red Sox won the pennant that season, finishing 20 games ahead of the ninth-place Yankees.

Rohr had only one more major league season, going 1-0 with a 6.87 ERA with the Cleveland Indians in 1968.

THE FIRST DESIGNATED HITTER TO BAT: APRIL 6, 1973

A young pitcher named Babe Ruth discovered his hitting prowess with the Boston Red Sox and later became a full-time outfielder with the New York Yankees. So it is with some irony that some 60 years later, a Red Sox-Yankees game on Opening Day of the 1973 at Fenway Park season inaugurated a new rule that would take the bats out of the hands of American League pitchers.

Yankee Ron Blomberg, a lifetime .293 hitter, was the first official "Designated Pinch Hitter," as the position was originally called. Before the game, he asked bench coach Elston Howard what to do as DH. "He said," Blomberg recalled, "'The only thing you do is go take batting practice and just hit.'

"When it was my time to hit," Blomberg said, "the bases were loaded. I was batting sixth in the Yankee order against Luis Tiant. I walked and forced in a run."

The DH was now a part of baseball history and baseball.

"I was left at first base," the brand-new first DH said. "And I was going to stay there because normally that was my position. Elston said, 'Come on back to the bench, you aren't supposed to stay out here.' I went back and said, 'What do I do?' He said, 'You just sit here with me.'"

Facing Luis Tiant, Blomberg went one-for-three. Boston DH Orlando Cepeda was less successful, going 0-for-six, but the Red Sox had no need for extra DH firepower in this game. They cruised to a 15-5 victory on 20 hits, including two home runs by Carlton Fisk, one a grand slam.

Blomberg was a product of the awful, some would say, woeful Yankees of the mid-60s. New York chose him with the first pick in the 1967 free agent draft after finishing in last place the year before. Blomberg also had hundreds of scholarship offers to play football and basketball.

A first-baseman-outfielder, Blomberg went three-for-six in his major league debut

on September 10, 1969. A very talented athlete, his lifetime batting average was just below .300. But by 1973, injuries had slowed him and limited his mobility, making him tailor-made for the new DH spot. While the DH is often associated with aging sluggers, this first designated hitter was only 24 years old.

"With Bobby Bonds in right field and three first basemen, I might as well have donated my glove to charity," Blomberg joked.

After the game, Blomberg's bat was shipped off to the Baseball Hall of fame in Cooperstown. "I went into the Hall of Fame through the back door," Blomberg says. "Everywhere I go, people always talk about me being the first DH in baseball."

He went on to have his best season in 1973, hitting .329 with 12 homers and 57 RBIs.

A sidebar to that game was that the first ball was thrown out by Ed Folger, a Red Sox minor leaguer who had his legs amputated following a farm accident the previous September.

YANKEE MASSACRE: JUNE 17-19,1977

It was a windy weekend at Fenway Park, and the 103,910 fans who had come to watch the Yankees battle the Red Sox for the lead in the American League East got their share of thrills—especially if they were Sox fans.

The Sox humiliated the Yankees, 9-4, 10-4 and 11-1. In the first game Catfish Hunter was shelled for four homers in the first inning. And then before thousands of gleeful Fenway Park partisans and a national TV audience, Yankee manager Billy Martin yanked Reggie Jackson out of the Saturday game claiming Jackson wasn't hustling. The two almost came to blows in the dugout as they screamed out their hostility to each other.

Martin was miffed that Jackson moved too slowly after a ball hit to right field and dispensed Paul Blair as Reggie's replacement. Jackson's exit was accentuated by loud booing throughout the park.

"When they don't hustle, I don't accept that," the hyper Martin said later. "When a player shows the club up, I show the player up."

The Sox showed the Yankees up in that second game, pounding five homers. Yaz hit two. Bernie Carbo belted a pair and George Scott slammed one.

The day of the final game of the series, the *Boston Herald American* headline read: "YANKS GO DOWN FIGHTING THEMSELVES." Denny Doyle homered for Boston with two men on in the fourth inning to continue the Red Sox barrage on Yankee pitching. It was only Doyle's first home run in 204 games. Carbo chipped in with another home run in the seventh inning.

In the final Red Sox plate appearances of the tumultuous series, Boston fans were screaming for more long-range hits. And they got them.

Jim Rice homered. Yaz followed with another homer. And George Scott, one out later, slammed another homer to cap the 11-1 runaway.

"The Yankee Massacre" or massacre of the Yankees by the Red Sox, set a record for most home runs in three games (16). Yaz had slammed four home runs and driven in 10 runs enabling him to take over the league lead in circuit clouts.

Some Yankee zealots claimed that Boston's rout was due to the strong wind that was blowing in Fenway that weekend. But BoSox rooters, elated at the sweep of their

Rick Burleson retires Reggie Jackson. (Photofest)

hated rival that gave Boston a 10-1 home stand record and the division lead, merely smiled: "The Yankees," a happy New Englander smiled, "had the same wind blowing all weekend and they didn't hit one home run."

BOSTON MASSACRE: SEPTEMBER 7-9, 1978

That season of 1978 was a study in contrasts for the Yankees and Red Sox. It seemed early on that Boston was by far the superior team. But as the season moved down through the dog days of August, the first-place Sox seemed to be chasing the second-place Yankees.

On the seventh day of September, Boston's lead was just four games over a charging Yankee team. The Red Sox had played 25-24 ball since their 14-game lead of July 24. The Yankees in that same time frame had won 35 of 49.

The man they called "Yaz," Carl Yastrzemski. (Photofest)

Worst of all were the nine errors committed by Boston.

"Boston's got the best record in baseball," Yankee super scout Clyde King said. "I could understand if an expansion team fell apart like this. It can't go on like this."

Beleaguered Red Sox manager Don Zimmer put his best pitcher out on the mound for the third game of the series. Dennis Eckersley had a 16-6 record and had won his last nine decisions at Fenway. The Yankees did Boston more than one better. Ron Guidry took the mound with his 20-2 record, popping fastball and dancing slider. Final score, 7-0 Yanks.

Boston catcher Carlton Fisk underscored his team's frustration: "How can a team get 30-something games over .500 in July and then in September see its pitching, hitting and fielding all fall apart at the same time?"

Reggie Jackson explained the Yankee turnaround: "This team is loaded with tough guys. This team is loaded with professionals."

Game four of the series pitted rookie Bobby Sprowl of Boston against Ed Figueroa. The Yanks had a 6-0 lead at the end of four and held on to win 7-4.

It was called "The Boston Massacre" and it was.

The Yankees pounded out 42 runs and 67 hits. Boston managed just nine runs and 21 hits. The Sox also committed a dozen errors. The Yankees won the four games by an average margin of over eight runs. For the long-suffering fans of the Boston Red Sox, it

Mike Torrez of Boston vs. Catfish Hunter of New York was the pitching match up in the first game of the four-game series.

After two innings, the Yanks led, 5-0. They led 7-0 after three. After four innings it was 12-0, Yankees. The final score that broke Red Sox hearts was 15-3.

The next day two rookies started against each other—Jim Wright for the humbled Sox and Jim Beattie for the high-flying Yankees. Boston was thrashed again, 13-2. In two games the Bronx Bombers had pounded out 28 runs to Boston's five, and out-hit the Sox 38-14.

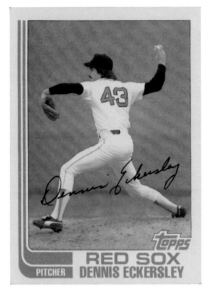

Dennis Eckersley (The Topps Company, Inc.)

Reggie Jackson (The Topps Company, Inc.)

Bucky Dent, "Bucky [bleeping] Dent" in Boston. (The Topps Company, Inc.)

was like an old-time horror movie replayed with the volume turned up. But there was still October 2, 1978 on the horizon.

BUCKY DENT'S HOME RUN: October 2, 1978

"When Bucky hit the ball, I said, 'That's good. That's an out,'" recalled Don Zimmer, the manager of the Red Sox at the time.

"And usually you know when the ball hits the bat whether it's short, against the wall, in the net or over the net. I see Yaz backing up, backing up, and when he's looking up, I still think he's going to catch it. When I see him turn around, then I know he's going to catch it off the wall. Then the ball wound up in the net. We went home the next day."

"When I hit the ball," Bucky Dent recalled, "I knew that I had hit it high enough

to hit the wall. But there were shadows on the net behind the wall and I didn't see the ball land there. I didn't know I had hit a homer until I saw the umpire at first signaling home run with his hand. I couldn't believe it."

Neither could the Red Sox.

Don Zimmer changed the Yankee shortstop's name to "Bucky F_____g Dent." Red Sox fans had even more salty phrases.

Dent's home run was the headline of headlines in that one-game playoff game on October 2 between the historic rivals at Fenway Park before 32,925. The Yankees had been down to the Sox in the AL East by 14 games on July 19. After frazzled Billy Martin was canned as manager, calm Bob Lemon took over and led the team to a 52-21 record.

Losing 14 of 17 in September, the Sox made a late-season run, winning their last eight games, catching the Yankees on the last day of the season. That set up this moment in Yankee-Red Sox time.

New York's superstar hurler Ron Guidry gave up two runs to Boston through six innings—a home run to Carl Yastrzemski and a Jim Rice RBI single. Mike Torrez, a former Yankee, was the Boston pitcher.

The top of the seventh inning started badly for Boston and got worse. Chris Chambliss singled. Roy White singled. Earl Russell Dent out of Savannah, Georgia, a nifty defensive shortstop but not much of an offensive threat, had batted but .243 for the season. Now he was coming to center stage. For the last 20 games he had batted a puny .140. But the Yankees were out of infield replacements. Regular second baseman Willie Randolph was injured. The only available midinfielder Fred Stanley was set to come in and replace Brian Doyle, who had been hit for earlier in the inning.

Dent, a lifetime .247 hitter, stepped in. Just hoping to make contact, the five-foot-nine Yankee peered out at Torrez, the six-foot-five Red Sox pitcher. Dent fouled the second pitch off his foot. The count was one and one. There was a brief delay as the Yankees trainer looked after Dent. Mickey Rivers, the on-deck-batter, pointed out that there was a crack in the handsome infielder's bat. Dent borrowed a bat from Rivers.

All set, Dent swung at the next pitch; the ball cleared the infield heading out to the left field wall. The wind and destiny moved the ball higher to its date with the Green Monster.

"Deep to left!" Bill White, the Yankees broadcaster shouted, "Yastrzemski will not get it!"

Yaz backed up. He had been in this position many times before. But he knew it was hopeless. The ball sailed into the 23-foot net above the Green Monster, the 37-foot wall in left field. "It's a home run!" Bill White screamed out. "A three-run homer by Bucky Dent! And the Yankees now lead by a score of 3-2!" White marveled at what had happened as the telecast continued: "The last guy on the ball club you'd expect to hit a home run."

It seemed that the entire Yankee bench was there waiting at home plate as Bucky Dent trotted around to score. "I remember how quiet the stadium was as I rounded third," Dent is fond of recalling. "You could hear the Yankee fans cheering. It was really eerie."

"I was so damn shocked," Torrez said. "I thought maybe it was going to be off the wall. Damn, I did not think it was going to go out."

The Red Sox, although many of their fans had totally lost hope, still had a chance in the bottom of the ninth. But Goose Gossage popped up Carl Yastrzemski with two on and two out. The final score was Yankees 5, Red Sox 4.

Not many remember that the victory in that game was earned by Ron Guidry, moving his record to 25-3, locking up the Cy Young Award for him.

The Yankee won the World Series that year, and Bucky Dent just kept right on trucking with his hero antics. He won the Series MVP award, hitting .417 with seven RBIs in the six-game series.

After the game ended, an enterprising buddy of Dent called the Red Sox, asking if the home-run ball was available. As it turned out the net had been littered with balls from batting-practice home runs. The worth of the Bucky Dent ball—perhaps valued in the seven-

Mike Torrez pitched for both the Yankees and Red Sox. (The Topps Company, Inc.)

figure range today—was unable to be identified amidst all the others there in the net.

As the years have passed—Bucky "Bleeping" Dent in Red Sox speak—has capitalized mightily on that moment. There was a part in a 1979 television movie *Dallas Cowboys Cheerleaders*. He runs a baseball school in the off season in Delray Beach, Florida that showcases a nearly full-size replica of the Green Monster, complete with a scoreboard freezing in time his Fenway moment of moments.

Like Ralph Branca and Bobby Thomson, the old Dodgers and Giant, Dent and Mike Torrez are sometimes an item signing autographs. Bucky likes to add the date 10/2/78 after his name.

An interesting sidelight is that the 1978 team was actually the fourth Yankees club that began the final month behind in the standings and finished first. The other three were the 1922, 1955 and 1964 teams. However, the 1978 team entered September down six and a half games and came from the furthest back to win.

SOX SEVEN-RUN EIGHTH TOPS YANKS: SEPTEMBER 19, 1981

The Yankees and Red Sox met at Fenway Park before more than 32,000 fans on September 19, 1981. Ron Guidry opposed Mike Torrez. Boston sought to break the Yanks' Fenway Park winning streak—nine straight.

Guidry coasted along, allowing just one run in seven innings, showing off the form that had enabled him to post an 80-2 career record against the Sox and three wins in three starts at the Fens. Torrez had pitched according to pattern, too. The ex-Yankee, with just one win against his former mates in 11 decisions, was pounded for eight hits and five runs in seven innings.

But Rick Miller hit a three-run homer in the bottom of the eighth inning off Yankee reliever Dave LaRoche, capping a seven-run rally, as the Sox prevailed, 8-5.

DAVE RIGHETTI: THE NO-HITTER: JULY 4, 1983

A holiday crowd of 41,077 was on hand at Yankee Stadium on Independence Day. Many of the fans wore Yankee hats that had been given away as a promotion for the game against the Boston Red Sox.

Dave Righetti had come to the Yankees in a multiple-player deal that sent Sparky Lyle to Texas. His major league debut was as an end of the season call up on September 16, 1979. But it was not until 1981 that he came back to the Yankees to stay.

The American League Rookie of the Year that 1981 season (8-4, 2.06 ERA), the player they called "Rags" won twice against Milwaukee in divisional play and once over Oakland in the LCS.

On this warm and sunny day, the 24-year-old Dave Righetti would make history, pitching a no-hitter against the BoSox. The handsome hurler walked four and struck out nine men, including Wade Boggs for the final out. Boggs, hitting .357 at the time, went down swinging on a hard slider.

Ironically, it would be Righetti's last season as a regular starting pitcher. The next year, he replaced Goose Gossage as the Yankees' closer, and in 1986 went on to set the then-

Yankee pitcher Dave Righetti letting the ball go.
(Photofest)

major league single-season save record of 46.

The Fourth of July no-hitter was the first by a lefthander in Yankee Stadium history, the first no-hitter by a Yankee pitcher since 1956, when Don Larsen tossed a perfect game. It was only the sixth regular-season no-hitter in Yankees history and the first since 1951. It was Dave Righetti's moment of moments as a New York Yankee.

BOSTON'S SHORT-LIVED REDEMP-TION: OCTOBER 16, 1999

"If you're a student of history, you have to love it," then Yankees pitcher David Cone said. "It's 1999 and the Yankees and Red Sox are playing in the postseason for the first time. It's an opportunity Boston fans have been waiting for since Babe Ruth. It's kind of eerie when you think about it."

In mid-October of 1999, the Yankees arrived in Boston for the third game of their best-of-seven American League Championship Series with the Red Sox, leading two games to none. In a highly anticipated pitching match up, New York sent former Boston ace Roger Clemens to the mound against new Boston ace Pedro Martinez. It had been three years since Clemens left Boston as a free agent, but the emotions were still raw for long-suffering Red Sox fans.

"I have thrown here before in different situations," Clemens said before the game. "This will be the biggest game obviously. I have so many emotions that I will have to curtail somehow."

After winning back-to-back Cy Young Awards with the Toronto Blue Jays, Clemens had been traded to the Yankees before the 1999 season. It was an off year for the Rocket, who

Wade Boggs became a Yankee in 1993. (Photofest)

"Roger, Roger." He fell behind early. A Jose Offerman triple off the right field wall, followed by a John Valentin home run over the Green Monster, put the Sox up 2-0 in the first inning. Boston made it 4-0 in the second on Offerman's single and doubles by Trot Nixon and Nomar Garciaparra.

In the third inning, Clemens gave up a single to Mike Stanley, and then was lifted after one pitch to Brian Daubach. Hideki Irabu came in to relieve for New York and gave up a home run to Daubach to make it 6-0. That made the final line for Clemens: two-plus innings, five earned runs, six hits and two walks.

The Red Sox weren't done. They continued pounding New York pitching, piling up 21 hits and coasting to a 13-1 victory—the Yankees' worst postseason loss ever. The game also snapped the Yankees' postseason winning streak at 12. Martinez was just as tough on the Yankees, striking out 12 while giving up only two hits and two walks in seven shutout innings.

But despite that emotional victory, the Red Sox didn't win another game in the series and were eliminated by the Yankees, four games to one. New York went on face the crosstown Mets in the World Series. Clemens lost his cool in that showdown, throwing a shattered bat at the Mets' Mike Piazza, but the Yankees wound up winning their second straight championship.

The Red Sox, as usual, had to delight in smaller pleasures. For the first time since the 1915 and 1916 seasons, they had made the postseason two years in a row. But the year

went 14-10 with a 4.60 ERA. Pedro, meanwhile, had seized the Cy Young mantle from Clemens in 1999, winning 23 games with a 2.07 ERA and 313 strikeouts—leading the league in all three categories.

"The ballpark was electric with anti-Yankee fever," recalled Congressman Ed Markey, a lifelong Red Sox fan from Malden, Mass. "It was our best chance, looking at our lineup, to break the curse, break this historical inability to beat the Yankees. The ballpark that night was alive with all of the hopes and all of the dreams of every Red Sox fan of all generations."

Clemens braced himself for a possible Fenway Park tirade. "You can't make people not boo you or like you if they don't, and you want them to come and get it out and let it out," he said. "That is what the Boston-New York situation is supposed to be. That is what's neat about it."

Boston fans didn't disappoint, booing Clemens and serenading him with chants of

1918 remained etched into the team's identity—the last time Boston won a World Series.

MIKE MUSSINA: NEAR-PERFECT GAME: SEPTEMBER 2, 2001

It was Yankees vs. Red Sox, September baseball between the two age-old rivals. Right-hander Mike Mussina against right-hander David Cone. Through eight innings, no score. Mussina, no walks, no hits given up. As the man they called "Moose" took a perfect game into the eighth for the third time, the Yankees dugout was quiet.

The inning started with a Tino Martinez single. Paul O'Neill slapped a sharp grounder. Second baseman Lou Merloni made an error.

Runners on first and third. Clay Bellinger pinch ran for Martinez. A hit by Enrique Wilson scored him and gave the Yanks a 1-0 lead.

In the bottom of the ninth, Troy O'Leary, pinch-hitting for Shea Hillenbrand, hit a liner that Bellinger, playing first base, dove for. He tossed the ball to Mussina. One out.

"I thought maybe this time it was going to happen," said Mussina, "considering that I thought that ball was through for sure."

Lou Merloni struck out. Carl Everett was in the clubhouse hitting off a tee; he got the call to pinch hit for Joe Oliver. The moody Everett, in a three-for-32 slump, was one-for-nine with seven strikeouts in his career against Mussina.

The switch-hitter fouled off the first pitch. He swung at strike two. Pitch number three to Everett was a ball. The next pitch was a high fastball. Everett fought it off, lofting a soft liner to left-center, between Chuck Knoblauch and Bernie Williams. It dropped—single.

Mussina knew immediately. "I thought it was a hit," he said. "I'm going to think about that pitch until I retire, but that was the pitch I threw." All Mussina could do was hang his head and give a little smile. "I've never been part of a no-hitter before as an opponent," Everett said. "It was very satisfying to get the hit. It was very satisfying to hit the high fastball."

The tense game came to an end when Mussina was able to get Trot Nixon to ground out to second baseman Alfonso Soriano. The Yankee pitcher then weakly pumped his fist as his teammates ran out onto the field.

Mussina finished with his fourth career one-hitter, striking out a season-high 13, nine of them on called third strikes. His wide break-

Paul O'Neill, a Yankee warrior from 1993–2001. (Photofest)

ing ball had the Red Sox off balance all night. The Yankee triumph gave them a three-game sweep over Boston, and tagged an eighth straight loss on the Sox, who tumbled to nine games back in the American League East.

"It was just a phenomenal game," Mussina said. "I was disappointed, I'm still disappointed. But the perfect game just wasn't meant to be."

In a move that ticked off Sox players, Red Sox general manager Dan Duquette minutes after the game relieved pitching coach John Cumberland of his duties. A furious Cumberland, who was promoted from bullpen coach to pitching coach just a month before when Joe Kerrigan became manager, told reporters that Duquette told him he was being reassigned to the team's training facility in Fort Myers, Florida.

"I'm not going," Cumberland said. "That's official, that's for damn sure. That's OK. We've had a lot of good people leave this organization, and now it's going to be me because I'm not going to be reassigned."

ROCKET'S REVENGE: SEPTEMBER 4, 2002

The Yankees came into the game with a six and a half game lead over the Red Sox, but manager Joe Torre was still nervous. New York had dropped its last three games, including the opener of a crucial three-game series at the Stadium to the BoSox. A loss would allow the Sox to get back within striking distance.

"I don't care how good your team is," Torre said. "There's always that little uneasy feeling when you lose a few games in a row."

On two previous occasions, pitcher Roger Clemens recalled, Torre had made a point of telling him he needed a strong outing. One was the deciding game of the 2001 division series with Oakland, the other Game 3 of the World Series that year, when New York trailed two games to none.

On this September day, Torre told Clemens, "Roger, we need you today."

"I heard him, loud and clear," Clemens said. "When the skipper says that, it's pretty nice when you can come through."

The 40-year-old pitcher came through against his former team, striking out the side in the first inning, finishing with 10 Ks, yielding just four hits and one walk in seven and one-third innings.

In the seventh inning, Torre and head trainer Gene Monahan visited Clemens on the mound.

"He was bending over," Torre said. "We didn't know if it was his back, his legs. He said: 'I'm 40 years old. I'm just trying to catch my breath.'"

Later Clemens reported that some of his teammates were laughing. He told them: "Wait until you all turn 40."

Johnny Damon was the last batter the former Red Sox Rocket faced. He hit a grounder to Derek Jeter who made a bad throw. That ended it for Clemens, who made an eighth-inning exit to a standing ovation from the 47,318 fans.

Clemens notched his 102nd career double-digit strikeout game—third most all-time—and won for the 19th time in his last 20 decisions at home. His .767 winning percentage at Yankee Stadium topped all New York pitchers with at least 30 wins.

The Yankees went on to win, 4-2, opening their lead over Boston to seven and a half games. The next day, New York took the rubber game of the series, 3-1, widening the lead to eight and a half games—effectively burying the Red Sox. It was yet another late-season collapse for Boston. At the All-Star break, the two teams had been locked in a battle for first place, with the Yankees clinging to a two-game lead.

For Roger Clemens, the victory against the team he started his career with had to be special. Since leaving the BoSox, Clemens had notched three Cy Young Awards and two World Series championships. Pain, more pain for the sad BoSox.

"There are only one or two guys over there that I went to battle with," Clemens said. "But you can tell the difference when we play the Sox because of the rivalry."

"He gave us everything he could have possibly given us," Torre said. "He's a horse. No question, he's a horse."

THE SEVENTH GAME: OCTOBER 17, 18, 2003

The match up was out of central casting: Pedro Martinez vs. Roger Clemens. In the mythic history of big games, none could compare. Through baseball history many superb hurlers were tabbed to start Game 7s, including Christy Mathewson, Walter Johnson, Dizzy Dean, Bob Gibson, Sandy Koufax, Clemens, John Smoltz, Curt Schilling. But two superstars like Pedro and Roger had never matched up with so much on the line.

Like two punch-drunk fighters, the Yankees and the Red Sox took the field at Yankee Stadium before 56,279 in 61 degree temperatures. Boston and New York had played 19 times during the regular season, six more times than in the postseason, a record 25 games in all. The two age-old rivals were tied 3-3 in the American League Championship Series. This was a winner-take-all Game 7, the first at Yankee Stadium in 46 years. The winner would go to the World Series.

For the Red Sox, a triumph would break their 85-year-old streak of not winning the World Series. Knowing this, many Yankees fans trotted out good-luck (bad-luck) charms and brought them to the game to keep the "Curse of the Bambino" going. One had made a pan painted with a four-leaf cover that he slammed with a spoon. The drum was attached to a sign: "Freddy Sez Yanks in Seven, don't look glum-chum." There were other fans who sported all kinds of variations of the Red Sox logo and the words "1918: RIP." The game got underway and to the dismay of Yankee zealots, Clemens was off his game. He gave up a second-inning two-run homer to Trot Nixon and a solo homer to Kevin Millar in the fourth. He was touched up for four runs in three-plus innings. Nevertheless, he was cheered by fans as he walked off slowly after Joe Torre took him out in the fourth inning. Mike Mussina, in his first career relief appearance, took the ball with no outs and runners on first and third. The Moose fanned Jason Varitek. Then he got speedy Johnny Damon to ground into an inning-ending double play. He pitched two more scoreless innings. Felix Heredia, Jeff Nelson and David Wells all followed Mussina on the mound, holding back Boston. Pedro Martinez was at the top of his game. Changing speeds, changing locations, moving the ball around, Martinez cruised. The only blemish was a bases-empty homer he yielded to Jason Giambi in the fifth. Then in the seventh, the stylish right-hander surrendered another solo homer to Giambi with two outs. The Boston lead was now 4-2. Pedro yielded two singles, then regrouped and fanned Alfonso Soriano on a 94 mph fastball to end the inning. Nomar Garciaparra hugged Martinez as they headed into the Boston dugout.

With his pitch count over 100 and relievers Mike Timlin and Scott Williamson at the ready, it seemed that Martinez, resting on the bench in the top of the eighth, was fin-ished for the night. Then David Ortiz homered to push the Red Sox lead to 5-2.

With the three-run lead, BoSox pilot Grady Little sent Pedro out to hurl the bottom of the eighth. Nick Johnson popped out. Five outs were all Boston needed to win the game and get into the World Series. It seemed "the Curse" was going to be broken. The Yankees, however, were not done. Derek Jeter doubled to right. Bernie Williams singled over shortstop to drive in Jeter. The Boston lead was now 5-3. Hideki Matsui, who had doubled twice off Martinez in the series, was next up for New York.

Little emerged from the Red Sox dugout, the right-hander Timlin and the left-hander Alan Embree were warm and ready. Little stood on the mound, talked to Martinez, and patted him down with encouragement. After the game was over the Boston pilot explained: "Pedro wanted to stay in there. He wanted to get the job done just as he has many times for us all season long and he's the man we all wanted on the mound."

The Dominican hurler got two strikes on Matsui. The Red Sox Nation relaxed for an instant. A fastball inside. Matsui pulled the ball down the right field line. It bounced into the stands—ground-rule double.

Yankee catcher Jorge Posada stepped in. The tying runs—Williams at third and Matsui at second—were in position. Timlin and Embree stared in from the bullpen. They were ready. But Little did not move. Pedro Martinez had thrown 118 pressure pitches. Pedro Martinez was who he wanted to pitch to Posada. Later Little would explain: "He had enough left in his tank to finish off Posada." Then things seemed to move in slow motion.

Joe Torre sat expressionless. Derek Jeter was animated on the top step of the Yankee dugout. "Stay back," he screamed to Posada. "Wait for your pitch." The count on Posada moved to 2-2. A fastball—inside. Posada swung and lifted the ball over second base. It wasn't much of a poke, but it fell in. Williams scored. Matsui scored. The score was tied. Little came out of the Boston dugout, and Martinez was out of the game. He had given up the three runs that tied the game on four straight one-out hits. Alan Embree and then Mike Timlin held the Yankees back as the game moved deadlocked 5-5 to the 11th inning. Mariano Rivera choked off the Red Sox in the ninth, 10th and 11th innings—the longest stint for the Yankee closer in seven seasons.

Boston knuckleballer Wakefield, victorious over the Yankees twice in the series, pitched a scoreless 10th inning. He came out to pitch the 11th inning.

Sitting in the front row was former New York City mayor Rudy Giuliani. Despite Wakefield's success against the Yankees, Giuliani was optimistic.

"I liked the idea of a going against a knuckleball pitcher like Wakefield," he said. "When a knuckleball pitcher makes a mistake, you hit a home run. If he just hangs one, the game's over."

As the Red Sox took the field in the bottom of the 11th inning, Giuliani turned to his wife Judith, and their daughter Whitney, and said, "You're going to see your first walk-off home run."

Aaron Boone, benched for not hitting, had entered the game as a pinch runner. Now he was leading off in his first at-bat of the game. The pitch from Wakefield was inside, below

Boone's hands. The time was 16 minutes past midnight, Friday morning. Boone swung and smashed the ball deep over the left-field wall. The big, old ballpark in the Bronx shook.

"The minute he hit it, I knew it was gone," Giuliani said. "I sit right behind the Yankee dugout, right on the field level. Having sat there for 20 years, very often, when people are jumping up, I will continue to sit because I know it's not going to go out. But that one, you could see he pulled it, and you could hear that he hit it very, very solid."

"I knew it was out. I finally put a good swing on it," Boone said later. The Yankees won, 6-5. The evil empire had triumphed again. New York had its fifth pennant in six seasons, its 39th American League pennant. It was the fifth home run in baseball history that ended a postseason series and the first ever in extra innings in a Game 7. Rounding third base, Boone threw himself into the arms of teammates waiting at home plate. Mariano Rivera was lifted onto the shoulders of teammates. The Yankees were jubilant in victory. The Red Sox were devastated in defeat. "Damn Yankees!" was the Friday front-page headline in the *Boston Herald* next to a photo of two Red Sox players—their heads hung in defeat.

The *Daily News* led simply with the banner headline of: "Boone Town!" *The New York Post* had its back page loaded with type: "Curse Lives as Aaron homer sends Yankees to Series" and "KA-BOONE!"

"I don't know about a curse, but I believe we have some ghosts in this stadium that have helped us out," Derek Jeter said. "We've just had some magical stuff that has happened to us tonight."

"We're not stunned at all because we knew we were competing with a very good team, a very professional team," Pedro Martinez said. "They're great players, they did what they had to do to win a ballgame. I respect them for that, I respect the way they play. There's nothing I could say bad against those guys."

"Like Derek told me, 'The ghosts will show up eventually,'" Boone said. "It couldn't be more satisfying," New York manager Joe Torre said. "This has to be the sweetest taste of all for me."

Boston led the majors with a .289 batting average, set a team record with 238 homers and set baseball's slugging percentage record of .491, nipping the .489 mark of the 1927 Yankees. "I'm thankful that it's me instead of one of my players taking the blame," Little said afterwards. "If we don't win the World Series, which is the definition of winning here, somebody's got to be that man and I'm just glad it's me instead."

Boston general manager Theo Epstein remarked: "You can dwell on what happened and wake up in the middle of the night screaming, 'Five more outs!' but I'm not going to do that," he said. "There's a choice. You can sit and dwell in perpetuity or have it inspire you to work harder to go and get it done next year. When we do win it, this will make it all that much sweeter."

Derek Jeter (Fleer)

A footnote to that seventh game took place on November 7 when Pedro Martinez stirred up some more "rivalry" controversy. He claimed he told Red Sox manager Grady Little that he was tiring. "I said, 'Get the guys ready in case I get in trouble,'" Martinez said of his conversation in the dugout after the seventh inning. There are those who maintain that Little was fired for staying with Martinez and not sending in a reliever after they talked.

TALKIN' RIVALRY

Celebrities, politicians, players, coaches, mangers, executives, fans, and media people all have their say in this free-for-all about what makes "The Great Rivalry" the great rivalry.

Like a face off in print, here are stories, asides, frontal attacks, poignant memories, insights, game accounts, vulgarisms, quips and rejoinders related by the famous, the not-so-famous, even the anonymous. Across generations and geography—Yankee loyalists and zealots and Red Sox Nation boosters and rooters all get into the act.

RUDY GIULIANI, *former mayor of New York City, named* Time Magazine's *'Person of the Year' in 2001 for his strong leadership and calming influence after the September 11 terrorist attacks.*

My very first baseball game, in 1950 or 1951, was between the Yankees and the Red Sox, with Joe DiMaggio playing for the Yankees and Dominic DiMaggio playing for the Red Sox. As a five- or six-year-old, I found that fascinating—that brothers would be on two different teams. It was really weird to me. I remember asking my father, "How come they're playing for different teams—are they angry at each other?" That was my first baseball game, so it sort of becomes the prototype of baseball for you. I knew those Red Sox teams really well, because we played them 18 times a year.

It's a great, great rivalry. It may be at this point in history the best rivalry of any in sport. There's no rivalry in professional sports that has as much history to it, going way back to Babe Ruth, Sparky Lyle, and more recently, the controversy they had about trying to get Jose Contreras. There have been so many times in which the two teams competed with each other by trading ballplayers, getting ballplayers. The rivalry becomes the most interesting, and the most intense, when they're both good. Maybe in the late '60s and early '70s, when the Yankees were struggling, the rivalry didn't have quite the intensity that it has now.

And it's been intensified by the fact that we play each other so many times each year. That's the way the Brooklyn Dodgers and New York Giants use to play, when the leagues were only eight teams each. That's the only rivalry that's ever matched it. Not now—I think the distance between Los Angeles and San Francisco has made that rivalry less intense. The Dodgers and the Giants, when they were both in New York, played 18 times a year. Well, the Yankees play the Red Sox 19 times a year now. That's a lot of games to develop a rivalry. And you really get to know each other. There are no surprises. There was no pitcher that the Yankees or the Red Sox could bring in that both teams hadn't seen.

The other thing about the Yankees and Red Sox that I really love is their uniforms haven't changed. My first game in 1950 or '51, the Yankees were wearing pinstripes, and the Red Sox were wearing that gray uniform with Boston written on it in red, with that B on their hat. Now, some teams have uniforms that look like space invaders, with purples and greens and oranges and who knows what. But the Red Sox and Yankees are still in the uniforms of Joe DiMaggio, Babe Ruth, Ted Williams. So you can just close your eyes and you think you're in traditional baseball. And the two organizations, particularly now the current Red Sox organization, have a sense of the tradition that they're dealing with. That is a very long tradition of baseball, and you've got to live up to it.

I remember once going with a friend of mine who was a Red Sox fan to a Yankees game in the late '60s or '70s. Rico Petrocelli was playing third base for the Red Sox. And my friend was a big, big Rico Petrocelli fan. He was cheer-ing him on, cheering him on. And the people in back were telling him to shut up, or they would throw him over the upper deck. And I told them to leave him alone, that he had a right to root for the Red Sox. So my friend kept cheering. I just balanced by rooting louder for the Yankees. We got creamed in that game.

Then I remember a game in the 1980s when Roger Clemens was pitching for the Red Sox. In the first three innings, the Red Sox got ahead 8-0. And friends that I was with wanted to leave, and go have dinner. And I said, "I never leave a baseball game." And just upon saying that, Dave Winfield hit a home run against Clemens, about 420 feet, and then the floodgates opened and by the end of the third inning, the Yankees were tied 8-8. And the game went to extra innings, and the Yankees won. I use that game as an example: Never believe that you're out of a game, and when you're losing by eight runs, the best way to win a game is to score one run. Because once you score one run, you never know what's going to happen.

I've been to many Yankees-Red Sox games over the years, but Game 7 of the 2003 championship series was the most exciting I've ever been to or seen. I watched the 1978 play-off game on TV, which was pretty close to the most exciting. But somehow this one was even more exciting. Maybe it all happened a little bit later, with the Yankees tying the game in the eighth inning. Maybe the whole thing had stretched on longer, past midnight. Remember, '78 was before the Red Sox has lost to the Mets in the World Series. There was more history that had built up by 2003. In the 1978 season, I don't think everybody went into that with this feeling of Yankee inevitability, Red

Sox are going to lose. It wasn't as developed. But since then, the Red Sox had virtually won a World Series against the Mets, and then lost. Then they lost the playoffs to us in '99.

Right before Aaron Boone hit the game-winning home run to win the seventh game, I turned around to my wife Judith, and to our daughter Whitney, and I said, "You're going to see your first walk-off home run." Now I wasn't sure it was going to be Boone, but I thought for sure that somebody would do it.

I liked the idea of a going against a knuckleball pitcher like Wakefield. When a knuckleball pitcher makes a mistake, you hit a home run. If he just hangs one, the game's over. And the Yankees had been seeing Wakefield for so long. That knuckleball has to be working every single inning, and on every single pitch. So I liked the idea of the Yankees facing him, where you know, no matter what a player tries to do, they're thinking home run. And I thought beforehand, wouldn't it be nice if Boone could do it, because he's been having a rough year, trying to get into being a Yankee. The minute he hit it, I knew it was gone. I sit right behind the Yankee dugout, right on the field level. Having sat there for 20 years, very often, when people are jumping up, I will continue to sit because I know it's not going to go out. But that one, you could see he pulled it, and you can hear that he hit it very, very solid.

And I actually thought going into the game that we would hit Pedro earlier. He may be the best pitcher in baseball, but on three days' rest, he's nowhere close to the best pitcher in baseball, because he has arm problems. This isn't a kid like Josh Beckett who we faced later in the World Series, who's 23 years old, and

could probably pitch every day. So I thought, this is not going to be 100 percent Pedro. This is going to be 60 to 70 percent Pedro. And I thought he pitched brilliantly, until he got into that eighth inning.

I'm not a Yankees fan who hates the Red Sox, not at all. If the Red Sox had gone to the World Series, I'd have been rooting for them very enthusiastically as an American League fan. With the single exception of the Mets, that I feel a loyalty to because they're in New York, I always root for the American League—that's where my team is. If the Red Sox had beaten the Yankees, it would have been difficult to deal with, but I would have rooted for them because it sort of makes you feel better about your team when the team that beats them wins the championship. I felt good in 2002 when the Angels won the World Series, because they had beaten us earlier. So at least we got beat by a really good team. I actually like the Red Sox. I like Boston as a baseball city. I think New York, Chicago, Boston and St. Louis are the best baseball cities in the world—I should say in the United States because I don't know what they're like in Japan.

When I go to games at Fenway Park, I don't get any of the fans' hostility because I think they relate to me somewhat differently because of September 11. I get a few yells, but not too much. I was at Fenway for the third and fourth games of the 2003 Series. I was also there for what would have been the fourth game, before it was rained out. So I had lot of chances to interact with the fans, because we were waiting around for the game to start. It was fine, there was no hostility. And then when the game starts, you can hear them yelling all kinds of stuff at the Yankee players.

But you hear the same stuff in the Bronx, which I think is stupid. I don't like that. I grew up as a Yankees fan, and this may come from having won so often, in which you were supposed to be gracious. My father taught me when a guy pitched a good game for the other team, you get up and give him a standing ovation when he comes off the mound, because you have to respect a great athletic performance, whoever does it. I get really annoyed when fans boo. I know we all do it—Yankee fans do it, Red Sox fans do it—and you're never going to stop it, it's part of the game. But I just don't like it.

Actually, it's more hostile for me in Shea Stadium than in Fenway. And it's fun hostile. It's because I'm such an outspoken Yankee fan, where a mayor is supposed to root for both teams—you know, pretend you root for both teams—and I never bought into that. I thought, well, I always want to be honest with people, and I'm a Yankee fan. I've been going to Yankee Stadium for so long, I couldn't fool anybody if I tried.

I identify with the Yankees, and the city of New York identifies with the Yankees, and vice versa. I thought that some of the revival of the spirit of the city happened when the Yankees won the World Series in 1996. People began adopting a more winning attitude. This is also true of Boston, Chicago and St. Louis— people identify with their baseball team more than they do any other sports teams. Baseball is to a lot of these American cities what soccer is to European cities. So when the team is doing well, it lifts the spirit of the city.

And I think New Yorkers have adopted some of the characteristics of the Yankees, and the Yankees have adopted some of the charac- teristics of New Yorkers. I'm sure I have too— I've been a Yankee fan all my life. You expect to win, you don't brag, you don't make predictions and jump up and down and have big victory celebrations when you win. When the Yankees won after 1996, it was wonderful to watch, because they took it for granted. Which is what you're supposed to do—we're here to win baseball games.

I don't think there's as much of a rivalry between the cities as there is between the Yankees and Red Sox. We're very different cities, we're not in a competition over a lot. We're very well established cities. Maybe the only rivalry we have sometimes is for big conventions. They're having the Democratic convention and we're having the Republican convention. And I'm satisfied with that division. I like Boston as a city, and I like the people, and I like going there. I've spent a lot of time in Boston.

I do feel sorry for the Red Sox. I have said the following, particularly if I'm with friends or groups from Boston and Chicago: If the Yankees and Mets don't make it to the World Series, then I hope for a Red Sox-Cubs World Series. I think there could be nothing better for baseball. I've never believed in the curse until 2003. Having watched the Yankee- Red Sox series, and being in Chicago for the sixth game of that series, somehow I think maybe there's something going on here we don't quite understand.

BUD SELIG, *Major League Baseball commissioner*

Any rivalry that intense and productive over the last seven or eight decades is very healthy. I think it's the greatest rivalry in sports.

FAY VINCENT, *commissioner of Major League Baseball from 1989-1992, replacing his friend, Bart Giamatti, who died of a heart attack.*

I grew up a Yankees fan in Connecticut. I will face up to it. Bart [commissioner Giammati, a lifelong Red Sox fan] would look up at me and say, "Can you believe this man is a Yankee fan?" He made it sound like I was a child molester. I used to say "But, Bart, we won, and you lost." Bart used to say that the line between Yankees fans and Red Sox ran right through center of New Haven. Everybody to the east was a Red Sox fan, and everybody to the west was a Yankee fan. DiMaggio was the big hero, but I was a terrific fan of Tommy Henrich—how could you not like somebody named Old Reliable? He was a terrific ballplayer, very bright.

I lived in Connecticut until 1968, then I moved to Maryland to work in Washington. Once I left Connecticut, I really gave up on the Yankees. It was hard to root for CBS—in those days CBS owned the Yankees. And then Steinbrenner. Now, I root more for the Red Sox in the American League and the Mets in the National League. I can't root for Yankees because of the payroll and Steinbrenner—it's like rooting for General Motors. I'd rather root for the underdog. If the Yankees don't win it's a mistake. They ought to win every year, they have so much money, and they buy all the great players.

I teased Giamatti many times about being a Red Sox fan. In 1986, he was the National League president, and the Red Sox played the Mets in the World Series. I teased him: "How will you root for your league's team?"

He replied: "From the waist up, I'm for the Mets. From the waist down, I'm for the Red Sox." You know, basically he was very much for the Red Sox. He was very disheartened when they lost that year.

A big part of the rivalry is that I think New England is very parochial, always feels that New York is better than Boston. Everything that Boston has, New York has better. So there's a natural tendency if you're a New Englander to look at New York as the bad guy. Boston is the underdog, let's go after the big guys. Boston and New England took on the rivalry against the best team in baseball.

THEO EPSTEIN, *Red Sox general manager*

The Curse of the Bambino doesn't exist. Just give us a couple of years and we're going to win a World Series and that'll satisfy those troubled people who continue to believe in curses.

LARRY LUCCHINO, *president of the Red Sox*

It's white hot. It's a rivalry on the field, it's a rivalry in the press, it's a rivalry in the front office, it's a rivalry among the fan base. It's as good and intense a rivalry as any you could have.

GEORGE STEINBRENNER, *Yankee principal owner*

That's B.S. [on Red Sox team president Larry Lucchino's "Evil Empire" remark on Yankee signing of Cuban defector pitcher Jose Contreras in December 2002]. That's how a sick person thinks. I've learned this about Lucchino. He's baseball's foremost chameleon of all time. He changes colors depending on where's he's standing. He's been at Baltimore and he deserted them there, and then went out to San Diego, and look at what trouble they're in out there. When he was in San Diego, he was a big man for the small markets. Now he's in Boston and he's for the big markets.

He's not the kind of guy you want to have in your foxhole. He's running the team behind John Henry's back. I warned John it would happen, told him, "Just be careful." He talks out of both sides of his mouth. He has trouble talking out of the front of it.

JOHN HENRY, *Red Sox owner*

There is nothing greater in sports than a great rivalry and this is truly one of the greatest rivalries in the history of all sports. I wouldn't call it overly obsessive, but I would call it great fun and a great challenge.

ARI FLEISCHER, *President Bush's press secretary from 2001 to mid-2003, a lifelong Yankee fan*

I think it's a perfect combination of history and geography. Boston and New York are not that far away. So you've got regions like Connecticut, where people can really pick which team they're for. Some towns are split right down the middle. Western Massachusetts is Yankees fans, eastern Massachusetts is Red Sox fans. There's the history of two teams in the American League East, usually going down to the wire.

And the fact that the Red Sox are always close through August, and then they fold. Which is obviously a source of great joy if you're a Yankee fan, and great misery if you're a Red Sox fan.

My favorite season as a baseball fan was 1978. Ron Guidry was 25-3 that year. I was 17 years old, and a huge Yankees fan. I was a freshman at Middlebury College in Vermont. And all of my friends who I had just met in college were all Red Sox fans. They all grew up outside Boston. We all went downtown to a bar to watch the one-game playoff. By the end of the game, all of my best friends that I just had made for about one month I lost. At the end of it, I printed up a sweatshirt that said, "We Beat Boston."

I still remember so much of that game vividly. It was one of the most exciting baseball games in my lifetime. I thought the Yankees were going to lose when the Red Sox jumped ahead. I was just nervous throughout. And then when Lou Piniella lost that line drive in the sun in right field, and then somehow he was able to recover and get it on a short hop, my heart was just boom-boom-boom-boom. Because if that ball had gotten by Piniella, it would have been a disaster. And then Bucky's home run. It was just one of the most intense, tight, exciting ballgames between two fantastic rivals.

And the rivalry in the '70s and early '80s was much more intense back then. Now at Yankee Stadium, they're nice to the Red Sox. I don't understand that. Back then, there were fights all the time in the crowd. I never got into a fistfight over the Yankees. But I remember at Yankee Stadium, if Red Sox fans wore their shirts or hats, they'd surely get beer poured on them or something thrown at them. You could count on it. Similarly if the Yankees went to Fenway, same treatment.

I went to a game the night after there was a giant, bench-clearing brawl at the Stadium. I was in high school, and it was either 1976 or 1977. It was tense. You could feel the rivalry in the air. Nothing happened on the ball field. But what I loved about it was there is nothing better in sports than a good, old-fashioned rivalry. There's nothing better than really having somebody to cheer for, and closely matched teams. And there's probably no better, longer rivalry than the Yankees and Red Sox. Even right now, it's great to be able to wake up and pull out the sports page.

At the White House, our chief of staff Andy Card is a Red Sox fan. I bust Andy's chops a little bit on it. But it's hard to get a Red Sox fan to take the bait anymore, because they themselves are so used to folding in August, that they're reluctant to get into it with you. President Bush is always giving me a hard time when the Yankees lose. He's such an avid baseball fan, as a former owner. He reads the box scores everyday, and he knows his stats. He gives me grief for being a Yankees fan. But he had tremendous pride in what the New York Yankees did in 2001. He threw out that World Series first pitch at Yankee Stadium, just weeks after the terrorist attacks. And when he came in the next morning for a meeting with senior staff, he said, "No matter what happens in my presidency, this will be one of the highlights of it." He could just feel that unbelievable sensation from the crowd, and it was still a moment where America was in post-September 11th seriousness. And they needed a perfect strike. And that was kind of a metaphor for making the country feel good, especially in New York. And he felt that.

He doesn't like the high-payroll approach in baseball. He enjoys busting my chops when it comes to my cheering for the Yankees. He's made fun of me at some public events about the Yankees too. When the Angels came to town the year after they won the World Series, he cited me as a Yankee fan in public remarks in the Rose Garden in front of the players.

I do politics for a living, and baseball is my love. And I would never want to confuse the two. I would hope that fans don't try to attach politics to sports teams. I don't care if the guy sitting next to me is a Democrat or Ralph Nader. If he's cheering for the Yankees, he's one of my guys.

Your heart has to go out to the Red Sox on one level. It's tough and it's frustrating to lose for so long. And ballplayers and fans are superstitious. So after it keeps going on for so long, there's a tendency to try to look for what could possibly be causing it off the field. I wish them luck, I hope they find something. I don't wish them a lot of luck. But I always cheer for the Red Sox to be there going down the wire. I like the rivalry, and I want the rivalry to be strong.

I remember I was in Nantucket in the mid-90s. The Yankees had been in a drought for a long time. It was August, and it was real exciting to pay attention to the Yankees that late in the season because they had a chance to make the playoffs—and at the same time pay attention to the Red Sox. Baseball is one of those sports where you watch the early games with interest, and you watch the later games with passion. There's no better crescendo in baseball than the Yankees and Red Sox.

MICHAEL DUKAKIS, *governor of Massachusetts from 1975 to 1979 and 1983 to 1991, was the Democratic presidential nominee in 1988, when he lost to George H.W. Bush.*

The first game I ever saw was in 1938, I was four and a half, and Lefty Grove was pitching for the Yankees at Fenway Park. Jimmie Foxx of the Red Sox that day hit a ball off the left field wall about as hard as I've ever seen. I mean, you could hear the smack of the ball against the wall. It was only a single, it was hit so hard.

But I also remember going to a Yankee-Red Sox game when I was in the eighth grade, 1945 or '46, when Boo Ferriss was the great young pitching sensation. This was our big excursion toward the end of the school year. The Yankees beat him 14-1. In fact, I can still remember the yellow 13 in the scoreboard during the inning—13 runs in one inning. Then they replaced it with a more permanent white one. I'll never forget that 13. By that time, Ferriss was long gone.

By 1978, when Bucky Dent hit the home run at Fenway Park in the one-game playoff, I was governor of Massachusetts. I could identify with the Red Sox that year. They had blown a 14-game lead, and I lost the Democratic primary to Ed King after leading by 40 points with five weeks to go. Not only was I feeling very upset about that, but then I had to watch Dent hit that pop fly into the screen. Dukakis and the Red Sox both went down the tubes together.

The games between the Yankees and Red Sox are always intense. I get a sense that the players feel it too. No matter who they are, or where they come from, how long or little they've been with the team, there's something

about those series. And my sense is that the Red Sox tend to play very well in Yankees series for the most part, whether it's at Yankee Stadium or here. And they're great games.

Interestingly enough, there's not a regional rivalry between New York City and New England. We're very close—there's a tremendous amount of traffic back and forth, a lot of people from New York go to school up here, and then go down to New York. There's a very strong bond between the two communities in all other respects.

The feelings up here in Boston are far stronger than they are in New York. I don't think there are a lot of people walking around in T-shirts saying "Red Sox Suck" in New York, but you see 'em everywhere here for the Yankees.

Red Sox general manager Theo Epstein's father Leslie spent some time in New York before coming to Boston. When Theo was hired as general manager, some reporter asked Leslie, "You spent a few years in New York before you came up here. Are you a Yankees fan?"

He said, "Oh no, I came to Boston, I fell in love with the city, I've been a Red Sox fan ever since. Being a Yankees fan is like voting Republican." That expresses my sentiments completely.

The Yankees got money—lots of it. And you know, they're out there, and they always do their thing, and nine times out of 10 they win, and all that kind of stuff. Whereas the Red Sox are scrappers and battlers, they've got to live off the land. The Yankees are the establishment.

We live 20 minutes from the ballpark. I'm a fan like everybody else. On the other hand, you always have to be prepared for the worst.

MARIO CUOMO, *former three-term governor of New York, was a minor league out-fielder in the Pittsburgh Pirates organization in 1952.*

Growing up in Queens in the 1930s, you had to be a Yankee fan for the following reason: You had three choices—one was the New York Giants in the Polo Grounds. As soon as anybody told you what the Polo Grounds were, you knew you could never be for the Giants.

Then it came down to the Brooklyn Dodgers or the New York Yankees. Now the Brooklyn Dodgers you immediately had to rule out, because you were from Queens. And therefore you hated Brooklyn. And the reason you hated Brooklyn was they got all of the publicity. If there were movies, and it was somebody from a borough of New York other than Manhattan, it was going to be William Bendix, and he was always from Brooklyn. There was never a story about a guy from Queens. We didn't start getting on the screen until television and Archie Bunker, and we hated it.

That left the Yankees as the only possibility. If you were Mario Cuomo, and they had a guy by the name of Joe DiMaggio, not to mention Frankie Crosetti and Phil Rizzuto, but mostly Joe DiMaggio, then you were for all-time fated to be a Yankee fan. The first baseball game I ever saw was with Joe DiMaggio. And I once saw Babe Ruth, believe it or not, face Walter Johnson. It was a World War II bond rally game, and Babe Ruth made an appearance. He was quite sick. He fouled off a couple, and then damned if he didn't hit one into the right field stands. They started cheer-

ing and demanding that he run; he didn't want to run. And they kept hollering. And so he pulled his cap down the way he would, and did that little short jog he did with his belly hanging out in front of him.

That's the kind of fan I was. I was absolutely mesmerized by the New York Yankees. They were everything and always were.

It's always been the same with the Red Sox. They always cave in August. I love to believe they're going to cave in August. I remember giving a speech at a big convention center, which is down the block from Fenway Park basically. And there was a baseball game that night. I was on my way to give this lecture. When I got there, the guy says, "Well what preparation do you need, Governor? We got a room, we got orange juice, we got this, we got lozenges, we got a bathroom?"

I said, "Is there some way you could set up a television set?" because they were playing the Yankees that night. And I remember mentioning that at the top of the speech and getting booed. Now, people had paid money to hear me speak, but as soon as I started talking about how eager I was to know how my team, the Yankees, was doing against the Red Sox, they started booing! Now, it was mostly playful, but that's what the rivalry has become.

The Red Sox start ahead and cave in August. That's the myth. And that's the myth I don't want to go away. It's like Santa Claus. I'm too old for Santa Claus, but I'm too young to give him up.

Having experienced both the glory of victory and the anguish of defeat, I've learned to enjoy winning. And that creates a decided advantage for the Yankees in my mind. The dominance of the Yankees over the Red Sox makes it fun to be a Yankee fan. It's nice to win. Now, I don't like the way they have won in recent years. I don't like the fact that we can wind up with a team that is three, four or five times as well-financed as other major league teams. And having been signed by the Pittsburgh Pirates myself, I always kind of look over at the National League, and look down at the Pirates in the National League. And they're usually down among the under-financed teams. That's unfortunate, frankly. But that notwithstanding, winning is a lot of fun.

As an avid sports fan, I very seldom went to a ballgame as governor. I really didn't like politicians at ballgames. And if I did go, as I did to a World Series game with Joe DiMaggio, I sat up in the boxes away from the people. Because people don't like seeing politicians, even politicians who had been ballplayers.

I've only been to Fenway Park once, back when I was 15 or 16. And all I could think of, as a right-handed hitter, who hit these monster fly balls—I mean I hit more fly ball outs than any first-year minor leaguer in history, I'm sure. I looked out at that wall, and I said, how unfair it is that I had to play without a Fenway Park. It reminded me of some of the minor league games. It had a little bit of the minor league in it—that kind of aberration. You don't normally see that in a major league park. I haven't been back to Fenway since I was a kid, because it's hard to sit through a whole game if you've been a player. I get edgy.

WALTER MEARS, *Pulitzer Prize winner, retired special correspondent and vice president with The Associated Press in Washington, D.C.*

I learned to hate the Yankees in the summer of '46, at the age of 11. My Dad took me to my first major league game. We sat a few rows behind the Red Sox dugout, and Joe Dobson beat Randy Gumpert of New York. The crowd around us was into the game and growling at the New Yorkers between cheers for Boston, so I joined in, and became a lifetime Sox fan, or as some say, victim.

Within a few years I was frequenting the bleachers at Fenway Park. Seats cost 50 cents, all unreserved, of course, and I could get there by bus, trolley and subway from Lexington for a quarter.

I was in the bleachers often in 1949. I was there for the two Yankee games in late September, after Boston had slipped about five games behind and then won 10 in a row to catch New York. I got to Fenway when the gates opened for the first of them, a Saturday I think, and was frustrated to find empty seats until an hour or so before game time. Both teams were better than today's All Stars—Ted Williams, Bobby Doerr, Dominic DiMaggio, Al Zarilla, Johnny Pesky etc., with Ellis Kinder shaking off his hangover and pitching a great game to pull Boston within one. Not easy against a lineup of Joe DiMaggio, Phil Rizzuto, Bobby Brown, Yogi Berra, Tommy Henrich.

Williams hit one out, DiMaggio [the New York one] answered with a shot over the wall in almost dead center, where the louvers are between the Wall and the bleachers. My favorite play was a foul pop off third base. Berra put his head down and ran at it like a steamroller. Bobby Brown, whose play it was, gracefully positioned himself to make the catch—until Yogi barreled into him, head first, and knocked him down like a linebacker. I can't remember who was batting, only that he got a hit on the next pitch. Boston won and trailed by a game.

Back the next day, with Mel Parnell pitching. I had my bleacher spot where Williams used to hit them, but none came near me. Parnell won his 25th and the pennant race was tied. Each team had one series to go before they met in two final games at Yankee Stadium. Boston went in to those games with a one-game lead, with Parnell and Kinder, who had become the entire pitching staff, going against Allie Reynolds and Vic Raschi.

The result was inevitable. Boston goes ahead, Yankees catch up and win game one. Tied. Same outcome the next day and New York wins the pennant. There was no TV to watch then, and I sat listening to the radio in Lexington as the Red Sox blew it. At 14, it seemed like the end of more than just a season. I remember saying to my father, "I think I'll just go for a walk," which I did, so that he wouldn't see me cry.

I think that's when I learned that there was no point in mourning the Red Sox. You just take it, knowing that they will come close and fall short. (I was at Shea on Bill Bucker night in 1986.)

In 1950, all I wanted for my birthday was an Opening Day seat at Fenway, which I got. Grandstand instead of bleachers that day. I was surrounded by Yankee fans, up from New York. One of them was crowing so much about how good they were that I bet him a dollar I didn't have that the Red Sox would win. Boston went ahead early, and was up, 9 to 0, at one point, when the Bronx loudmouth left Fenway. Good thing for my un-financed bet, as the Yankees came back and kept coming, finally winning the game 15-10. Jack Kramer had just come over from the Browns and was supposed to be the next great thing on the pitching staff. He came in to try to stop the

bleeding and threw his first pitch into the stands just to the third-base side of the backstop.

There was nothing to match '49 until the Bucky Dent game in '78. I only saw TV on that one, but it leads to a story you may or may not have heard. Tip O'Neill went to Rome that fall and saw the Pope. When he came back he was at some function with Yaz and told him the Holy Father had spoken of him. Yaz wanted to know what the Pope had said. Tip replied, "He said, 'How the hell could Yastrzemski pop out in the last of the ninth with the tying run on third?'"

SHERWOOD BOEHLERT, *Republican congressman, Cooperstown, N.Y.*

I grew up in Utica, 233 miles from New York City and about 275 miles from Boston, so I could have turned out a Red Sox fan. There were some Red Sox fans where I grew up. But we had a radio station where the Yankee games were available, but the Red Sox weren't. And I was a proud New Yorker. Boston might as well have been on the other side of the world. And we had a very heavy Italian-American population. My hometown, growing up, was more than 50 percent Italian-American, so Joe DiMaggio was God.

I first really got interested in professional baseball in 1945, when I was nine years old, and have rooted for the Yankees ever since.

The Red Sox just have a history of lousy decisions, lousy breaks, nothing seems to go right for them. They never get a break. I mean, look at what happened to Bill Buckner. If I live to be a thousand years, I'll never understand the sale of Babe Ruth to the Yankees—the Red Sox owner had a greater passion for Broadway than he did for baseball, apparently.

Even then, Ruth was one of the great players of the game. I think a lot of Red Sox fans, and even players, believe in the Curse of the Bambino. And therefore, it adds something extra to the requirement that they excel to overcome the Curse of the Bambino.

I'm not passionate about the Yankees-Red Sox rivalry, even though many Red Sox fans are. It's easy to be more gracious in victory, because we usually come out on top. I can't conceive of a Red Sox fan rooting for the Yankees under any circumstances. I can conceive of Yankees fans—I'm one—who will root for the Red Sox over another team.

I'm glad I turned out a Yankees fan, because I've had a lot fewer disappointments in my life. You might think it's silly for a 20-year veteran of Congress, a committee chairman, who serves on the Intelligence Committee, who deals with big issues, to say that baseball's important to him. But it is. It adds an extra dimension to my life.

My wife and I have a 53-inch screen TV—only because of baseball. We wear our Yankees hats, and we get sunflower seeds, and we get a bowl, we spit 'em in there, we have a couple of beers, and we have fun.

My office is decked out with caps from every major league team, and my reception area is adorned with memorabilia from the Hall of Fame, including autographs on the wall from Hall of Famers.

ED MARKEY, *Democrat congressman, suburban Boston*

As a boy, I remember Ted Williams battling Mickey Mantle every year for the batting championship. It was an epic event every time the Red Sox played the Yankees, even if we knew the Yankees were better, because we knew that Ted Williams was a better hitter than Mickey Mantle. Ted Williams had the most perfect swing in the history of baseball.

I grew up in Malden, just outside Boston, and got into baseball in the mid-50s. When you're a boy, your identity, except for your family, and your church and the school that you go to, is very wrapped up in baseball. So how well your team did against the Yankees defined our athletic consciousness outside of our own neighborhoods.

When we were down at the park, one team was the Red Sox and one team was the Yankees—because they were the team to beat. The pitcher would pretend he was Whitey Ford, and the best player would be Mickey Mantle. And then the Red Sox would be Jackie Jensen and Jimmy Piersall and Ted Williams and Sammy White. And that would become our rich fantasy baseball life—a real-life rotisserie league. To make it interesting, somebody had to be the Yankees. It was easier to convince boys to become Yankees in a baseball game than the Knicks in a pickup basketball game.

I enjoyed the rivalry with the Yankees, and then I rooted for the Yankees against the National League teams in the World Series. I admired Mickey Mantle, Whitey Ford—I admired the individual players. As a unit, the Yankees were the rivals. But I was an American League boy, and I was loyal to my league against the National League. Except I rooted for the Milwaukee Braves against the Yankees in the 1957 and 1958 World Series, because they had been the Boston Braves and so many of them had played in Boston.

When I was 20, I went to a Yankees-Red Sox game at Fenway Park early in the 1967 season. Billy Rohr was pitching. He was coming off his major league debut, an Opening Day one-hitter at Yankee Stadium. And now, we're in Fenway Park, and we're up against the Yankees. The ballpark was electric. This was our chance to vanquish the Yankees. And Billy Rohr in the early part of that season became the symbol of our renaissance—the lefthander we so needed over all those years. He won that game, too, 6-1. By the end of the year he had been lost, but the Red Sox went on to win the pennant.

I was at the Roger Clemens-Pedro Martinez playoff game in 1999. The ballpark was electric with anti-Yankee fever. Again, we felt our redemption was at hand. It was the two greatest pitchers in baseball, matched up in our home ballpark. It was our best chance, looking at our lineup, to break the curse, break this historical inability to beat the Yankees. The ballpark that night was alive with all of the hopes and all of the dreams of every Red Sox fan of all generations. For that one night, they were all fulfilled. We won 13-1. Every Red Sox batter was perfect. It was the dream game of every Red Sox boy or girl, come to life, for one shining moment, one shining night. Even though the Yankees wound up winning the series.

Boston fans love the rivalry with New York. We love the fact that for 50 years, the Celtics have been beating the Knicks. And the Red Sox always have good teams. There was only a brief time, from 1959 to 1966, when the Red Sox didn't have good teams—going all the way back to maybe the mid-30s.

Dan Shaughnessy, who wrote the book *The Curse of the Bambino*, is a good friend of mine. We didn't think of the curse when I was a boy. But I have to admit that by the time you reach 2004, the mystic cords of baseball

history do seem aligned conspiratorially to deny the Red Sox their rightful place at the pinnacle of baseball history.

Of course the Curse of the Bambino doesn't relate just to the Yankees. It relates to the inability of the Red Sox to win the World Series against St. Louis in '46, Cincinnati in '67, and the Mets in '86. New Yorkers might think that the curse only relates to them, but it doesn't.

I had tickets for the Bucky Dent game in 1978, but I was in Washington for congressional business. I should have flown back to go to the game. Even though the Red Sox lost, these are historical moments, and they are the source of great amusement, and storytelling for Boston and New York fans. It's a great story either way. If Bucky Dent's home run wins the game, it's a great story. If Yaz catches it, and the Red Sox win, it's a great story. It's the game itself, it's the love of the highest level of competition between two cities. And it carries over to the Patriots beating the Jets and the Celtics beating the Knicks, or vice versa. There's a special relationship that exists between the two cities.

We have two passions in Boston—politics and sports. At the top of the sports mania is the Red Sox. We enjoy the fact that we actually each year have the hope that this is the year. I'm not exactly sure what Red Sox fans would do the year after we've won. In a way, that's how we view the Knicks fans.

In Congress, the New York and New England lawmakers are constantly betting each other, or talking about the rivalry. But it's all fun. Real-life trumps the make-believe of baseball. It's a good diversion from our more important business of aligning against the right-wing Republicans from the Deep South that want to undermine the New Deal that New York and Boston are so strongly identified with.

Sometimes, when we're in an energy debate, one of the Texans will say, "You're just a Yankee."

And I'll go, "Don't ever insult me that way." They view us all as Yankees.

LESLIE EPSTEIN, *director of the creative writing program at Boston University, novelist, father of Theo Epstein, Red Sox general manager*

I moved to Boston in 1978 just in time for the tremendous collapse and Bucky Bleeping Dent's team. I don't know why, but the Red Sox have sort of become the team for the literati. So there is a literary reason for liking the Red Sox—they are a literary person's team.

I think the reason I liked the Red Sox most of all was that they have been the chief rival of the Yankees, and I so hated the Yankees. I say that rooting for the Yankees is like voting Republican. Yet, I actually like this Yankee team of the last few years. The players seem so nice that they are hard to root against. But I actually don't like the idea of a baseball team like the Yankees spending twice as much money as its nearest rival. I think it's bad for baseball, bad for sportsmanship.

I raised Theo to be anti-Yankee. When Theo got the job as general manger of the Red Sox, the job he was after from the beginning, everyone was saying he was too young and that was the big focus of attention. I told the *Boston Globe*, "What is all the fuss about? When Alexander the Great was Theo's age he was general manager of the world."

My daughter is married to a Yankee fan who is wavering now because of Theo. Our little grandchild has a Yankee boody and a Red Sox shirt.

His getting the position has completely dominated our lives this summer of 2003. I am not a writer this summer. I read three newspapers in the morning and get interviewed a lot, though Theo wants me to get interviewed a lot less. When we go to the games, he will sit 15 rows away and will not acknowledge that he has a family there because it makes him look younger.

Someone asked me, "What will Theo do if he is able to get the Red Sox to win the World Series?" I said, "Maybe he will be the first Jewish Pope."

DAN SHAUGHNESSY, Boston Globe *sports columnist*

The rivalry is a big part of the fabric of the community in New England. But the rivalry is a bit one-sided. I am always reminded of the scene in *Casablanca* when Peter Lorre turns to Humphrey Bogart and says: "You despise me, Rick."

And Bogart says, "If I gave it any thought I probably would." Sometimes I think that's how Yankee people, fans and players think about the Red Sox. I just think that the Red Sox fans think more about the Yankees than the Yankee fans think about the Red Sox.

My book *The Curse of the Bambino* came out in 1990 and that particular phrase in popular use started with the book. But probably the reason that Boston has not won is that they have not been good enough.

I am not as a journalist a fan of either team—I root for the story. In my lifetime the

'78 playoff game was the highlight of the rivalry. The Red Sox had a two-run lead in the sixth, seventh inning. This guy Bucky Dent had hit four home runs all year. This guy hits a pop fly that would not have been a home run in any other ballpark. It is a signature moment in the rivalry.

BILL MADDEN, New York Daily News *baseball writer*

Passions seem to always run a bit freer whenever these teams are involved. It was really at fever pitch in the late 1970s with Graig Nettles, Bill Lee, Munson, Reggie, and Billy Martin would always add to the mix.

It has been a little weird for me to see players like Clemens, Boggs, in and out of Yankee-Red Sox uniforms or the reverse as the case may be. Before the era of free agency these two teams hardly ever in recent years traded with each other.

JIM KAAT, *former pitcher, current broadcaster*

Now it's a fan's rivalry. Once you play, players get caught up in the fans and they really inspire the players to feel it.

ALAN SEGAL, *sportscaster for WBZ Radio, Boston*

Basically for the first 14 years of my life growing up in Boston and seeing my first game in 1959—the rivalry to me was that the Yankees were always good and the Red Sox were always terrible. That all changed in 1967 with the Impossible Dream and the Red Sox winning. That year was also the first baseball fight I ever saw: Rico Petrocelli and Joe Pepitone. I was 14 at the time and that really got me into the rivalry. By 1978, I had graduated from Northeastern and had been in the media for a year. I gotta admit that Monday afternoon brought tears to me. I had just come home from Temple and the family was gathered around the TV set watching the game. Joy in the beginning when Yaz hit the home run and a lot of bad emotion at the end when Yaz made the final out. I was thinking—the Red Sox are never going to beat this jinx, this team, the Yankees.

It has really said something that players from the Red Sox have had to go to New York to win a world championship. But the new owners in Boston in some respects have heightened the rivalry. They want to beat the Yankees so much that they have taken the franchise and the city with them.

The rivalry is bigger and more important for the Red Sox fans to beat the Yankees than it is for the Yankee fans to beat the Red Sox—not that they don't want to beat them. But it is an obsession here in Boston. It is not an obsession in New York.

ALEX ARIAS, *former Yankee infielder*

What's funny about playing in the rivalry is that you saw it on TV or from the stands all your whole life, and then you're in the thick of it. I think to the players, we just go about our business playing the Boston Red Sox. But the fans are the ones that really make the rivalry.

The fans in Boston are pretty nice. I think every time a Yankee team goes there, the Boston fans want to beat them, but I think they have a lot of respect for the team. You know, they want a lot autographs from the ballplayers.

MIKE BARNICLE, *former* Boston Globe *columnist*

Baseball isn't a life and death matter, but the Red Sox are.

JOHN CHEEVER, *novelist*

All literary men are Red Sox fans. To be a Yankee fan in literary society is to endanger your life.

ROGER CLEMENS, *pitcher, Red Sox and Yankees*

In the mid-to-late '70s, it may have been more intense. But when the teams are at the top of the division battling for first place, it makes it more of a rivalry. The fans enjoy it. They get into it for sure.

When you're not out there working, and you're in the dugout looking around, there are an awful lot of good fights in the stands. The fans are pretty intense about it.

MICKEY MCDERMOTT, *former Red Sox pitcher*

Everybody knows God's a Yankee fan.

AARON BOONE, *Yankee third baseman*

Like Derek told me, "The ghosts will show up eventually," (talking about the home run he hit to give New York the 2003 American League championship).

TONY CLONINGER, *former pitching coach Red Sox, former Yankee coach*

The fans love it. The players say it's another game, but I have a tendency to think that they put a little emphasis on it. I think the fans put more of an emphasis on it than the players do.

It was mixed emotions coming over to the Red Sox after about a decade with the Yankees. But people will tell you once they cross that line, they'd run over my mother to try to beat you. It's a professional sport. And if you walk between those lines, you want to beat whoever you're playing. A lot of the guys on the Yankees are like my family.

No matter what the players said, the Yankees always respected the Red Sox, They had the type of ball club that no matter what the standings, they played hard. It might have outwardly seemed like just another game, but the Yankees respected that team a lot.

The fans at Fenway were always cordial toward the coaches. It was the players they were on. We called that fence behind the bullpen the "Steve Howe fence" because he got into it with a fan out there once, and the next time we came in, that fence was up.

DAVID CONE, *pitcher, Yankees and Red Sox*

I've seen the passion of this rivalry on a first-hand basis, and it's one of the reasons that attracted me to sign with Boston. Without a doubt, the players feed off that rivalry. We see it, we see the passion in the fans and how much it means to them.

BOBBY DOERR, *former Red Sox infielder*

It's not so much being knocked down, but it's the idea of knocking me down for something someone else did. That's what gets me. *(May 2, 1948, Doerr was knocked down by Yankee reliever Joe Page after Ted Williams and Vern Stephens hit back-to-back homers.)*

CASEY FOSSUM, *former Red Sox pitcher*

It seems like the division always comes down to us and the Yankees in the American League East. Pretty much every time we play them, it's to gain ground on them or to move ahead of them. It's a big game when we play them because we're always the top two teams. It's not that we hate the guys or we hate New York, but we want to win. It's pretty intense.

Everybody steps it up a notch. I know when we played those guys, it seemed like Roger Clemens especially reached back extra. Sometimes you watch him dominate, and then the next game in Toronto, I don't even know if he lasted five innings. For him, having played for the Red Sox, and them not resigning him, I think it might be a little more incentive to stick it to us every time.

The best game I saw was in 2001 when Mike Mussina had a perfect game until the ninth inning, and David Cone probably pitched one of the better games of his career, too. It was at our place, and we were pretty much eliminated from the playoffs, but still, we wanted to beat the Yankees. It was probably the most well pitched game on both sides that I've ever seen. It was just so intense. There were two outs in the bottom of the ninth, and Mussina had a perfect game. I'd never seen everybody on the top step of the dugout, just hanging on the pitch. That's when Carl Everett broke it up with that bloop single over the shortstop.

As a pitcher, when you look at their lineup, they've got one of the best in the league. So, you've got to concentrate on everyone. You can't take any one of their guys for granted. It makes me focus more, it makes me concentrate more knowing that all those guys are superstars. You can't lose your concentration, or you'll pay for it. It seems like the games between the Red Sox and Yankees are always good games, and rarely is there a blowout.

HARRY FRAZEE, *former Red Sox owner*

No other club could afford to give the amount the Yankees have paid for Babe Ruth. And I do not mind saying I think they are taking a gamble. The Boston club can now go into the market and buy other players and have a stronger and better team than if Ruth had remained with us.

NOMAR GARCIAPARRA, *Red Sox shortstop*

I grew up in California, so I didn't know much about the rivalry, until I got to the Red Sox, where you just feel it. It's definitely a huge rivalry, it's definitely there, one of the bigger ones in sports. You can feel it when we play there, you can feel it when they play us at Fenway. When we had the playoffs in '99, I felt the intensity—when we played there, how crazy it was. It was a fun series to be a part of. I don't worry about comparisons to Jeter. I don't compare myself to anybody, or worry about comparisons. I'm just a small part of the team.

JASON GIAMBI, *Yankee first baseman*

I'm excited about being part of this series. It's all it's cracked up to be. I'm excited just coming to the ballpark. I know the fans get it going when the two teams go head to head.

JEREMY GIAMBI, *Red Sox DH*

Until you really experience it, you can't explain it. Weeks before the media starts talking about it. You are not concerned about the next two teams coming it. It's the Yankees and the rivalry on the weekend. It's more than playoff atmosphere. It's probably more like a World Series atmosphere—18 games a year.

With Jason and me there is an added twist—brother vs. brother. It's a throwback to the days of backyard baseball.

STEPHEN JAY GOULD, *writer, philosopher*

I finally came to realize the unique nature of Red Sox pain—not like Cubs pain (never to get there at all), or Phillies pain (lousy teams, though they did win the Series in 1980), but the deepest possible anguish of running a long and hard course again and again to the very end, and then self-destructing one inch from the finish line.

BILLY HERMAN, *former Red Sox manager, 1964-1966*

Boston has two seasons: August and winter.

GEORGE V. HIGGINS, *author*

The Red Sox are a religion. Every year we re-enact the agony and the temptation in the Garden. Baseball's child's play? Hell, up here in Boston, it's a passion play.

STEVE KARSAY, *Yankee pitcher*

When you sit in front of the TV as a youngster, you watch the Yankees play, and you kind of understand what kind of rivalry there is between those two teams. I was six years old when Bucky Dent hit the home run in Fenway Park that beat the Boston Red Sox in the 1978 playoff game. To see him hit that ball and deflate the Red Sox was fun for a New Yorker. You're always pulling and rooting for your team to go as far as they can. But I grew up in Flushing, Queens, near Shea Stadium, so most of my friends around the neighborhood were Mets fans.

I think the rivalry is as intense as ever. With us going to Boston and Boston coming to Yankee Stadium, the fans really get into it. Every series is electric. And every series is put above all else. If you're playing the Royals, it's not really a big deal. If you're playing Cleveland, it's OK. But when the Red Sox come to town, the stadium's packed, and it's fun to play in those games. It's like playoff-type atmosphere.

I get a little more juiced for those games. You get caught up in it a little bit. You get caught up in the excitement, and how fans react. They love when you beat Boston, and it's a good feeling when you're out there getting the job done. It's a hostile environment in Fenway Park. I have friends from Boston, they're Yankee-haters. Just walking into the stadium, walking into the town, you know the eyes are all over you and you're not very well liked in that part of the woods.

One game, I was warming up in the bullpen and they threw a crab—a big stone crab, with a big "B" on its back for Boston. It was the symbol of Boston. You're just sitting there, and the next thing you know, you see this big crab come crashing down. You get stuff thrown at you all the time, but you try not to pay too much attention. The security's good down there, and they try to keep 'em off us as much as possible.

One game stands out in the 2002 season, where we wound up coming from behind a couple of times at Yankee Stadium. We won the ballgame when a base hit to right field got by Trot Nixon. I think that was a big game for us. They had a chance to sweep us in that series, and then we ended up winning two out of three and really deflating their chances of making a run for the playoffs.

I've heard people say that Babe Ruth gave it a little kick to the right so it would miss his glove. It's a little joke that we talk about in the locker room. The more people talk about the Curse of the Bambino, the more you start believing it. It's kind of a myth and a legend, but it's kind of coincidental that they haven't won a World Series since they sold him to the Yankees.

DEREK JETER, *Yankee shortstop*

Any time you play Boston, especially when both teams are in first and second place, people are gonna build it up.

CHUCK KNOBLAUCH, *former Yankee infielder-outfielder*

I know I was really excited the first time. You hear about it in the media. The fans are all into it. That was the big thing for me the first time we played in that series against the Red Sox.

BILL LEE, *former Red Sox pitcher*

The Yankees—Billy Martin's brown shirts.

GRADY LITTLE, *former Red Sox manager*

I think it's probably more intense than any rivalry in all of sports. Both teams don't necessarily have to be winning. Both teams could be fourth and fifth in the Eastern Division of the American League, and the rivalry between the Yankees and the Red Sox would be the same.

The fans and the strong media markets in both cities make it the great rivalry that it is. The intensity level of both clubs rises up a level when they play each other, whether it's at Fenway Park or Yankee Stadium—it doesn't matter. And you can visually see it. The coaches are just like the players. It's exciting, and it means so much to a lot of people.

DEREK LOWE, *Red Sox pitcher*

It's different now than when teams had the same guys for 10 years. Teams have 15, 18 new guys every year. The media wants us to have a rivalry, and if all 25 of our guys were from New England and their 25 guys were from New York then you'd have one. But we've got guys from Montana.

The players definitely take the rivalry seriously, but the game's different now. Before, it was more of a hatred between players. But now, everyone's friends. So it's a different type of rivalry. They're always fun games to play, and for the fans, it's by far the biggest game of the year.

When we play the Yankees, you're nervous—but it's a good nervous. Especially in Yankee Stadium—there's no better place to play than there. The crowd is so electric, and it takes time to get used to pitching in those games. If you never did it before, you'd be extremely nervous and maybe couldn't settle down. I've had some very bad games there. I really haven't pitched that good there over the course of my career. When things are going south, they can go south in a hurry there. It's a different type of atmosphere. It definitely can affect your pitching. You speed up, maybe you're not the same, you get going too fast, the adrenaline takes over and you try to overthrow. All of those things come into play. And they're such a veteran team, they take advantage of it, and they get you most of the time.

The best game I ever saw was a Pedro-Clemens game a couple of years ago, 1-0. It was as close to a World Series game that I can relate to. When you pitch against them, it's a challenge, because they're probably the best team that's been around for years.

LOU MERLONI, *Red Sox infielder*

I grew up in Framingham, Massachusetts, a big Red Sox fan. In 1978, I was a seven- or eight-year-old kid, that's when I was first getting into baseball and became old enough to watch the games. That whole season, the way they battled each other, made me realize how intense this rivalry is. When they played that one-game playoff at the end of the season, I was at home watching it with my dad. When Bucky Dent hit that home run over the Green Monster, I just couldn't believe it—that Bucky Dent, a guy who doesn't hit any home runs, and he's the guy that hits that home run, with all of the other guys they have in that lineup.

You just knew you had to hate the Yankees. When you started rooting for the Red Sox, you were told right away, you gotta start hating the Yankees. If you're a Red Sox fan, you hate the Yankees. It's that simple. At the same point, as much as you hated them, you respected them. I used to love to watch Willie Randolph and Graig Nettles and those guys, and Reggie Jackson.

When the Yankees were coming to town, those dates were circled on everybody's calendar. The city is different; they're just different games. I remember my dad trying to get tickets every time the Yankees played, and we'd go to those games, and they were just so much fun. Then I'd watch them play the Twins, and it would just totally be a different game, a different crowd, a different energy in the stands.

At Yankee-Red Sox games, there'd be a crowd of Yankees fans fighting in a section over from you, and people yelling and screaming and throwing stuff at each other, and my father always trying to keep an eye on me, not let me go too far, because he knew how crazy those games could be.

I remember everybody hated Reggie Jackson. They'd boo him to death. You'd get into it and just follow the crowd. Those were the great days, when the rivalry was really hot, before the free agency, every year the same guys battling each other. Now, it's more of a competitive rivalry. These days, in the game of baseball, you play against teams with guys that you have played with in the past. So it's tough to really go out there and hate them personally. That was more back in the '70s, it was more of a hatred. You know, they played them every year, and they were sick of it, the same guys. Now, the rivalry is more out of respect. To the fans, it's still a heated, heated rivalry.

But there's no doubt, the Yankee-Red Sox games are still more intense than other games, the players get up a little bit more. I love playing at Fenway, but my second favorite place to play is Yankee Stadium. I just know, when we go to Yankee Stadium, how crazy it is, how much fun it is. When the game is over, you look back and say, "That's the way every single game should be." It's great to have those fans so into it. It's unbelievable. I love it. There's nothing better than being involved in a Yankees-Red Sox game. Helping the team beat the Yankees—that's one of the best feelings.

My rookie year, 1998, we were winning 11-1 at Yankee Stadium in a game that Pedro Martinez was pitching. They came back, and it was 11-8, and it was bases loaded and one out in the eighth inning. Pedro was already out of the game, and Dennis Eckersley was pitching, I was playing second. Jorge Posada hit a one-hopper, line drive up the middle. I dove, I caught it, and from the ground flipped it to Nomar, and he turned a double play. We ended up winning the game. It was one of the better plays I've ever made.

And it's always more special when you do it against the Yankees, because you know the intensity, the rivalry, the attention of those games, you just have that every time you go out there and play.

I think Nomar and Jeter—those two are discussed everywhere you go. You hear Jeter's better, you hear Nomar's better. And the rivalry heated up even more when Roger Clemens ended up in New York, because he was here for so long. And now the Red Sox fans have Pedro, and he's the man. When those two get together, it's like no other game.

GRAIG NETTLES, *former Yankee third baseman*

And now for the varsity. *(A snide remark made by Nettles at Fenway Park after the Red Sox had completed infield practice and New York was set to take its turn.)*

PEDRO MARTINEZ, *Red Sox pitcher*

I wish I'd never see them again. I wish they'd disappear from the league. I don't believe in curses. Wake up the damn Bambino, maybe I'll drill him.

MEL PARNELL, *former Red Sox pitcher*

I was known as a Yankee killer. My best year against them was 1953. I beat them five times and shut them out four times. You just played a little harder against them.

JOHNNY PESKY, *former Red Sox player, coach and manager*

Never sell the Yankees short. They played great the last three months. They'll never play that well again as long as they have assholes. *(As Red Sox coach in 1978 when the Yankees went 52-22 and won the pennant.)*

MORDECAI RICHLER, *author*

In Boston we believe the world will break your heart some day, and we are luckier than most—we get ours broken every year at Fenway Park.

CURT SCHILLING, *Red Sox pitcher*

I just know that I am looking forward to having a ball in my hand whether it be Fenway

Park or Yankee Stadium and pitching in that first game as a Red Sox against the Yankees.

I like the thought of playing in the biggest rivalry in sports in front of some incredible fans. I have been a part of a Yankee matchup with other clubs, but the Yankee-Red Sox rivalry transcends sports. It's so much bigger than everything else in sports. Being a part of that was certainly an attraction to all of this.

I want to be part of bringing the first World Series in modern history to Boston, I guess I hate the Yankees now.

GEORGE SCOTT, *former Red Sox first baseman*

Of course it's embarrassing. *(Speaking about the 1978 season.)*

MIKE STANLEY, *former Yankee and Red Sox player*

It was not something I was aware of until I actually put on the pinstripes for the first time, and I got that *full* sense of it. Unless you're from Boston or New York, you don't really understand it until you grow up in it or play on one of these two teams. It's so intense and so electric, you can just walk around a ballpark, and if you don't know which team is in, you'll be able to tell when the Yankees come to town. And the same goes for the Stadium. People mark off these days on their calendar, and they're going to miss work if it's in the middle of the week—it's so intense. You can sense it as soon as you come to the ballpark. Extra media on the field and in the clubhouse—you know it's a Yankee-Red Sox series.

We played them in '99 in the ALCS. That was as intense and as great a series as you can

possibly get. The rest of the times, they're just hot, intense battles. No brawls or anything like that.

Here in Boston, they're a little bit more frustrated. People in New York have a lot more firepower to throw at you if you're a Red Sox fan going there, a little bit more confidence there. Here, there's more hatred toward the Yankees because of what they've been able to obtain the last few years.

TIM WAKEFIELD, *Red Sox pitcher*

You can't get caught up in the rivalry between New York and Boston. It's just a matter of us winning ballgames, no matter who the opponent is.

JERRY REMY, *former Red Sox player, broadcaster*

As an announcer I love these games. The buzz in the stadium is different. You know the attention in the whole city is different. You know the atmosphere is different. You know the ratings will be great.

MIKE STANTON, *former Yankee and Red Sox pitcher*

When I got traded to Boston in 1995, we were nine games up when the Yankees came to town, and everyone was on the edge of their seats. I was like, "Guys, we're nine games up!" But it was the Yankees. It didn't matter.

JOE TORRE, *Yankee manager*

Here we go again. Believe me, we don't look forward to it. This is a rivalry no matter whether we're fighting for fourth place or first place. I was with the Cardinals for six years, and five more as a manager, and the Cubs rivalry was pretty special. But I don't think it possesses the intensity that this one does.

JASON VARITEK, *Red Sox catcher*

We play 'em so many times, that every game we win is a memory. It's made up by the fans. They're the ones that create it, and they bring us into it. We enjoy playing the Yankees. We enjoy the competition. They've been at the top of our division since I've been here. To be the best, you've got to beat the best.

If we can find a way to take a couple of titles from them, it'll be even stronger.

TED WILLIAMS, *former Red Sox outfielder*

If I could run like Mantle I'd hit .400 every year! (*After he lost the 1956 batting race to Mickey on the last day of the season.*)

CARL YASTRZEMSKI, *former Red Sox outfielder*

I'd say Mantle is the greatest player in either league.

STEVE WULF, *ESPN columnist and* Sports Illustrated *writer*

The Yankees belong to George Steinbrenner, and the Dodgers belong to Manifest Destiny, but the Red Sox, more than any other team, belong to the fans.

TOM ZACHARY, *former Red Sox pitcher*

I gave Ruth a curve, low and outside. It was my best pitch. The ball just hooked into the right field seats, and I instinctively cried 'Foul!' But I guess I was the only guy who saw

it that way. (On yielding Babe Ruth's 60th home run)

DON ZIMMER, *former Red Sox manager, former Yankee coach*

I didn't even know there was a big rivalry until I came to the Red Sox. But I found out soon enough. I was coaching at third base in 1974 at Yankee Stadium, and the fans were throwing so much crap on the field that I had to put on a helmet for protection. The players don't really hate each other. It's really a rivalry of fans.

In the '70s, it was real hatred. The rivalry is definitely not as intense as it used to be. Even the fans are not as boisterous as they were in the '70s, even though we'll fill the house at Yankee Stadium and in Boston. Today it's still a good rivalry, but in '76, '77, '78, there were some players that hated each other. It was like a war. Now, there's no hatred between the players, mainly because you don't even know who half the players are, the way baseball switches around. In the '70s, the Yankees and Red Sox had the same teams for seven years. Maybe once in a while, one guy would be changed.

I don't think Fisk and Munson got along that well. But I didn't get caught up in that. Who was I going to get mad at—Bob Lemon, the Yankees manager, one of the nicest guys in the world?

MARK SHERMAN, *Associated Press reporter, Washington, D.C.*

In the early '70s, when I was about 10 years old, my brother took me to a twi-night Yankees-Red Sox doubleheader at the Stadium.

By the later innings of Game 2 it was really cold. And there was a lot of drinking going on in the stands. So many fights broke out that night that the NYPD was removing people through the dugouts. That's the only time I've seen that.

The Yankees-Red Sox one-game playoff in 1978 took place on Rosh Hashanah. Which meant that: one, I'd be home from school and two, something would have to give because we normally didn't watch TV on Rosh Hashanah, a very holy time in the Jewish religion. That morning at synagogue, all the talk was about the game and someone said that surely God wouldn't want us to miss it. And so it was decreed (not by the rabbi) that we had been given a special dispensation to watch the game, from the first pitch to Nettles's catch of Yaz's foul pop to end it.

THOR HANSEN, *New York City*

I'm a Yankee fan. They're winners. The way the Red Sox play is like the repeated sailing of the Titanic.

AL SCHOCH, *Minneapolis, Minnesota News Network anchor*

When Luis Gonzales's flair hit the back of the infield dirt at the BOB, I knew my love affair was over. I had followed the Yankees seemingly forever. I grew up with Horace Clarke, cut my teeth on Lou Piniella, celebrated with Reggie Jackson, suffered through the days of Steve Kemp, and was rejuvenated with Paul O'Neill.

But living in Minneapolis, just a short hop from the Metrodome, it was such a kick to follow the forever-undermanned Twins. Now they were winning again, with the same group of guys that came up together in the late 1990s. Remember the joy we all felt when Roy White and Bernie Williams began to win after so many years in the system and on struggling teams? Same thing here. Sure, I don't miss a game when the Yankees come to town for their one trip a year, but my loyalties are now with the local nine.

I got married in May 2002, and our honeymoon back east took us to Boston, Portland and Cape Breton Island in Nova Scotia. A trip to Boston means a game at Fenway Park. I saw the schedule. Yankees and Red Sox. There were no arguments. After settling into the Holiday Inn Fenway, I arranged a pair of seats from a ticket broker down Brookline Avenue. My seats, front row, next to the right field foul pole.

I did not wear Yankee merchandise to the game. It was my honeymoon, and I wasn't going to tempt misfortune. The 11 people tossed from the bleachers alone showed I made the right choice. The game rocked along and the BoSox went up 2-0 on Mussina. No big deal. I was enjoying the moment, and the Yankees were just wallpaper. Then Soriano hit one toward right that Trot Nixon got a glove on and deflected into the bullpen. Posada hit one into the screen. Something deep inside was taking over. Instead of watching with amusement, I reverted to my old self and got behind the Bombers one more time. Ron Coomer hit one onto Yawkey Way. The Coom-dog. Former Twin who played his lone All-Star game on that very field. This was a night for the ages.

After Giambi hammered one off the center field camera wall for three more runs, I was in full throat. My Yankee roots had taken over. The Red Sox fans had no answer, and I let them know. Eighth inning, Ventura hits for Coomer. A soaring drive down the right field line. I gaze up into the starless night and watch the flight of the ball directly over my head, around the foul pole, into the hands of half-a-dozen fans. Three runs. I jumped up, stood on the top of the wall, wrapped my arm around the foul pole and pointed to everyone where the ball went.

That night on ESPN, you can see this guy in a white long-sleeved T-shirt, wearing a maroon and gold Minnesota cap (the "M" stood for "married" that week), waving Ventura's blast fair. My days following the Yankees through thick and thin are over. But being a Twins fan still allows me to hate the Red Sox.

BARRY I. DEUTSCH, *Ft. Lauderdale, Florida, banking consultant*

I was, and always have been, a Yankee fan, but I could never work up a major dislike of the Red Sox. My start is right around 1948-49. I think the Sox came in second by one game in 1949 and I remember how exciting it was but, as I sort it out, there were four reasons behind my failure to hate the Red Sox. Most important, I knew they would never win. I just knew that their role in life was to be the losers. They were supposed to threaten, but they could not win. Second, Dominic played for the Red Sox back then and the idea of rooting against any DiMaggio just seemed wrong to me.

Then there was the supporting cast. For me and my friends, who we liked and who we did not like had a lot to do with their baseball cards and how the guys looked on those cards; and on their names. The Red Sox had guys like Birdie Tebbetts, Johnny Pesky, Buster Stephens, and Ellis Kinder, and those were cool names.

Finally, there was that other team, the one I really did not like—the Cleveland Indians. They had beaten us in 1948 and they were good in 1949, too good. I just hated Bob Feller. He was the guy who made our guys look bad. And Bob Lemon. What kind of name was that? And Mike Garcia. Some people said he was an even better relief pitcher than Joe Page. They were wrong.

Now, as an adult who travels a lot and gets to see ballgames all over, I have a new reason for not hating the Red Sox. The sidewalk food outside of Fenway provides the best dinner available in the majors, and that includes the sushi in Seattle, the bratwurst in Milwaukee and the barbecue in Baltimore.

MIKE NOLA, *Tallahassee, Florida, Shoeless Joe Jackson Virtual Hall of Fame webmaster*

Being from the South...can't say that I like the Red Sox. But, I can say I HATE the Yankees. As a Northern friend of mine once told me, "Real Yankees root for the Red Sox!" I personally just root for anyone playing the Yankees.

LAURA L. MINICHIELLO, *Hanover, New Hampshire, fan*

My father, who is in nursing home in Gloucester, Massachusetts, has been a Sox fan for many years (he grew up in Boston as a young boy and used to save up his money and go to Fenway to watch games). In 2002, on Father's Day, Fenway opened to dads and their kids. Well, my brother, Mark, from Connecticut (also a huge Sox fan due to dear old dad) came up with the idea of bringing dad to the park. My brother asked me to meet him at noon at Fenway. I found a parking spot and as I turned the corner to the park, there is my brother and in a wheelchair (with a Red Sox flag on the back) is dear old dad. We ran him around the bases in his chair and had him "play" every position on the field. His favorite was shortstop Nomar. As we left the park that day, my dad said it was one of the best days of his life.

My boys (Nate and Matt) are big Sox fans. Loving every weekend game they can watch (because they can stay up late because there is no school the next day). In April 2002, as a surprise to my sons, I awoke them very early on a Sunday, to take them to the Yankees/Red Sox game. We arrived at the park around 6:30 AM and waited for the box office to open (to purchase standing room only or obstructive view tickets) at 9:00 AM. My husband stood in line and the boys and I decided to walk around outside of the park and look for something to eat. I ran into a security guard and chatted about the upcoming game and the fact that this was the first time my boys had ever been to Fenway. This guard said his job was to escort the players into the parking lot and field as they entered. He was kind enough to call my boys over when Shea Hillenbrand arrived at the park. However, I had nothing to give my boys to have Mr. Hillenbrand sign. Searching my purse, while my boys are pleading for anything to have Mr. Hillenbrand sign, I found a bill from our propane company. My boys, not caring what I had, handed Shea the company bill and he

signed it! Just as soon as Fenway opened to allow the crowds of people in, we jumped in line. We found our seats, which were the "obstructed view" seats. Since it was 45 minutes before the start of the game, I saw the seats right down behind the batter were empty. I thought I could bring the boys down and have them sit there and watch the players warm up and when the owners of the seats arrived, we would move. Although my sons are huge Sox fans they were watching the Yankees warm up. My son, Matt, who had just turned 7 at the time, was so impressed with Derek Jeter. There was a crowd of individuals yelling out 'Jeter sucks!' repeatedly. My sons couldn't understand why anyone would be so rude.

All of a sudden, out of my seven-year-old, whom I should mention is only 46 pounds, yells: "Derek Jeter, you are the best!" Mr. Jeter stopped what he was doing and came over. "Thank you for telling me I'm the best' Enjoy the game.' It was a moment Matt (and Nate) will never forget.

AL SCHLAZER, *Clermont, Florida, former college athletic director*

Growing up in Brooklyn and rooting for the Brooklyn Dodgers was very special to me. I was privileged to be able to be a true Dodger fan who to this day still bleeds Dodger Blue. Getting out to Ebbets Fields to root for the Bums, being a part of the Happy Felton Knot Hole Gang, the Dodger Symphony, Red Barber on the radio, and all the exciting players that played for them in that era was something very special.

I quickly learned to hate the New York Yankees because they always were able to deflate my ego as they constantly overpowered the Dodgers. The only team in the American League, I felt was strong enough to compete with the Yankees was the Boston Red Sox. Therefore, I decided to become a Red Sox fan and rooted for them to knock off the Yanks. I was sure that Ted Williams, Bobby Doerr, Dom DiMaggio, Vern Stephens, Mel Parnell, and company would do the job.

Unfortunately, it didn't come to be, even when the Red Sox held a 14-game lead in 1978 they finally succumbed to the Bronx Bombers in a one-game playoff.

They had some great battles though, and the rivalry has proven to be outstanding. Their constant battles have left me with many memories. Better than 50 years has passed since the time of my Yankee hatred, but has lasted through the many years.

The New York Yankee pinstripe uniform was the uniform that I grew to hate at an early age. I even learned to dislike WPIX, Channel 11, in New York, because the Yankees were on that station. What made it worse was that I had to learn all the numbers of the players as the Yankees never put their names on the jerseys.

I learned to dislike No. 9 the most because that player was tough and mean, an ex-marine. That player was Hank Bauer, the right fielder. It always seemed that he would come up in a key situation and come through with the big hit.

I did meet him in Orlando not too long ago. He actually was a super guy, but I did tell him how I disliked him all these years for what he consistently did when he played against the Dodgers. He had a good laugh. It wasn't funny back then if you lived and grew up in Brooklyn.

RUSS COHEN, *Glassboro, New Jersey, communications director, Sportsology.net*

As a tortured Met fan I turned to the Boston Red Sox as my alternate team to root for. They were a likable bunch with Carlton Fisk, Carl Yastrzemski, and Dwight Evans to name a few. I was no fan of the Yankees but my dad was. Now the battle lines were drawn in a classic 'I know more than you do, Dad' contest. Both of us were looking forward to the Yankees-Red Sox one-game playoff on October 2, 1978 (one day before my 15th birthday). This game had particular significance since the Red Sox had a 14-game lead over the Yankees on July 19, and I was loving life until the Yankees caught them!

We both sat down to watch the game each hoping that the other's hopes would be squashed. My dad was so confident that the Yankees were going to win this game that he decided to work on the roof midway during the game. After the weak hitting Bucky Dent homered over the Green Monster I ran outside to tell my dad, he smiled and kept on working. From that day on I learned that rooting against the Yankees usually put me in the losers' circle.

ROB EDELMAN, *Amsterdam, New York, author of* Great Baseball Films

Growing up in Brooklyn in the late 1950s and '60s, my awareness of the Boston Red Sox—let alone any Red Sox-New York Yankees rivalry—primarily was linked to the movies. I knew that Jimmy Piersall played for the Red Sox as much because of the film *Fear Strikes Out* as for his presence in box scores or on baseball cards.

Babe Ruth did not begin appearing on screen (*Headin' Home, The Babe Comes Home, Speedy, The Pride of the Yankees*) until he started swatting homers in New York. *Fear Strikes Out* aside, movies were made about Yankees (starting with *Rawhide, The Pride of the Yankees, The Babe Ruth Story* and *Safe at Home!*), rather than players from Boston. Mickey Mantle, Roger Maris and Yogi Berra—not Carl Yastrzemski, Frank Malzone and Pete Runnels—had cameo roles in the 1962 Cary Grant-Doris Day comedy *That Touch of Mink*.

Around 1978, I attended my first Yankees-Red Sox game. I do not remember the date. But I do recall that Yankee Stadium was packed. Ron Guidry was on the mound for the home team, and pitched with pinpoint control. Of course, the Yankees won.

Outside the stadium, t-shirts with "Boston sucks" emblazoned across the front were being hawked by vendors. I thought they were a novelty and bought one, for perhaps $5 or $10. After the game, I went to a party in Brooklyn's Park Slope with the shirt under my arm. To my amazement, one of the guests offered me $50 for it. Thinking I unwittingly had purchased what might become a valuable artifact, I declined his bid. Today, I have no idea what became of the shirt.

I recalled this incident a couple of years ago at Fenway Park, when I noticed quite a few citizens of Red Sox Nation wearing "Jeter Sucks" t-shirts. What fascinated me was that the Red Sox opponents that day were not the Yankees, but the Toronto Blue Jays.

MIKE WEBB, *Willingboro, New Jersey, fan*

I live near Philadelphia now, and am thus forced to follow the local teams in the four major sports. But I always tell people I am a Red Sox fan. It's almost like a religion—you're born into it, and first place, or last place, or whatever place—you're in it. I don't think it came from my dad, exactly. I don't know where it came from. It's just there, and it feels like it's always been there.

But it's hard to hate the Torre Yankees—they're a great bunch of mostly solid professionals. Who could not love the way Derek Jeter plays the game? As a baseball fan, I respect the Yankees and what they have accomplished. But I will never, ever, root for them, ever.

My second favorite professional team is whoever is playing the Yankees...I had to reuse a friend's line when the Yankees and Mets were in the World Series—"Root For? I can only hope the stadium roof falls on both of them!"

My first memory of any kind concerning The Great Rivalry is the time I was charging across my front lawn coming home from school, banging open the screen door, running to the television. Yaz is up—runners on base. Gossage pitches—he pops it up. HE POPS IT UP! Of course, through volume after volume of baseball books, I now know about Yaz in the stretch in '67, Lonborg on two days' rest, Pesky holding the ball, Aparicio stumbling around third—all that stuff.

But it started in 1978 for me.

Besotted with a girl, I went to a party the night of Game 6 in 1986. I came home to watch the extra innings. I don't remember much except the funereal gloom at school the next day, and my friends wouldn't talk to me after Game 7.

I had told them the Mets were a good team, watching them on WOR on cable all summer and they didn't believe me. My friend Josh was not a sports fan, and he died before they got to the World Series. He asked me why the Red Sox were so bad, and I told him the young pitchers, like Clemens and Bruce Hurst, would be ready soon and would help them win. I was right, but he was gone.

There's something about coming up the ramp at Fenway and seeing the field. It's a green that's too green, and the uniforms are painfully white. My wife liked to joke about John Valentin. "Doesn't his wife know how to wash his uniform?" because he always seemed to be dirty.

Seeing Pedro pitch at the height of his power in 1999 was truly, truly awesome to behold. Just toying with people, making it seem like they'll never get a hit. Makes you feel like you saw Cy Young or Walter Johnson. Pedro's relief outing in 1999 in the playoffs was awe-inspiring. Changeup after changeup after changeup. That playoff loss didn't sting as much as some of them have. Yes, there were horrible calls. But great teams overcome. These Red Sox aren't great—not yet.

As a Mets fan, even I was sucked in to the intense Yanks-Sox rivalry. The irrational extent of the Sox fan's hatred of the Yankees overshadows and negates the heated rivalry with the Mets. Do the names Mookie Wilson and Bill Buckner ring a bell? I was at Fenway Park during the 2000 season for a series vs. the Mets. Outside the gates they were selling "Yankees SUCK" t-shirts. When I reminded the chowderheads that they were playing the Mets, they disdainfully replied: "It's Noo Yawk, same difference." If they can't tell the difference between a Mets and Yankees fan,

no wonder they can't ever win a championship!

SKIP MCAFEE, *Columbia, Maryland*

I was a nine-year-old Yankee fan in 1947 when my father took me to my first game at Yankee Stadium. I wore my mini-Yankee pinstripes with No. 3 on the back. Upon entering the stadium, I was first struck by the greenness of the field (I believe this is a common happenstance for first-timers). We had reserved seats, but somehow my father had arranged for me to approach the visitor's dugout before the game to meet with Red Sox manager Joe Cronin and slugger Ted Williams.

What I will always remember is: one, the congeniality, kindness, and warmth displayed by Ted when we shook hands and talked briefly, and two, how conflicted I felt walking back to my seat knowing that I was supposed to root against the Red Sox. I don't recall the outcome of the game, but I do recall how a legendary figure took the time to talk to a youngster as if nothing else in the world mattered at that moment.

RICHARD "LEFTY" SEPULVEDA, *fan*

Well, I was at one game and had fun yelling out "Boston sucks'" like so many other Yankees fans do. Of course, I mean this in jest only. But some folks take this term and the rivalry a bit too seriously. I had had a few brews and was using the comfort station and was just on my way out when some Yankee fan had something really naughty to say about the Sox. A Sox fan objected to his comment.

Then, just as I opened the door to leave the comfort station you could hear "WHACK!" The Yankee fan slugged the Sox fan and there was some shouting as another Sox fan got pummeled. Mind you, these rooms have a cavern-like sound effect so that the "whack" and the shouting can sound VERY loud when they occur.

Boy am I glad I got out of that room when I did! I wonder whatever happened to those poor Sox fans!

Let's have some fun but, come on, don't ever take that stuff so seriously!

I attended about two or three Yanks-Sox games at the Stadium and each time there were several fights. Nope, that's not my idea of fun. But I'm sure other folks will confirm that those games generated loads of action outside of the ball field!

Oh, those Yanks-Sox games had more action outside of the ball field than a dispute between the Hatfields and McCoys!

FRANK, *Boston, Massachusetts*

My wife Kathy works at the airport and one day recently a visitor came in and, while he was signing in, she noticed he had this really nice ring. It said "Red Sox World Series."

"Oh, you played for the Red Sox?"

She looks down at the signature but didn't recognize the name; it said: "Bob Montgomery." He used to be a catcher for the Sox.

Montgomery said, "Sure, I used to play with Carl Yastrzemski, and Carlton Fisk."

"Oh, I wish my husband were here, he loves baseball." Kathy says.

"Oh, is your husband a Red Sox fan?" Montgomery asked.

Kathy laughs and says, "No he is a Yankees fan. Mickey Mantle was his favorite as a kid. He was born and raised in Boston and he was always a Yankee fan."

Just then Montgomery reaches into his briefcase and says, "I have something for your husband." He whips out a photo and asks, "What's your husband's name?"

"Frank," she says.

Then he writes, "To Frank, Thanks for all your support. Bob Montgomery."

And the great part is anyone who sees this picture thinks I am his biggest fan or that we are old pals and go way back. "Thanks for all your support."

How do you like that? Insulted by a big leaguer.

HARRY KAPLAN, *Cranston, Rhode Island, sales consultant*

I have been a diehard fan since I was seven years old. I go back to when Boston blew the two-game lead in 1949 to the Yankees. I am a frustrated Red Sox fan who does not believe in the Curse of the Bambino. I think it is the curse of Tom Gawky. This is the reason for all the chokes over the years. It is the man paying back the red flops for racial discriminations—giving Jackie Robinson a token workout in 1945 and not letting him take a shower at Fenway, the statement made by a confirmed racist Pinky Higgins as the manager in 1950 that no black man would ever play on his ball club. They treated Jim Rice, Luis Tiant, Reggie Smith and Ellis Burks like they were pond scum.

My greatest Red Sox moment was the sixth game of the World Series when Fisk hit the home run in the 12th inning, plus the catch by Dewey Evans in right field.

My greatest Yankee-Red Sox moment was the fight between Thurman Munson and Pudge Fisk at Yankee Stadium. Those were the good old days.

They had the second highest payroll in 2002 and they still fell apart in August and September. But I think the Red Sox today are on the right track with the new owners who did us all a favor and got rid of jerk Dan Duquette.

DAVE PINTO, *Longmeadow, Massachusetts, fan*

This seems like a silly one, and I don't know if anyone else will recall it. On August 16, 1985, Joe Cowely vs. Oil Can Boyd at Yankee Stadium. The Red Sox had taken a 4-2 lead in the seventh on Rich Gedman's second home run off Cowely. Yankees come back to 4-3 in the eighth with a home run by Pags, then tie it in the ninth inning on a single by Hassey, bunt by Randolph, and a single by Pags.

We then go to the bottom of the 11th. Score still tied at four, Crawford pitching for the Sox. He gets Mattingly and Griffey Sr. to ground to second base. Winfield doubles. They intentionally walk Pasqua. Butch Wynegar then draws a walk to load the bases for Willie Randolph. The Red Sox bring in Bob Stanley. Randolph then takes four pitches, each of which he falls away from as if they are about to hit him. The umpire falls for this, and calls each of them a ball. At least one of them was a strike. It was brilliant on Randolph's part, to think he could drive in the winning run without taking the bat off his shoulders!

ARTHUR DILLON, *Lebanon, New Hampshire, procurement specialist, Hypertherm*

As a Midwesterner born and raised I'm a Detroit Tigers fan and a fish out of water in the midst of "Red Sox Nation." On August 4, 2001, I was in New York and got good seats for the Yankees-Angels game. It was my first visit to Yankee Stadium. Taking our seats I knew I was in the home of the greatest baseball franchise the world has ever known. Looking at the grass, I realized that Tigers Ty Cobb, baseball stars and gentlemen Hank Greenberg, Charlie Gehringer, and my own childhood hero—Al Kaline, had played right there, right in front of us, against Ruth, Gehrig, Ford, and Mantle.

Roger Clemens pitched that day, Derek Jeter played shortstop, and New York won 5-4. As long as they're not playing Detroit, I can be a Yankees fan.

HANK FESTA, *Studio City, California, freelance writer*

I was too young to care in '67. But I lost it back in '75 and '86. No doubt the bad luck and the jinx lives on and is as supernatural as the legacy of the Kennedys. Beantown baseball in October is like that childhood crush that never came to fruition. But you mature into adulthood, you get over it and fall for other teams. Not one to let the curse spoil my overall enjoyment of the sweet science, I switch fan support in the postseason. And teams I adopt like the Angels tend to win it if Boston can't, which is bittersweet.

Because you can never go home as they say, one should not define one's fan persona solely by the record of the hometown team.

Especially if you were born in one place and raised in another. A Bostonian bicoastal transplanted L.A. native, I remind Big Apple fans that the Dodgers won it all in 1963, the year I was born in a sweep of the Yanks in a Fall Classic pitching clinic featuring what may well have been the greatest team performance on the mound ever in October. So there.

But Boston has become more famous for losing than the Yanks are for winning. Boston today isn't the same hub of the universe I grew up in. Thus my loyalty has suffered the slings and arrows of time, distance and age.

I've always said that if they can't win in real life, then Boston might as well in the movies. Then again, an epic screenplay I penned is still gathering dust. Too many big shots in Hollywood are Yankee fans. Like the Sox chances, the jinx never ends—no matter what our field of dreams.

STEVE SILVA, *Boston, advertising professional*

October 14, 1999: AL championship Game 2 at Yankee Stadium, Yankees 3, Red Sox 2. Even though I'm a third generation Red Sox fan, this was my first trip to Yankee Stadium. My best friend, a Red Sox fan from Boston who relocated to the City, got us a pair of tickets. I threw on my hat and jacket and just bee-lined down "95" right to the Bronx and into the Stadium's parking lot.

I met my friend Jim across the street from the Stadium, in a very small bar next to venerable Stans. It was more like a pizza shop that sold beer, but it was wall-to-wall people before the game. They put your beers in paper bags so you take them out on the street.

I had my "1967 American League Champion" jacket on with a traditional Red Sox "B" cap. We were leaning on the counter, having a beer in the bar when suddenly the chant "assHOLE... assHOLE" kept getting louder and louder behind us.

I asked Jim, "Who the hell are they yelling at?"

He answered, "You."

I was then hassled a bit and warned "not to wear that shit into the Stadium." But I did anyway. A third-generation Red Sox fan isn't going to wear his team colors during his first trip to Yankee Stadium for a playoff game? Give me a break. Turned out their bark was worse than their bite. They tossed a few items my way, but no real trouble on that 45-degree night until Paul O'Neill drove in the winning run with a seventh-inning single as New York's playoff win streak reached 12 games.

Boston reliever Rheal Cormier said: "Unfortunately, the ball went behind the shortstop where nobody was." Pedro Martinez and the Red Sox went on to crush the Yankees and Roger Clemens in Boston for game three, 13-1. But the old towne team lost the next two, and the series. Same old song and dance for long-suffering Red Sox Nation.

MATT ZELEK, *Boston, software professional*

I am a Massachusetts-based Yankee fan who attended the Yanks/Sox playoff game in '78. I was lucky enough to have a friend who was at Fenway the day before. He left the game to stand in line at the box office in about the fourth inning, when he realized that the Yankees were going to lose to the Cleveland Indians and Rick Waits (for about the sixth time that year) and that the Sox were going to hold on and win their game. That set up the one-game playoff the following day at Fenway. I quickly accepted his invitation—despite the punishment of being benched for the Tuesday Harwich/Nauset high school game for missing Monday practice.

There was so much tension in the stands as fans were anxious but also nervous for the game to start. I remember seeing Ron Guidry warm up in the bullpen before the game. He was pitching on three days' rest—can you ever imagine Pedro volunteering to do that—and could not have weighed more than 145 pounds at game time.

Yet in the bullpen, I remember the warm up catcher, I think it was Elrod Hendricks, having to wear a mask since Guidry was firing bullets. In fact, between him and Goose Gossage I don't think a pitch was thrown at less than 90 mph all day, since neither pitcher was gonna get beat in this game on a changeup or hanging curve.

Other great baseball memories that day were: a Yaz clutch rip on a Guidry fastball early in the game—he did not choke as some say on his final at-bat. He was lucky to make contact on that Gossage fastball the way the shadows were at that time.

Sweet Lou's blind stab in right field, I was 50 feet from him, and it was a blind stab as I am sure he only grabbed it from the sound of it about to go by his ear.

The eerie silence after Bucky's home run and my feeling of euphoria at seeing all the annoying Red Sox fans' hopes crushed. Nettles catching the final out below his left shoulder as if wanting to prolong the Sox fans' agony as that pop-up hung in the air for what seemed an eternity.

To this day, despite all the World Series championships and other great Yankee moments, for me, that Nettles catch off the shoulder ranks as the best.

BRAD TURNER, *Providence, Rhode Island, semi-retired businessman*

As a former diehard Sox fan, some of my worst moments were watching late-inning leads disappear as Yogi Berra poled low balls into the Sox bullpen. It was a time of good hit, no pitch, so they often got our expectations up only to see the Yanks prevail. And then they sent us Joe McCarthy to be our manager! And we reciprocated by sending Sparky Lyle.

SAMUEL PERSON, *Bonita Springs, Florida, retired accounting professor*

My recollections of the Yankees and Red Sox are not so much about rooting for one against the other, but rather the excellence both have demonstrated throughout the years. This is said notwithstanding the ironies that have given rise to the "Curse of the Bambino," as if there could be such a thing.

I first became a serious baseball fan in 1941, the year two all-time greats—one Yankee and one member of the Boston Red Sox—were leaving marks unparalleled to this day.

No doubt the excitement generated by Joe DiMaggio's 56-game hitting streak and Ted Williams's march to a .406 batting average cemented my love for the game.

Despite the fact that I lived in Brooklyn from 1940 on, I was always a Yankee fan. Perhaps this is so because I had been born on 172nd

Street and the Grand Concourse in the Bronx—literally in the shadow of Yankee Stadium.

Of all the accumulated memories of Yankee-Red Sox twists and turns, the 1978 season stands out the most. During that summer, my wife and I took our sons to Cooperstown. We stayed overnight, and I vividly recall hearing a radio broadcast of a Yankee game. As I turned off the radio following a Yankee loss, it was with the belief my season was ending early. Little did I know one of the greatest comebacks in baseball history would soon unfold!

It will be ages before fans forget that the Yankees roared back, and weeks later, having closed all the ground, the Yankees went to Boston for the one-game playoff for the 1978 American League pennant. It culminated with Bucky Dent's home run off Mike Torrez (a Yankee the year before) to win it for the Yankees.

And so it continues. In 2002, the Red Sox destroyed the Yankees early in the season, only to collapse as summer waned and autumn arrived.

There is ample reason to believe the rivalry, the tradition, and the excellent competition will continue as long as baseball does. And, yes, maybe the Red Sox will win a pennant again.

FRANK A. POSSEMATO, *Boston, teacher, writer*

As far as I can see the rivalry is a fairly one-sided one. For many seasons, in many decades, the Yankees have had other things,(like World Series games) to worry about, while the Red Sox cling to the rivalry—

sort of like how every school wants to be rivals with Harvard.

Even during slower years Yankee fans had the memory of not all that distant world championships, while you would be hard pressed to find someone with fond memories of the Sox 1918 win in Boston. The Red Sox are like Sisyphus, endlessly pushing the rock up the hill year after year, soldiering on in the face of disappointment and somehow, on a good season, getting people to hope with them. So "statistically" I would think the Yanks won the rivalry long ago. But, if baseball, or sports for that matter, can be seen as a metaphor for life, for the human condition, then the Red Sox are the best team in baseball: better than the Yankees, better than anyone.

The Yankees are great if you can leap tall buildings in a single bound or win 114 games in a season. But for anyone who knows what it's like to wait for next year, the Red Sox are your team.

JOE SINGER, *Boston, Massachusetts, fan*

It's not a real rivalry—it's just petty jealousy. I've always liked the Yankees. When I was a little kid the Yanks were awesome, they had Reggie Jackson and Ron Guidry, and this was in the pre-Clemens days so who did the Sox have on that? I mean Jim Rice was the man, but come on! The Sox are my favorite team though, but the Yanks are my second favorite and I don't see anything wrong with that.

These people with their "Yankees Suck" T-shirts ought to be wearing a T-shirt that says, "I'm a townie jackass with no class and an IQ I can count on my fingers" instead. Seriously, if they spent as much time complaining about the Sox's owners as they did blaming the Yanks maybe the ticket prices wouldn't be so high.

SAM BERNSTEIN, *Brooklyn, New York, retired furrier*

The Yankees are still the rich man's team. They're snobs. Boston is human and not so good, but they can surprise you. I do not like George Steinbrenner. He's too haughty, too high and mighty. He represents what the Yankees have always been like. There's too much arrogance there. I like the Red Sox because they remind me of an old-time team. Their uniforms, their ballpark, is the way baseball was. The Sox are natural. The Yankees are plastic, a store-bought team with a man who thinks he's a king who owns them. That's why I root for Boston and root against the Yankees even though I've lived almost all of my life in New York City.

CIRCO TUDISSCO, *Brooklyn, New York, fan*

One thing I could always count on was watching the Bronx Bombers on a Sunday afternoon. Pop and my brothers would tune in to hear the Scooter describe the action. Rizzuto would suffer along with each strike and give a sincere "Holy Cow" when the Yanks homered. Needless to say, so did my loyal Yankee family.

Even though I have been brainwashed by Yankees pinstripes all my life, I admire the Boston Red Sox. Their attitude toward baseball is the way a team develops character. Boston's teams seem to play for the love of the sport; they have heart and great fans. Boston and New York fans are die-hard, hard on a player when he fails and right there to cheer when he succeeds.

TOM GENEROUS, *Wallingford, Connecticut, fan*

I was a senior at Brown in the spring of 1963, when the Sox were somewhat interesting after years of poor teams. Yaz, Radatz, Mombo, as I recall, made the team a contender for a good part of the season. That was also the year of the police dog—Birmingham, Alabama, most notably, but even the Providence police used their dogs against Brown students who walked downtown the wrong way through the bus tunnel one May evening on a lark.

Not to be outdone, the Boston police cleared the bleachers one night of a Yankee game with its K-9 corps. Several of my college chums and I had gone to the game, and were sitting close behind the Sox bullpen. We were drinking beer, to be sure, since you could and we did bring our own in those days. But we were shocked when some creeps in the center field section began throwing empty cans at Mickey Mantle. As the game progressed, the cans became empty. They made what I have to admit was an entertaining sound and sight as they tumbled end-over-end, spewing foam and fizz en route to Mantle of the incredibly thick neck. I forgot exactly what intervening steps were taken, but in the final moments of the incident, I think we were standing on the field in the right field corner, watching the Boston blue with dogs on leash, sweep back and forth, until no one was left in the bleachers. We scrambled over the fence into the right field sections, and we watched the rest of the game, but not before we had shouted, "Birmingham, Birmingham" at the cops.

The event was born of several conflicting things: some genuine hatred of the Yankees and Mantle, some Fenway bleacherism and all the besotted and bestoned things it has always meant, and some puckish joy at the sound and sight of a flying beer can.

ANONYMOUS

I remember those Yankee fans back at school, at Harvard. They were small, peculiar-looking people with horn-rimmed glasses who had never played any sport and had to identify with a superior force. They'd come in to the TV room at Lowell House and emit shrieks of glee whenever the Yankees scored.

SCOTT RUSSELL, *New York City, fan*

I was an 11-year-old growing up in the South Bronx who cried when the Dodgers were pulled out by O'Malley to California. I asked my father, "Is there any owner in baseball who looks at the sport the way I do?" My father answered, "Tom Yawkey." And the Red Sox have been my team ever since.

WALTER C. ROBERTSON, *Hempstead, Long Island, New York, fan*

I have been a Yankee fan since 1932. Red Sox-Yankee games have always been fierce competition. I remember the fight between Jake Powell and Archie McKain in 1938. I remember in 1939 how the Red Sox, led by their manager and shortstop Joe Cronin, beat the Yanks five straight at the Stadium to cut the lead to a few percentage points. But the Yanks went on to win their fourth straight flag.

Then there were the Williams homers and the Williams shift, with George

Sternweiss, the second baseman on the Yankees, playing in short right field. But of all the games played, I will always remember Saturday, October 1, 1949—Joe DiMaggio Day. Each fan was given a photo of Joe. I still have mine. Allie Reynolds started for the Yankees against Mel Parnell, with the Sox needing just one win in the final two games to clinch the pennant. Earlier, Parnell had made the statement that the batboy could pitch tomorrow, the last game of the season.

The Yankees won on October 1, and on October 2 they won again, and one of the pitchers used by the Red Sox was not the batboy but Mel Parnell. I always thought about Joe McCarthy. He could have been only the second manager to win the pennant with three different teams. A playoff in 1948 and the final game of 1949 denied him the chance.

BILL MAESFIELD, *Staten Island, New York, fan*

I'll always come to Yankee Stadium and wear this Boston cap. I'm a New Yorker but as a very young kid the first game I ever saw was at Fenway Park. I fell in love with the team, but each year they come up short. I get beer thrown at me. I've had a couple of fights. I don't take the hat off. Some day the Red Sox will really come through.

BO FIELD, *Kearney, New Jersey, fan*

I hate the Yankees and love the Sox. One of my friends got hit right in the mouth at the Stadium for wearing a Boston cap. I still wear mine. When I leave the stadium, I put it in my pocket. I made earrings with the pictures of Red Sox on them in 1968. I'm afraid to wear the earrings to Yankee Stadium. I put them on after I'm in my seat. I live about 50 miles from Manhattan. I've never been to Fenway, but I'd love to be there one day to see a game. I love the Red Sox because of Ted Williams. He was my idol growing up, and I think he was the most marvelous person God ever put on the face of the earth when it comes to baseball. Ted made me a Red Sox fan.

ERIC PORTNOY, *Brookline, Massachusetts, sales*

The great thing about moving from Rhode Island to Brookline, Massachusetts was our new proximity to Fenway Park. It was nothing for my brother Bobby and I to get on the trolley and make the 10-minute ride to the ballpark, to see as many games as we could especially when the Sox play the Yankees. Our grandfather had been a big Sox fan since he came to this country in the 1920s. He remembered everything, all the old stars, even when Babe Ruth played for Boston. So it's been kind of a family tradition rooting for the Red Sox. It's rooting for New England as opposed to New York.

SAM SKOLER, *Quincy, Massachusetts, former businessman*

I came to America in the 1920s. Almost immediately I became interested in baseball, especially because of the Boston Red Sox. The team was not too good, but sitting in the bleachers in Fenway Park was a thrilling experience. I went with my friends, my sons, later on with my grandsons. In the beginning, I sat in the bleachers, but as the years moved on, I moved closer and closer to home plate. Half of my family settled in the Boston area, the rest in New York so there was always this rivalry over where we chose to live. The Yan-

kees represented New York, a little too big, a little too proud. Boston is my kind of town. The Red Sox are Boston.

ANONYMOUS, *Lynn, Massachusetts*

I grew up in Boston and one of the reasons I have detested the Yankees so much is that they have beaten us with so much regularity. Every time the Yankees beat us here in Fenway, it's special frustration. The Dent home run was the worst moment.

GARY WILLIAMS, *Bergenfield, New Jersey, fan*

Every year I go to Yankee and Red Sox games at the Stadium and at Fenway. I wear my Boston cap. At the Stadium people always yell at me. They tell you to shove it and do this and do that with it. They say we are losers, that the Red Sox don't win. I'll always remember that lucky pop fly home run by Bucky Dent. I'll never forget it as long as I live, I won't. I cried all winter. It could have been Fred Stanley or somebody else. It was a cheap fluke thing. I grew up around here and the Yankees have always been so successful I can't understand why younger people go for them. I know it runs in the family but they have been standing for too much success for too long. I just like to see the little guy win. The Red Sox should win for a change. It burns me the way free agents all seem to want to play in the city of New York—why?

JIMMY JOHNSON, *Raleigh, North Carolina, fan*

I don't say I hate the Red Sox. I just have always been a Yankee fan. My father was a Yankee fan, and it's more or less been a tradition. Yankee, Yankee, Yankee! I was seven years old before I knew there was another team. Mickey Mantle was my hero. He could play.

DAN MACKIE, *feature writer and columnist,* Valley News, *West Lebanon, New Hampshire*

My name is Dan. I'm a Red Sox fan. I am powerless over my addiction.

It began with a few baseball cards in the early 1960s in Cranston, Rhode Island. Some of my friends had Mickey Mantles and Whitey Fords. Ptooh! Yankees. I tossed them away and hoarded Pumpsie Greens and Eddie Bressouds.

I never thought this would be a problem. I thought I could control it. In early years, I did. The Red Sox stunk. Most years they finished just ahead of Cleveland, who I think started every season with 20 losses. The Yankees were good, like General Motors, IBM, the American Way.

I shoulda known better than to dabble with the Red Sox. They last won a world championship in 1918. Sometimes it seems there's a better chance they'll find crop circles cut in Fenway's green, cursed grass than a championship banner.

But like I said, I'm a fan. I started to like a player or two: Pete Runnels, the sometimes batting champ, Dick Stuart, Dr. Strangeglove, a hard-hitting, hard-fielding first baseman. I started to feel there's a teeter-totter balance to the universe. The Red Sox lose. The Yankees win. One sits low. One sits high.

Through the years my regard for the Red Sox grew and my contempt for the Yankees, who sat atop the teeter-totter, simmered. The Sox almost won in 1967 and 1975, and then, in 1978, assembled a powerful team built around Yaz, Jim Rice and Freddy Lynn. Luis Tiant, contortionist, hula dancer, big-game pitcher, was a master of deception. Bill Lee, a leftie who tossed anti-establishment philosophy and junk ball pitches, the Zen splitter, was terrific, too.

By 1978 I was a grown person and could have chosen another path. But I read the box scores, listened to the radio, watched games on TV. I got in deeper and deeper.

Anyway, this is all history, like the fall of the Roman Empire, or Enron. Despite being 14 games behind the Sox in July of '78, the Yankees, who had a terrific team of their own that year, caught up, fell behind, caught up again, and forced a one-game playoff. Bucky Dent won it with a wind-assisted popup that barely got out of the infield, and then, through a harmonic convergence—the Jet Stream, Babe Ruth in heaven, a minor earthquake in the Philippines, gravity from Mars and Pluto, a kid stomping his foot in the Bronx, high pressure over the Northeast, a jet landing at Logan Airport, a pigeon flapping its wings, a whale spouting off the coast of Finland, a heavy lady in the third row waving her program and yelling "Get Out, Get Out," all these forces and more aligned—a little white ball floated further and further, up and over the Green Monster, light as a feather, then fell like a stone into the net, the home run net.

I hit bottom. I swore them off. I said I'd turn my life over to a higher power. Unfortunately, the higher power turned out to be Roger Clemens. He was a false god.

I am a Red Sox fan still. I hate the Yankees. A Yankee loss is as good as a Red Sox victory. That's sweet bile, I know, but it's all I have. And I mainline optimism, addictive as opium, every spring.

It comes on in a rush: Hey, the Sox are looking pretty good. They're looking real good. The Yankees' pitchers look a little long in the tooth. If Pedro's healthy and we pick up a big bat or two...

My name is Dan. I'm a Red Sox fan.

SHEILA C. PERRY, *Orford, New Hampshire, fan*

It's hard to believe a girl from the Boston suburbs could have given birth to a Yankees fan, but it's true. The good news is I'm batting .500 because the Yankee fan, Tyler, has a younger brother, Eric, who is a Red Sox fan.

Tyler is now 12 and an honest-to-goodness Yankee FAN. I guess I read too many books on Lou Gehrig, Babe Ruth, Jackie Robinson and Joe DiMaggio in his formative years. The Movie *61** didn't help either. Who couldn't like Roger Maris and at least respect Mickey Mantle in the film?

Yes, I took Tyler and Eric to Fenway Park when they were little. They've already been three times in their short lives. I didn't get to go into Fenway until I was 13! But I got to ride the "T" into Kenmore Square with my brothers and we sat, of course, in the bleachers. I told my sons about the '67 World Series heartbreaker with "Yaz" and the '86 heartbreaker. I've told them about the great Red Sox traditions with the Green Monster and the bleacher fans.

Both boys love baseball. They both play in Little League. Ty's the only Yankee fan in the extended family. He's earned the respect of several aunts and uncles because he won't waver in his mindset. Sad thing, it's not like he has reason to. The Yankees are a good team—the best money can buy. But, baseball isn't really all about winning. It's about hope in the spring and angst every fall for what might have been. Yeah, right.

In 2002, I took my boys, one of my brothers and my godson to Yankee Stadium. The parking was cheap! Ten dollars in New York as opposed to $25 in Boston. We had the best seats $15 could buy; we were up behind home plate—three decks up, and one row from the very top! But we could see the pitches much better than from the bleachers at Fenway Park. The crowd around us was very nice. I mean, we didn't irritate the many Red Sox fans who also traveled to see their team. And, we didn't irritate the Yankee fans because there was one of them in the middle of us! And yes, we all cheered as loudly as we could for our respective teams.

Eric kept dancing thinking maybe he'd be on the "Fan Cam" that Yankee Stadium is famous for. But really, I wasn't surprised when he wasn't—he had on his No. 5 Garciaparra Red Sox shirt and a Red Sox baseball hat. I had been warned about letting him wear his fan clothes; "Are you sure it's safe for him to wear that in New York?" Sure it was! He was with a kid wearing a No. 2 Jeter shirt and a Yankee cap.

At the game, there was quite a bit of bitter changing back and forth between fan groups. Several fans, on both sides, were—deservedly—thrown out of the stadium. After an hour and a half rain delay (we didn't care, we were under the roof and dry) we watched our Sox beat them Yankees.

It was beautiful. This game was the first game in a series of "must wins." However, Boston lost the other two (or was it three?) games it needed to win to stay in contention.

So, despite our glorious moment, the Yankees eliminated us from the playoffs and Tyler had the last gloat.

The problem is Red Sox fans remember moments of glory; Yankee fans have so many moments of glory, they can't keep them straight!

I don't pretend to like the Yankees for Tyler's sake. I admire Derek Jeter, Joe Torre and Jorge Posada. I do like Don Zimmer (but he has some Red Sox history, so that's OK.) When I do laundry, often the No. 5 Garciaparra shirt is swimming in the suds with the No. 2 Jeter shirt.

Baseball is fun, it's exciting. It's heartbreaking. It's entertaining! Hey, you've never heard my father try to explain to Tyler why Ted Williams was a better player than Babe Ruth or Mickey Mantle. Tyler is just as tenacious as his grandfather. The "conversation" is fabulous to listen to.

As hard as many in my family have tried, Tyler won't convert; we've given up. I suppose dogged determination is a good trait in a child. If you can be a Yankee fan in my family, you can be a Yankee fan anywhere. We cheer loudly whenever the Yankees lose. He loves it when the Red Sox blow it—which they've done every year of his young life. There is always next year, though.

DAVID GOODFRIEND,
Arlington, Virginia, fan

One game that really sticks in my mind was in 1979, a summer Saturday game, the year after Bucky Dent's home run. I went with my best friend, who I still play with in a band, who I call "old man." We drove to Fort Lee, New Jersey, took a bus across the George Wash-ington Bridge, and then waited for the subway.

I'm a lifelong Yankees fan, but "old man" was wearing a Red Sox hat. I was only half-kidding when I told him that when we switched trains at 145th Street, he was in for some shit. He thought I was joking, but as soon as we stepped on the train I took a hard right to get away from "old man."

The whole train exploded with obscenities directed at him. To his credit, he stood his ground, but I could tell he was a little shook up.

That game was the last time I saw Thurman Munson. Right before the game, as he stood behind home plate having a catch, he positioned himself so he was right next to the Red Sox rookie catcher, Gary Allenson, who was listening intently and nodding. It looked to me that Thurm was giving one of his archenemies some baseball advice. And that was the first thing I thought of when Munson died that summer.

The game was a tight one, Luis Tiant on the hill for the pinstripes against his old teammates. It was a tie game in either the eighth or ninth when Carl Yastrzemski came up for the Red Sox. I will never forget it. Tiant hung one, and before Yaz even swung, the whole crowd just groaned—they knew it was gone before he even started to swing. Yaz parked it in the right-field stands and the hated Sox won. A great day, except for the score.

I have always said my biggest regret in life was not watching the Bucky Dent game with "old man," but I did get some satisfaction a month after the 1978 season. My car broke down before a gig, and we had to use "old man's" car. His trunk was filled up, so we had to clean it out before we could load the equipment. The trunk was just piled with old newspapers—the *Washington Post* sports sections for the entire months of September and October. All the stories of the Sox collapse, day by day. I will never forget going through those papers, one by one, and torturing "old man" by reading the game accounts out loud. I didn't get to see the Bucky game with him, but that was some sweet revenge reading those papers.

There used to be a great rock 'n' roll club across the street from Fenway Park called the Boston Tea Party. The first few times I went there the Sox fans began taunting us for our long hair (at one point in my life I did have hair). We walked right over and beat the living shit out of the Sox fans. This happened twice, although I remember the second time a couple of Sox fans said something about our hair and jumped us. We beat the shit out of them, too. After that, I do not ever remember getting bothered at the Tea Party. I think the word got out to the idiot Sox fans that maybe these long hairs were not pacifists and should not be messed with.

Anyway, as a longtime Sox-hater I do have one little soft spot in my heart for them. I have won a lot of money through the years thanks to the Sox!

CECILIA TAN, *Cambridge, Massachusetts, writer*

The Duel: May 28, 2000, Boston Red Sox at New York Yankees. Yes, my friends, I was there. It was always going to be a special game, because all Yanks/Sox battles are. But it was also a rare Sunday night game, on a three-day weekend, slated to air nationally on ESPN. The hype machine was at full steam, especially since it became obvious as the game neared that the pitching rotations would pit former Red Sox ace Roger Clemens against the current man of that title, Pedro Martinez. Cy Young winner vs. Cy Young winner, new generation vs. old. Hope for the Red Sox Nation vs. their cast-out champion. Add the fact that the Red Sox and Yankees were see-sawing the lead in the AL East.

It might have been May, but the game was as important as October. Think back for a moment what the world would have been like if the Red Sox had kept Roger Clemens, instead of driving him to Toronto. They can't pin that one on Harry Frazee.

Clemens had been having a Jekyll and Hyde year with the Yankees. His previous start he had been touched for six eared runs in only four innings. Earlier in the month the lowly Tigers had lit him up for six runs in four and two-thirds. But he'd also posted some wins that month, one with nine strikeouts, once giving up only one run. No one knew which Roger Clemens would be on the mound that night—the seething mass of aggression who challenged every hitter, or the psyched-out pitcher who had been driven from the Fenway mound when facing Pedro in the previous year's American League Championship Series.

Meanwhile, you could be sure which Pedro you were going to get. Pedro saves his Jekyll/Hyde act for the days he doesn't pitch. On his off days, he's a jokester, always making his teammates laugh and goofing around in the dugout. But on the days he starts, Pedro is all business. And in May 2000 he had not yet acquired the reputation for fragility that marred later seasons with the Red Sox. He was the Ace of Aces, the best pitcher in baseball.

The later-than-usual start time had not

deterred any of the crowd as every ticket was sold and 55,339 turned out to witness the match up. The excitement in the air made it feel like a postseason game. Thousands of flashes went off on the first several pitches, for each pitcher, like some holiday fireworks show.

It looked from the very first inning like the seething-mass Clemens had decided to make an appearance. Jeff Frye led off the game with a comebacker right to Clemens who leaped from the mound to get it. Right fielder Trot Nixon came next and after looking at a ball, had a heated verbal exchange with Clemens. Clemens gesticulated and yelled— it was later reported that he shouted, "Get the bat off your shoulder, kid!" Nixon didn't take kindly to the remark, but let the record show that he actually did look at strike three, so perhaps Clemens was merely trying to give a rookie some helpful advice. Yeah, right. Daubach popped up to Jeter to end the top of the inning.

Now the riddle for the Yankees became how to solve Pedro Martinez. It appeared the Yankees wanted to keep it simple. Just try to hit the damn ball. Knoblauch did so, but back to the first baseman. Jeter had more success, poking a single. O'Neill also hit the ball hard, but, sadly, into a 6-4-3 DP. Score 0-0.

By the time the ninth inning rolled around, the score was the same. In the top of the inning, John Valentin grounded out. Jason Varitek grounded out. Clemens was one out away from pitching nine shutout innings, having given up only three hits. But Jeff Frye finally got lucky, and although he hit his third comebacker of the night, this one whacked Clemens on the hip and rolled away—it was rightly scored a single. Because Trot Nixon

came to the plate, steamed over the shouting match, his two strikeouts, and being left on third, Nixon wanted to do the one thing that wouldn't leave him standing on third, or any-where. On a 2-1 count, he waited for the fastball that would challenge him, got it, and deposited the ball in the seats.

Two-run home run. I wish I could tell you Yankee Stadium fell silent, but no, it was just as loud: thousands of Sox fans cheered their luck, and 50,000 Yankee loyalists heaped abuse on Nixon for having the cheek to take Clemens deep. Besides, we had last licks. And once Brian Daubach grounded out, Yankees fans were sure a miracle was in the making.

Knoblauch led off the inning, and you could tell Pedro wanted blood, now that he had the lead. The high pitch count and the overexcitement were a little much for the tough Dominican, though, and he hit Knoblauch. Derek Jeter handled it with his usual aplomb, and went three-for-four by poking another single. Paul O'Neill was Pedro's ninth strikeout victim, but with two men on, one out, and Pedro tiring, things still looked good for the Yankees. Bernie hit the ball high, he hit the ball far, but that pesky Trot Nixon hauled the ball in on the warning track.

It could have been a three-run homer, but instead it was the sac fly that moved Chuck to third. Jeter then stole second. Jorge Posada came up. Pedro, with two strikes on the bat-ter, hit him with a pitch and loaded the bases.

Tino Martinez came to the plate. Two outs. Bottom of the ninth. Bases loaded. Down 2-0. Pedro on the mound. The nation watch-ing, unable to leave their seats through the entire, unbelievable pitchers' duel. Before the game, during batting practice, Tino had walloped a ball over the wall in left center, into Monument Park.

I know because I happened to be standing there gawking the monuments when it sailed over, and I happened to be the one who grabbed it before anyone else. I held that ball in my hands and prayed that he could do it again.

But it was not to be. Tino grounded to second, as the wily Pedro escaped from the jam with a 2-0 win. The crowd was stunned. Red Sox fans were hugging each other, not believing that they had, for once, managed to hang onto victory even as the jaws of defeat were closing in around them. Yankees fans stumbled home, consoled only by the fact that, even if the Yanks had lost, they had just witnessed one of the greatest games in the history of baseball.

DAN EASTMAN, *Cornish, New Hampshire, fan*

I had just finished sixth grade: the year was 1949. And I was about to enter upon the first of what to become 53 years to date of rise, fall, of livin' and dyin' with 'my' team, the Boston Red Sox!

Oh, yes I remember the bitter end of that '49 season when my beloved Red Sox led the New York Yankees by one game for the American League pennant with but two games left to play. And we had out two best pitchers all set: Ellis Kinder, who won 23 games that year, and Mel Parnell the brilliant southpaw who had won 25! But the Yankees had four excellent pitchers in Ed Lopat, Vic Raschi, Allie Reynolds and fireman Joe Page.

The Sox lost Game 1. The next day, Parnell pitched beautifully but the Red Sox

bats were silent until late in the game and the Sox trailed 1-0. So Parnell was removed for a pinch hitter. The Yankees subsequently scored additional runs.

But the Sox came back thanks to Bobby Doerr and scored a few runs themselves. Alas, rally was not enough and the Red Sox lost, 5-3.

My sister cried and cried. We both were heartbroken. My mother tried to comfort us with, "Don't cry, just wait 'til next year."

Little did we realize then what would be ahead of us for the next more than 50-plus years.

HARDY ASTLEY, *Lyme, New Hampshire, retired health care professional*

I was born in Belmont, Massachusetts—Red Sox country. I have a picture of my Dad cutting across the railroad tracks to go to Fenway Park—probably after work. I don't remember going to a game when I lived in Massachusetts, but all my uncles were Red Sox fans and they hated the 'Damn Yankees.' When I was nine years old, my family moved to the Upper Valley of New Hampshire where I followed the Red Sox on the radio. I have always followed the scores, trades and standings in the newspapers.

Games with the Yankees are always exciting, but boy do I hate it when the Yankees win. Oh well, maybe next year!

JOAN ASTLEY, *Lyme, New Hampshire, retired health care professional*

My first memory of baseball is when I had the measles. I was quite ill with a high fever and had to remain in bed for at least a week. My only distraction was the Red Sox on radio—Curt Gowdy introduced me to baseball and to the rivalry between the Sox and the Yankees. I think it was during spring training that year that I was sick because I remember they were playing in Florida.

After I recovered there wasn't much time for baseball. I finished school and went on to nursing school and spent six months of my training in Boston—just around the corner from Fenway Park. I could hear the fans cheering, but I still didn't get to go to a game.

After school, after Hardy was discharged from the army, we were married in June. What did we do? No—not Disney World, we went to a Red Sox game.

At some point we took Hardy's brothers (they were both much younger) to games. One of those games was with the Yankees, and the Red Sox lost.

Hardy always gets depressed and/or disgusted when the Yankees beat up on the Sox or even get a good lead in a game. If this happens, he will stop watching and go out and mow the lawn.

Oh well, maybe next year!

AUBREY T. HANBICKI,
Washington, D.C., Naval Research Laboratory

When I was a kid growing up, I was only peripherally aware of baseball. Basically, my only exposure to it was every fall when my father would watch the World Series. And then I would only get to see the first couple innings before having to go to bed. Sometime midway through the 1978 season, however, that changed.

I remember one lazy summer afternoon when I decided to sit in front of a game with my father—the first game that I ever saw from start to finish. Ron Guidry was pitching and he was un-hittable. At the time, I didn't think it was unusual that he was striking out everyone in the park.

In fact, it seemed quite natural that the strikeout would be the obvious conclusion to most at-bats because it looked really hard to hit a ball thrown so hard. It was only my father's reaction that made me realize an 18-strikeout game was something quite unusual.

His enthusiasm infected me and we watched many games that summer. As I started to learn the rules and then the finer points and nuances of the game from my father, I came to understand how beautiful a game this was. Plus it was a great bonding experience. The experience became even richer later that season when the Yankees started winning. This was when I was first introduced to the dreaded Red Sox.

At first I was crushed every time the Yankees lost; being so young and new to the sport I didn't really realize how long the season was. Each game seemed to be of epic significance. As it turns out, every game that season was of major significance. As the season progressed and my now-beloved Yankees started closing in on the BoSox, I began to live the rivalry. I read dozens of books ranging from the *Baseball Encyclopedia* to the history of the Yankees-Red Sox rivalry. All the while I never really believed that the Yankees could overcome the likes of Jim Rice, Fred Lynn, and Yaz.

These guys were so good, they didn't seem human. Why couldn't the Yankees have players like that (except of course we had Guidry)? In retrospect, the Yankees did have great players, but seeing them every day meant I saw them fail 70 percent of the time.

I barely remember Bucky Dent's home run or the subsequent playoff against Kansas City. The season as a whole though, made especially magical because of the intense rivalry with Boston, stands out foremost in my mind. In subsequent years, my passion for the Yankees and passion against the Red Sox grew. My father would take my brother and me to the Stadium several times a year, including a trip near our birthday.

Being born in September, it seemed like the Yanks would always be playing the Red Sox on my birthday and the Yankees seemed to inevitably lose. Even if they were on a roll and would win two out of three in the series, that one loss always seemed to come when we were at the stadium. This didn't help to endear the boys from Beantown to me.

Then a strange phenomenon began to happen. Players that I spent years of my youth rooting against, and who I most associated with Boston, started to play for New York. Some of the best years of my youth were spent mocking and disliking Wade Boggs, for instance. Then one day he is suddenly in pinstripes. What was I supposed to do? Eventually, I decided that, to remain a loyal Yankee fan, I had to disassociate myself from the players and root for the team. As long as there were pinstripes on the field, I knew who to root for. Unfortunately, that took away a lot of my zeal for the rivalry.

By the time Roger Clemens started playing for George Steinbrenner, it no longer mattered to me that he had worn Red Sox. Partly because he had been laundered through Toronto, partly because I liked him as a player and athlete, partly because he left Boston on bad terms, and partly because this was no longer a unique occurrence, I accepted him immediately as a Yankee.

KEVIN McCAFFREY,
Framingham, Massachusetts, communications specialist, Bose Corporation

"YANKEES SUCK" were the words that greeted me when I reached the top of the staircase of the T station. It was on hats, on t-shirts, on buttons, and bumper stickers—the vendors hawked their goods by shouting the words gleefully. One particularly visible shirt even added a little bit more inappropriateness to the mix. The front was furnished with the "Yankees Suck" message while the back informed lookers-on that "Jeter Swallows." Who would have thunk it? I thought he dated Mariah Carey?

Even more disturbing than the existence of the merchandise itself was the fact that dozens of young Red Sox fans begged their fathers to buy them something from one of the carts—something, anything, as long as they could join the popular crusade against the dreaded Yankees.

I held my tongue as I walked past one after another of these carts and headed toward our normal pregame meeting place—Copperfield's, which was never as insane as the overcrowded Cask 'n' Flagon or the Boston Beer Works, even for Yankees games. Our group for the game was a good mix: myself and one other Yankee fan, a neutral baseball fan, and a Red Sox fan. We knew we were walking into the lion's den, but we'd done it before and we'll certainly do it again.

I've lived in Boston for seven years now (four during college and three after). Each year we always try to get tickets for these big games.

Every year it gets harder. There is just so much at stake, too much history between the two teams—the Bucky Dent home run, the Boggs and Clemens defections, and the recent square-offs in the playoffs—thanks to the wild card—are only the very recent examples. It's a rivalry that transcends the mere sport; it's personal. It's Boston vs. New York. It's the Italian guy from Brooklyn vs. the Italian guy from the North End. It's New York City's finest vs. the Boston Police Department. It's the ghost of Mickey Mantle vs. the ghost of Ted Williams. And, even though it's just one game out of 162, and one of several head-to-head match-ups in a season, you have to love what happens.

As soon as you get close to Fenway you can sense that the Red Sox are not playing the Devil Rays or the Tigers today. The Fenway Faithful are fired up and justifiably so.

With the shadow of 26 Yankee championships hanging over their heads, two recent eliminations from the playoffs, and the memory of a ground ball through the legs of Bill Buckner against the other team from New York stealing their last, best chance to exorcise the demons, it's no wonder they're so venomous.

The game started out like the rest I had attended. The home team was cheered, the visitors were jeered. Sox fans leaned in close to the visitor's bullpen and heckled the Yankee starter. One thing became apparent, however: we had friends in the crowd. Here and there the cry of "Let's go Yankees" would go up. It wouldn't last long as the "Yankees suck" chant would quickly overpower it, but we were not alone. Then as the first few Yankee runners crossed the plate, the Yankees fans got

louder and the Red Sox fans got quieter. As the Yankee lead opened up, the Yankees fans started getting bolder and a few scattered chants of "1918" started up. It's almost too easy, but when the opposing team tells you all about how big your payroll is, and who carries out what bodily function on your team, you have to retaliate somehow. This give-and-take is half the fun of the game. Sure the game itself is interesting and usually close, but the interactions in the stands are what really entertain you.

As the game progressed, the Red Sox faithful were slumping just like their team. But then as fate would have it (and believe me, Red Sox fans are big believers in that concept), the Yankee starter tired. He stopped making good pitches and started making good hitters. As more and more Red Sox drew walks and hit singles, our once insurmountable lead diminished. So, Joe Torre came out to call in his bullpen to mop up. In trotted the Yankee reliever, but this wasn't one of the big three, it was a seldom-used sidewinder, normally brought in during garbage time. That's OK, I thought, the lead was big enough to hold even if he did falter.

As he began warming up on the mound the Red Sox fans began taking a renewed interest in the game, and we sunk in to our seats in slight dismay. The pitcher was not exactly instilling confidence in the Yankees who had braved Fenway that day. One pitch hit the dirt; another was high enough that the catcher had to stand up to catch it. Yet another pitch sailed so high it hit the metal netting behind home plate. The sound that pitch made was like a wakeup call to the entire place.

This game was not over. The Sox fans

screamed insults and taunts at the reliever who must have known by then that it just wasn't his day. One more high pitch that nearly sailed to the backstop was enough. Fenway Park was on its feet now and the fans were re-energized. Like a pack of wolves circling the injured elk, knowing that it was weakened, they waited.

The first Red Sox batter drew a walk on pitches nowhere near the strike zone, the second did the same. At this point the Red Sox fans that we had been jawing with were giving it back pretty good. "This guy's wicked good huh?" "Nomahhhh's better," and of course the ever-popular "Yankees suck…Yankees suck" chant. What could we do? Our bullpen was failing us fast, and by the time Torre came back out to pull the wild thing, the score was close.

The next reliever didn't do much better and by now the crowd was whipped in to a frenzy of Yankee-hating madness. It was almost frightening to see. I had lived in this city for quite a few years and been to at least one Yankees-Red Sox game a year but this I had never seen. It was the result of years of frustration coupled with the feeling that the Yankees were vulnerable and the Red Sox were sticking it to them good.

The Red Sox won the game that day and in dramatic fashion too. They mounted a huge comeback, cracked what had previously been a very stalwart Yankee bullpen, and defeated their archrival. The fans had enjoyed every moment of it. The Red Sox fans that is. On that day the Yankee fans were outdone. The Red Sox fans got to gloat on the way out of the stadium and as we made our way past the sidewalk vendors there was renewed vigor on their part to hawk their variety of "YANKEES SUCK" wares. And now everyone was buying it, everyone from young boys and girls to young men to grownups. The vendors were getting rich off the comeback.

We left losers that day, but we were already thinking what every Red Sox fan had grown accustomed to thinking—wait until next year. It's not easy to leave the games on days your team loses because you hear about the game the whole ride home, but it sure is sweet on the days you win—and that's what going to Fenway to see the Yankees play the Red Sox is all about.

There is a sign on an overpass of Storrow Drive, the road that runs along the Charles River on the Boston side, that used to say Reverse Curve to warn drivers of a dangerous curve in the road as it twists to conform to the rivers path. Since the Red Sox squared off with the Yankees in the ALCS it has read "Reverse The Curse," thanks to the creative handiwork of some Red Sox fans. Every time the city repaints the sign, someone returns to reiterate the message.

DOUG ALONGI, *Boston, Massachusetts, account executive*

For a true Yankee fan, there is nothing like watching a Yankee Red Sox contest from the bleachers in "Not So Friendly Fenway Park." Both excitement and a feeling of uneasiness fill the air for those brave enough to don a cap containing the hated interlocking NY.

What I never realized prior to moving to Boston was how personal Sox Nation takes this rivalry. The tired chant of "Yankees suck" is just as likely to be heard in May when the Royals visit Fenway as it is when the Yankees come calling in September. The true hatred of the dreaded Yankees was never more evident in the bleachers of Fenway than it was on the night of September 2, 2001.

This game was being played in front of a national audience on the Sunday of Labor Day weekend. Mike Mussina took a perfect game into the ninth inning that evening, the only thing between him and history was Carl "Jurassic" Everett. Jurassic was a nickname given to Everett by the Boston faithful who accurately deemed his personality to be similar to that of a dinosaur. The only thing Sox Nation despises as much as a Yankee, is a Red Sox player gone bad, and in Carl Everett, Sox fans had found themselves a poster boy.

Mussina found himself one strike away from a perfect game and was facing the least popular Red Sox player in Everett. Yet all of Fenway's faithful were on their feet pulling for Everett as if he was a Kennedy. To Yankee fans' dismay, Everett served a base hit to left sending all of Fenway into hysteria. The cheers that came out of Fenway at that moment sounded more like those that follow the last out of a World Series Game 7. Walking out of Fenway that evening, it hit me.

Red Sox fans root against the Yankees as much as they cheer for their beloved Sox.

PETE CROOKER, *Yankee hater*

I was born in 1938 and raised in Bath, Maine, a great baseball town back in the 1940s and early 1950s. I have always believed that I came from my mother's womb a Yankee hater.

Growing up in pre-television time, the radio was my link to the outside world and my path to Major League Baseball. And when I went to my elderly grandmother's house, if there was a Sox game being played, it was on her radio too.

As a child I was able to hear so many games because of daytime baseball. And our holidays—Memorial Day, the Fourth, Labor Day—always carried the doubleheaders, which could drone on in the background of any activity, as long as you were in the vicinity of an electrical outlet.

My friends, my schoolmates and I all despised the Yankees. Beating or losing to the Athletics, Senators, Browns, Tigers, Indians or White Sox did not cause much of a reaction either way—but any series against the Yankees could result in an extreme emotional rollercoaster ride.

No kid would have dared to show up in a hat bearing an NY (or any other team for that matter). When I opened up packs of Fleers or Topps, I often quickly tore up any Yankee cards. Sometimes we would place them on a board and toss or flip our jack knives at them. Mantle, Berra, Raschi, Reynolds, or Rizzuto—they all were bums.

In 1947, my dad took me to Boston to see my first big-time games. The drive down Route One along the coast was a long one, but well worth it, of course. After entering the ballpark of my dreams we took seats in the left-field grandstand, right above Ted. Oh, the wonder of it all! Years later I could not remember how the Saturday and Sunday games came out.

Last year while in Cooperstown, I visited the Hall of Fame Archives and read the *Sporting News* until I found the summaries. The Sox won the first, but the Yankees took the one the next day. DAMNED YANKEES!

The sight of pinstripes on a uniform—even on a high school team—causes me to cheer for the other side!

My New York license plate is "SOX 9."

JOE PICKERING JR., *Bangor,*
Maine songwriter (All song lyrics are from the
CD, Baseball Songs Sports Heroes *© 2001*
King of the Road Music, BMI Publisher.)

"THE MYSTERY OF THE WORLD"
A Red Sox Fan's Explanation

New England holds its break from summer into fall

Our Sox climb to first place and then blow it all

Why the Sox lose with glory's the mystery of the world

No one's ever solved it so I'm giving it a whirl

They say the Sox can't win because of Babe Ruth's curse

Well, ladies and gentlemen it's much, much worse

Don't blame the Sultan of Swat the great Babe Ruth

God's not a Red Sox fan, and that's the awful truth

God knows why the Sox lose at the end of the year

Why do the Yankees win? The same reason I fear

Lord, are you a Yankee fan, don't tell me if you are

No Sox fan can stand it that's going too far

Repeat Chorus

All you Red Sox fans across the U.S.A.

And those up in Canada who stay up to watch them play

Sox fans in Mexico all the world too

Even you down under who play ball with the kangaroo

Fans round the world pray for a series win

Pray hard royal rooters from the Vatican

Oh God don't hear our prayers with a deaf ear

May all the saints sing 'Let the Sox win this year!'

Wait 'til next year!

The New York Yankees are baseball's mortal sin

Their greed's so great they always need to win

How can their fans stand it year after year

How boring it must be to cheer without fear!

"BABE RUTH'S CURSE I"

Our Red Sox now lead by a country mile

Still fear grips our hearts the crowd wears no smile

Babe's curse is with us all clouds grow dark

It's World Series time at old Fenway Park

That's not distant thunder I hear from the sky

But Mister Babe Ruth stepping down from on high

Babe's coming to play with his bat and his ball

To make sure we don't win the Series this fall

Joe DiMaggio, Ted Williams, Dom DiMaggio. (Photofest)

Chorus

Hey Mister Babe please give us a break

How much more can the Red Sox fans take

In the annals of baseball none can be worse

Than the terrible tale of Babe Ruth's curse

In the Series of '18 Babe strode to the mound

And proceeded to mow the Chicago Cubs down

But that's the last Series the Sox ever won

Soon Babe Ruth was traded, the dirty deed done

The Babe grabbed the train and left sad old Beantown

To build up the Yankees and tear the Sox down

All the fans agree, the trade was a sin

But it wasn't our fault Babe so please let us win!

FOR THE RECORD

BOSTON RED SOX

A.K.A.: Boston Somersets 1901-1902, Boston
Pilgrims 1903-1906

Nicknames: Speed Boys 1901-1902, Plymouth
Rocks 1901-1902, Boston Puritans 1901-1902,
BoSox, Americans

Franchise: Charter franchise

Ballparks: Huntington Ave. Grounds 1901-
1911, Fenway Park I 1912-1933, Braves Field
1915-1916 (World Series), 1929-1932 (Sun-
days), Fenway Park 1934-

BOSTON RED SOX
CHAMPIONSHIP HISTORY

World Series Champions
1903, 1912, 1915, 1916, 1918

American League Champions
1903, 1904, 1912, 1915, 1916, 1918, 1946,
1967, 1975, 1986

American League East Champions
1975, 1986, 1988, 1990, 1995

American League Wild-Card
1998, 1999, 2003

NOTABLE RED SOX ARTIFACTS AT THE
BASEBALL HALL OF FAME

- Gold Glove Award given to Hall of Fame left
  fielder Carl Yastrzemski, 1971
- Triple Crown trophy awarded to Carl
  Yastrzemski in 1967
- Silver Bat awarded to Carl Yastrzemski for win-
  ning the 1963 American League batting title
- Ball hit by Hall of Fame outfielder Ted Will-
  iams for his 500th career homer, June 17, 1960
- Ball signed by Ted Williams and Dom
  DiMaggio
- Sunglasses worn by Ted Williams
- Ball from Mel Parnell's no-hit game, July 14,
  1956
- Red Sox uniform pants worn by Hall of Fame
  shortstop Lou Boudreau, 1952
- Hall of Fame second baseman Bobby Doerr's
  fielder's glove
- Agreement selling Hall of Famer Babe Ruth to
  the New York Yankees, 1919
- Bat used by Hall of Fame outfielder Harry
  Hooper
- Ball thrown by New York's Jack Chesbro in the
  second game of a doubleheader on October 8,
  1904 for a wild pitch, allowing the winning
  run to score and delivering the American
  League pennant to Boston

Don Zimmer and Johnny Pesky (Frommer Archives)

- Pipe and case belonging to Hall of Fame hurler Cy Young

RED SOX HALL OF FAME PLAYERS

Player	Years with Red Sox
Luis Aparicio	1971-1973
Lou Boudreau	1951-52
Jesse Burkett	1905
Orlando Cepeda	1973
Jack Chesbro	1909
Jimmy Collins	1901-1907
Joe Cronin	1935-1945
Bobby Doerr	1937-1944, 1946-1951
Dennis Eckersley	1978-84, 1998
Rick Ferrell	1934-1937
Carlton Fisk	1969, 1971-1980
Jimmie Foxx	1936-1942
Lefty Grove	1934-1941
Harry Hooper	1909-1920
Waite Hoyt	1919-20
Fergie Jenkins	1976-77
George Kell	1952-1954
Heinie Manush	1936
Juan Marichal	1974
Herb Pennock	1915-1922
Tony Perez	1980-1982
Red Ruffing	1924-1930
Babe Ruth	1914-1919
Tom Seaver	1986
Al Simmons	1943
Tris Speaker	1907-1915
Ted Williams	1939-1942, 1946-1960
Carl Yastrzemski	1961-1983
Cy Young	1901-1908

RED SOX HALL OF FAME MANAGERS

Manager	Years with Red Sox
Ed Barrow	1918-1920
Lou Boudreau	1952-1954
Frank Chance	1923
Jimmy Collins	1901-1906
Joe Cronin	1935-1947
Hugh Duffy	1921-22
Bucky Harris	1934
Billy Herman	1964-1966
Joe McCarthy	1948-1950
Cy Young	1907

BASEBALL IN BOSTON

- The first major league team in Boston was the Boston Red Caps, who played in the inaugural National League season of 1876 and later became the Boston Braves.
- Fenway Park opened on April 20, 1912, the same day as Detroit's Navin Field, which later became Tiger Stadium.

- From 1901 to 1952, Boston hosted two major league teams: the Red Sox (also known as the Americans, Somersets and Pilgrims) and the Braves.
- Modern fans know the Red Sox/Yankees rivalry as a one-sided affair, with New York having won 26 World Series titles while Boston hasn't won since 1918. But prior to 1921, the Red Sox were the more successful franchise, having won six of the first 18 American League pennants while New York finished no higher than second place. In a seven-year stretch (1912-1918), the Red Sox won four World Series titles behind star players Tris Speaker, Harry Hooper, Joe Wood, Babe Ruth, and Duffy Lewis.

RED SOX RETIRED UNIFORM NUMBERS

1	Bobby Doerr
4	Joe Cronin
8	Carl Yastrzemski
9	Ted Williams
27	Carlton Fisk

RED SOX WIN-LOSS RECORD

(1901-2003)
Wins: 8,165
Losses: 7,753

RED SOX RECORD SEASON-BY-SEASON

Year	Record	Average	Finish
2003	95-67	.586	2nd
2002	93-69	.574	2nd
2001	82-79	.509	2nd
2000	85-77	.525	2nd
1999	94-68	.580	2nd
1998	92-70	.568	2nd
1997	78-84	.481	4th
1996	85-77	.525	3rd
1995	86-58	.597	1st
1994	54-61	.470	4th
1993	80-82	.494	5th
1992	73-89	.451	7th
1991	84-78	.519	t2nd

Year	Record	Average	Finish
1990	88-74	.543	1st
1989	83-79	.512	3rd
1988	89-73	.549	1st
1987	78-84	.481	5th
1986	95-66	.590	1st
1985	81-81	.500	5th
1984	86-76	.531	4th
1983	78-84	.481	6th
1982	89-73	.549	3rd
1981	59-49	.546	5th
1980	83-77	.519	4th
1979	91-69	.569	3rd
1978	99-64	.607	2nd
1977	97-64	.602	t3rd
1976	83-79	.512	3rd
1975	95-65	.594	1st
1974	84-78	.519	3rd
1973	89-73	.549	2nd
1972	85-70	.548	2nd
1971	85-77	.525	3rd
1970	87-75	.537	3rd
1969	87-75	.537	3rd
1968	86-76	.531	4th
1967	92-70	.568	1st
1966	72-90	.444	9th
1965	62-100	.383	9th
1964	72-90	.444	8th
1963	76-85	.472	7th
1962	76-84	.475	8th
1961	76-86	.469	6th
1960	65-89	.422	7th
1959	75-79	.487	5th
1958	79-75	.513	3rd
1957	82-72	.532	3rd
1956	84-70	.545	4th
1955	84-70	.545	4th
1954	69-85	.448	4th
1953	84-69	.549	4th
1952	76-78	.494	6th
1951	87-67	.565	3rd
1950	94-60	.610	3rd
1949	96-58	.623	2nd
1948	96-59	.619	2nd
1947	83-71	.539	3rd
1946	104-50	.675	1st

Year	Record	Average	Finish
1945	71-83	.461	7th
1944	77-77	.500	4th
1943	68-84	.447	7th
1942	93-59	.612	2nd
1941	84-70	.545	2nd
1940	82-72	.532	4th
1939	89-62	.589	2nd
1938	88-61	.591	2nd
1937	80-72	.526	5th
1936	74-80	.481	6th
1935	78-75	.516	4th
1934	76-76	.500	4th
1933	63-86	.423	7th
1932	43-111	.279	8th
1931	62-90	.408	6th
1930	52-102	.338	8th
1929	58-96	.377	8th
1928	57-96	.373	8th
1927	51-103	.331	8th
1926	46-107	.301	8th
1925	47-105	.309	8th
1924	67-87	.435	7th
1923	61-91	.401	8th
1922	61-93	.396	8th
1921	75-79	.487	5th
1920	72-81	.471	5th
1919	66-71	.482	6th
1918	75-51	.595	1st
1917	90-62	.592	2nd
1916	91-63	.591	1st
1915	101-50	.669	1st
1914	91-62	.595	2nd
1913	79-71	.527	4th
1912	105-47	.691	1st
1911	78-75	.510	5th
1910	81-72	.529	4th
1909	88-63	.583	3rd
1908	75-79	.487	5th
1907	59-90	.396	7th
1906	49-105	.318	8th
1905	78-74	.513	4th
1904	95-59	.617	1st
1903	91-47	.659	1st
1902	77-60	.582	3rd
1901	79-57	.581	2nd

BOSTON RED SOX PRESIDENTS

John Henry	2002-present
John L. Harrington	1989-2001
Jean R. Yawkey	1977-1988
Thomas A. Yawkey	1933-1976
Robert Quinn	1923-1932
Harry H. Frazee	1917-1923
Joseph J. Lannin	1913-1916
James R. McAleer	1912-1913
John I. Taylor	1904-1911
Henry J. Killilea	1903-1904
Charles W. Somers	1901-1902

BOSTON RED SOX MANAGERS

2004-	Terry Francona
2002-2003	Grady Little
2001	Joe Kerrigan
1997-2001	Jimy Williams
1995-1996	Kevin Kennedy
1992-1994	Butch Hobson
1988-1991	Joe Morgan
1985-1988	John McNamara
1981-1984	Ralph Houk
1980	Johnny Pesky
1976-1980	Don Zimmer
1974-1976	Darrell Johnson
1973	Eddie Popowski
1970-1973	Eddie Kasko
1969	Eddie Popowski
1967-1969	Dick Williams
1966	Pete Runnels
1964-1966	Billy Herman
1963-1964	Johnny Pesky
1960-1962	Mike Higgins
1960	Del Baker
1959-1960	Billy Jurges
1959	Rudy York
1955-1959	Mike Higgins
1952-1954	Lou Boudreau
1950-1951	Steve O'Neill
1948-1950	Joe McCarthy
1935-1947	Joe Cronin
1934	Bucky Harris
1932-1933	Marty McManus

1931-1932	Shano Collins
1930	Heinie Wagner
1927-1929	Bill Carrigan
1924-1926	Lee Fohl
1923	Frank Chance
1921-1922	Hugh Duffy
1918-1920	Ed Barrow
1917	Jack Barry
1913-1916	Bill Carrigan
1912-1913	Jake Stahl
1910-1911	Patsy Donovan
1908-1909	Fred Lake
1907-1908	Deacon McGuire
1907	Bob Unglaub
1907	Cy Young
1907	George Huff
1906	Chick Stahl
	Jimmy Collins

RED SOX PLAYER SALARIES, OPENING DAY 2003

Manny Ramirez	$17,185,177
Pedro Martinez	$15,500,000
Nomar Garciaparra	$10,500,000
Johnny Damon	$7,500,000
John Burkett	$5,500,000
Jason Varitek	$4,700,000
Trot Nixon	$4,000,000
Tim Wakefield	$4,000,000
Derek Lowe	$3,625,000
Todd Walker	$3,450,000
Alan Embree	$3,000,000
Ramiro Mendoza	$2,900,000
Bill Mueller	$2,100,000
Jeremy Giambi	$2,000,000
Kevin Millar	$2,000,000
Mike Timlin	$1,850,000
Bobby Howry	$1,700,000
David Ortiz	$1,250,000
Doug Mirabelli	$805,000
Damian Jackson	$625,000
Chad Fox	$500,000
Shea Hillenbrand	$407,500
Casey Fossum	$324,500
Brandon Lyon	$309,500
Dicky Gonzalez	$300,000
Robert Person	$300,000
Matthew White	$300,000

NEW YORK YANKEES
A.K.A.: New York Highlanders 1903-1912

Nicknames: New York Porchclimbers 1903-1904, New York Burglars 1903-1904, New York Invaders 1903, Greater New Yorks 1900s, New York Hill Toppers 1903-1912, Bronx Bombers

Franchise: Relocated from Baltimore Orioles 1901-1902.

Called Highlanders after a famous British Army regiment named Gordon's Highlanders, and because home ballpark Hilltop Park was located on a hilltop overlooking Washington Heights.

Called Yankees first by sportswriters Mark Roth of the *New York Globe* and Sam Crane of the *New York Journal*. Name in print for the first time on June 21, 1904 in *Boston Herald*.

BALLPARKS
Hilltop Park 1903-1912, Polo Grounds V 1913-1922, Yankee Stadium I 1923-1973, Shea Stadium 1974-1975, (new) Yankee Stadium 1976-

NEW YORK YANKEES CHAMPIONSHIP HISTORY

World Series Champions
1923, 1927, 1928, 1932, 1936, 1937, 1938, 1939, 1941, 1943, 1947, 1949, 1950, 1951, 1952, 1953, 1956, 1958, 1961, 1962, 1977, 1978, 1996, 1998, 1999, 2000

American League Champions
1921, 1922, 1923, 1926, 1927, 1928, 1932, 1936, 1937, 1938, 1939, 1941, 1942, 1943, 1947, 1949, 1950, 1951, 1952, 1953, 1955, 1956, 1957, 1958, 1960, 1961, 1962, 1963, 1964, 1976, 1977, 1978, 1981, 1996, 1998, 1999, 2000, 2001, 2003

American League East Champions
1976, 1977, 1978, 1981, 1994, 1996, 1998, 1999, 2000, 2001, 2002, 2003

American League East First-Half Champions
1981

American League Wild-Card
1995, 1997

NOTABLE YANKEES ARTIFACTS AT THE BASEBALL HALL OF FAME

- Bat used by Tino Martinez to hit the bottom of the ninth game-tying home run in Game 4 of the 2001 World Series vs. the Arizona Diamondbacks on October 31
- Signed baseball from Roger Clemens used in his 20th victory of the 2001 season when he improved his record to 20-1. The ball is signed "God Bless the USA" to honor the memory of those in the September 11, 2001 tragedy
- Batting helmet worn by Derek Jeter in the 2000 World Series, when he won the Most Valuable Player award as the Yankees defeated the New York Mets
- Bat used by Chad Curtis to hit the game-winning home run in Game 3 of the 1999 World Series, October 26 against the Atlanta Braves
- Cap, ball, ticket, and beanie baby giveaway doll from David Wells's perfect game, May 17, 1998
- Bat used by Hall of Famer Mickey Mantle to hit his 500th career home run, May 14, 1967
- Glove used by Hall of Fame catcher
- Yogi Berra to catch Don Larsen's perfect game, October 8, 1956 in the World Series against the Dodgers
- Pen used by Hall of Fame outfielder Joe DiMaggio to sign his $100,000 contract on February 7, 1949
- Ticket to Lou Gehrig Day, July 4, 1939

- Key ring belonging to Hall of Fame first baseman Lou Gehrig
- Yankee Stadium locker used by Hall of Fame slugger Babe Ruth
- Bats used by Ruth to hit his 57th, 58th, and 60th home runs, 1927
- Glove used by Ruth in the 1926 World Series against the St. Louis Cardinals
- First ball thrown by New York governor Alfred Smith at Yankee Stadium dedication ceremony, April 18, 1923

YANKEES HALL OF FAME PLAYERS

Player	Years with Yankees
Frank Baker	1916-1919, 1921-22
Yogi Berra	1946-1963
Frank Chance	1913-14
Jack Chesbro	1903-1909
Earle Combs	1924-1935
Stan Coveleski	1928
Bill Dickey	1928-1943, 1946
Joe DiMaggio	1936-1942, 1946-1951
Leo Durocher	1925, 1928-29
Whitey Ford	1950, 1953-1967
Lou Gehrig	1923-1939
Lefty Gomez	1930-1942
Clark Griffith	1903-1907
Burleigh Grimes	1934
Waite Hoyt	1921-1930
Catfish Hunter	1975-1979
Reggie Jackson	1977-1981
Willie Keeler	1903-1909
Tony Lazzeri	1926-1937
Mickey Mantle	1951-1968
Bill McKechnie	1913
Johnny Mize	1949-1953
Phil Niekro	1984-85
Herb Pennock	1923-1933
Gaylord Perry	1980
Phil Rizzuto	1941-42, 1946-1956
Red Ruffing	1930-1942, 1945-46
Babe Ruth	1920-1934
Joe Sewell	1931-1933
Enos Slaughter	1954-1959
Dazzy Vance	1915, 1918

| Paul Waner | 1944-45 |
| Dave Winfield | 1981-88, 1990 |

YANKEES HALL OF FAME MANAGERS

Manager	Years with Yankees
Yogi Berra	1964, 1984-85
Frank Chance	1913-14
Bill Dickey	1946
Clark Griffith	1903-1908
Bucky Harris	1947-48
Miller Huggins	1918-1929
Bob Lemon	1978-79, 1981-82
Joe McCarthy	1931-1946
Casey Stengel	1949-1960

BASEBALL IN NEW YORK CITY

- The first major league team in New York city was the New York Mutuals, who played in the inaugural National League season of 1876.
- The first game was played in Yankee Stadium on April 18, 1923. Bob Shawkey threw a three-hitter for the win, and Babe Ruth hit a three-run homer, the first in stadium history. The attendance was 74,217.
- From 1903 to 1957, at least three major league teams competed in New York: the Giants, Dodgers, and Yankees. In 1914 and 1915 the Brooklyn Tip-Tops were the fourth major league team in New York, playing in the Federal League.

YANKEES RETIRED UNIFORM NUMBERS

1	Billy Martin
3	Babe Ruth
4	Lou Gehrig
5	Joe DiMaggio
7	Mickey Mantle
8	Bill Dickey, Yogi Berra
9	Roger Maris
10	Phil Rizzuto
15	Thurman Munson
16	Whitey Ford
23	Don Mattingly
32	Elston Howard
37	Casey Stengel
44	Reggie Jackson

YANKEES WIN-LOSS RECORD
(1901-2003)
Wins: 8,896
Losses: 6,901

YANKEES RECORD SEASON-BY-SEASON

Year	Record	Average	Finish
2003	101-61	.623	1st
2002	103-58	.640	1st
2001	95-65	.594	1st
2000	87-74	.540	1st
1999	98-64	.605	1st
1998	114-48	.704	1st
1997	96-66	.593	2nd
1996	92-70	.568	1st
1995	79-65	.549	2nd
1994	70-43	.619	1st
1993	88-74	.543	2nd
1992	78-86	.469	t4th
1991	71-91	.438	5th
1990	67-95	.414	7th
1989	74-87	.460	5th
1988	85-76	.530	5th
1987	89-73	.549	4th
1986	90-72	.556	2nd
1985	97-64	.602	2nd
1984	87-75	.537	3rd
1983	91-71	.562	3rd
1982	79-83	.488	5th
1981	59-48	.551	3rd
1980	103-59	.636	1st
1979	89-71	.556	4th
1978	100-63	.613	1st
1977	100-62	.617	1st
1976	97-62	.610	1st
1975	83-77	.519	3rd
1974	89-73	.549	2nd

Year	Record	Average	Finish	Year	Record	Average	Finish
1973	80-82	.494	4th	1929	88-66	.571	2nd
1972	79-76	.510	4th	1928	101-53	.656	1st
1971	82-80	.506	4th	1927	110-44	.714	1st
1970	93-69	.574	2nd	1926	91-63	.591	1st
1969	80-81	.497	5th	1925	69-85	.448	7th
1968	83-79	.512	5th	1924	89-63	.586	2nd
1967	72-90	.444	9th	1923	98-54	.645	1st
1966	70-89	.440	10th	1922	94-60	.610	1st
1965	77-85	.475	6th	1921	98-55	.641	1st
1964	99-63	.611	1st	1920	95-59	.617	3rd
1963	104-57	.646	1st	1919	80-59	.576	3rd
1962	96-66	.593	1st	1918	60-63	.488	4th
1961	109-53	.673	1st	1917	71-82	.464	6th
1960	97-57	.630	1st	1916	80-74	.519	4th
1959	79-75	.513	3rd	1915	69-83	.454	5th
1958	92-62	.597	1st	1914	70-84	.455	t6th
1957	98-56	.636	1st	1913	57-94	.377	7th
1956	97-57	.630	1st	1912	50-102	.329	8th
1955	96-58	.623	1st	1911	76-76	.500	6th
1954	103-51	.669	2nd	1910	88-63	.583	2nd
1953	99-52	.656	1st	1909	74-77	.490	5th
1952	95-59	.617	1st	1908	51-103	.331	8th
1951	98-56	.636	1st	1907	70-78	.473	5th
1950	98-56	.636	1st	1906	90-61	.596	2nd
1949	97-57	.630	1st	1905	71-78	.477	6th
1948	94-60	.610	3rd	1904	92-59	.609	2nd
1947	97-57	.630	1st	1903	72-62	.537	4th
1946	87-67	.565	3rd				
1945	81-71	.533	4th				
1944	83-71	.539	3rd				
1943	98-56	.636	1st				
1942	103-51	.669	1st				
1941	101-53	.656	1st				
1940	88-66	.571	3rd				
1939	106-45	.702	1st				
1938	99-53	.651	1st				
1937	102-52	.662	1st				
1936	102-51	.000	1st				
1935	89-60	.597	2nd				
1934	94-60	.610	2nd				
1933	91-59	.607	2nd				
1932	107-47	.695	1st				
1931	94-59	.614	2nd				
1930	86-68	.558	3rd				

NEW YORK YANKEES PRESIDENTS

1993-present	George M. Steinbrenner
1992	Daniel McCarthy
1990-1991	Robert Nederlander
1980-1990	George M. Steinbrenner
1978-1980	Albert L. Rosen
1973-1977	Gabriel H. Paul
1966-1973	Michael Burke
1948-1966	Daniel R. Topping
1945-1947	Leland S. MacPhail
1939-1944	Edward G. Barrow
1915-1938	Jacob Ruppert
1907-1914	Frank J. Farrell
1903-1906	Joseph W. Gordon
1902	John J. Mahon
1901	Sidney W. Frank

NEW YORK YANKEES MANAGERS

1996-	Joe Torre
1992-1995	Buck Showalter
1990-1991	Stump Merrill
1989-1990	Bucky Dent
1989	Dallas Green
1988	Billy Martin
1986-1988	Lou Piniella
1985	Billy Martin
1984-1985	Yogi Berra
1983	Billy Martin
1982	Clyde King
1982	Gene Michael
1981-1982	Bob Lemon
1981	Gene Michael
1980	Dick Howser
1979	Billy Martin
1978-1979	Bob Lemon
1975-1978	Billy Martin
1974-1975	Bill Virdon
1966-1973	Ralph Houk
1965-1966	Johnny Keane
1964	Yogi Berra
1961-1963	Ralph Houk
1949-1960	Casey Stengel
1947-1948	Bucky Harris
1946	Johnny Neun
1946	Bill Dickey
1931-1946	Joe McCarthy
1930	Bob Shawkey
1929	Art Fletcher
1918-1929	Miller Huggins
1915-1917	Bill Donovan
1914	Roger Peckinpaugh
1913-1914	Frank Chance
1912	Harry Wolverton
1910-1911	Hal Chase
1909-1910	George Stallings
1908	Kid Elberfeld
1903-1908	Clark Griffith

YANKEES PLAYER SALARIES, OPENING DAY 2003

Derek Jeter	$15,600,000
Raul Mondesi	$13,000,000
Bernie Williams	$12,357,143
Mike Mussina	$12,000,000
Andy Pettitte	$11,500,000
Jason Giambi	$11,428,571
Mariano Rivera	$10,500,000
Jorge Posada	$8,000,000
Roger Clemens	$7,061,181
Sterling Hitchcock	$6,000,000
Hideki Matsui	$6,000,000
Jose Contreras	$5,500,000
Steve Karsay	$5,000,000
Robin Ventura	$5,000,000
Jeff Weaver	$4,150,000
David Wells	$3,250,000
Bubba Trammell	$2,500,000
Antonio Osuna	$2,400,000
Chris Hammond	$2,200,000
Todd Zeile	$1,500,000
Juan Acevedo	$900,000
Alfonso Soriano	$800,000
John Flaherty	$750,000
Enrique Wilson	$700,000
Jon Lieber	$550,000
Chris Latham	$400,000
Nick Johnson	$364,100
Jason Anderson	$300,000

Information courtesy of the Boston Red Sox, the New York Yankees and the National Baseball Hall of Fame.

	BOSTON	NEW YORK
Nicknames	Beantown	Big Apple
Clam Chowder	New England	Manhattan
Signature Food	Baked Beans	Pizza
Original Name	Boston Americans	New York Highlanders
Playing Fields	Fenway Park	Yankee Stadium
Current Attendance Capacity	34,898	57,478
Park Features	The Green Monster	Short porch in right field
	Manual scoreboard	Monument Park
Anthem	"Dirty Water" ("Oh, Boston")	"New York, New York"
Signature National Anthem Singers	Barenaked Ladies	Robert Merrill
Titles Through 1918	5	0
Titles Since 1918	0	26
World Championships	5	26
American League Pennants	10	38
Slogan	"Reverse the Curse"	"Winning is Essential"
Hall of Famers	28	33
Best DiMaggio	Dom	Joe
Best Player Ever	Ted Williams	Babe Ruth
Best Pitcher Ever	Cy Young	Whitey Ford
2003 Slogan	"Cowboy Up!"	"Let's Go Yankees!"
Celebrity Rooters	Matt Damon	Billy Crystal
Politico Zealots	Michael Dukakis	Rudy Giuilani